Bad Choices in Our Food System

Bad Choices in Our Food System

By

Lydia Zepeda

Cambridge
Scholars
Publishing

Bad Choices in Our Food System

By Lydia Zepeda

This book first published 2021

Cambridge Scholars Publishing

Lady Stephenson Library, Newcastle upon Tyne, NE6 2PA, UK

British Library Cataloguing in Publication Data
A catalogue record for this book is available from the British Library

ISBN (10): 1-5275-6466-5
ISBN (13): 978-1-5275-6466-4

To Steve, never patient, though helpful,
and sadly, rarely wrong

TABLE OF CONTENTS

List of Figures x

List of Tables xi

Abbreviations xii

Chapter 1 Bad Choices 1
- Introduction 1
- Exercise: Honor a home cook 7
- References 7

Chapter 2 What is our food system like? 9
- What foods do we produce with our food system? 13
- What does our food system mean for our health? 15
- What is the contribution of our food system to the global economy? 17
- Looking at the US food system: what do we produce and subsidize? 18
- US consumers' expenditures on food 25
- What is your food system like? 26
- Exercise: Questions to ask yourself about your 24-hour photo food diary 31
- References 32

Chapter 3 How did we get here? 38
- A brief history of the US agricultural policy 38
- The rise of the international agro-food industry in the 19th century 45
- Brands in the 20th century 47
- The consolidation of food and beverage companies 51
- Is this what consumers wanted? 57
- Changes in household food expenditure over time 59
- Where are we now? 62
- Exercise: Tally your food expenditures for a week 63
- References 63

Chapter 4	The other costs of our choices	74
	Health impacts of our food system	74
	The environmental impacts of our food system	79
	Social justice impacts of our food system: US policy and farmers	86
	US agriculture and its workers	95
	Do US agricultural policies ensure people get acccss to food?	98
	Then who benefits from the US food system?	100
	Exercise: Look in your refrigerator	102
	References	102
Chapter 5	Where are we going?	114
	Will there be enough food?	116
	What about the environmental impacts?	119
	Will our food be safe?	121
	How will we get our food?	124
	What will we eat? Retailers nudge consumers	132
	Telling us what to eat: culture, diets, and media	134
	Our food system	139
	Exercise: Keep a 24-hour time diary	140
	References	141
Chapter 6	Why do we choose the foods we do?	148
	The economics of food demand	148
	The economics of behavior change	151
	Why do people eat what they do? The psychology of changing food choices	154
	Shaping consumer preferences	163
	We eat what we are given to eat	169
	Exercise: Set a food goal with someone	171
	References	171
Chapter 7	How do we fix this?	177
	Reliance on non-profits to privatize public problems	180
	The scope and limitations of non-profits	184
	Non-profits cannot solve health issues created by government policies	187
	We need to change the policies that cause the problems in the first place	192
	Exercise: Look at the policies	193
	References	193

Chapter 8 No really, how do we fix this? 197
US agricultural policy: Farm Bills, farm operators and what is produced 198
End policies that subsidize unhealthy foods, pollute, and promote fewer, bigger farms 201
Our unhealthy food environment is created by current policies 206
The US Farm Bill 210
What if the Farm Bill promoted health, the environment, and farm incomes? 215
Exercise: Voice your support or opposition to policy 217
References 217

Chapter 9 Epilogue 225
Why we blame the individual 230
Why we look for local solutions and why we avoid policy solutions 233
Exercise: Support a group working for change 235
References 235

LIST OF FIGURES

Figure 2.1 Global plantings of the top 12 crops, 2016 (million hectares) 11
Figure 2.2 Comparison of nutritional versus agricultural land use allocation 19
Figure 2.3 Increase in net cash income of farms due to US government payments (percentage) 22
Figure 2.4 Top 25 government payments to farmers by state, 2017 23
Figure 2.5 Percentage of US government payments by commodity program 24
Figure 3.1 Percent of US household expenditure spent on food away from home, 1909-2017 61
Figure 4.1 Prevalence of overweight, obesity, and diabetes, adults and adolescents, 1988-2016 (percentage of the population) 76
Figure 4.2 Number of US farms, 1850-2017 88
Figure 4.3 Average US farm size, 1850-2017 (hectares) 90
Figure 4.4 Government subsidies per farm by farm size (hectares) 2012 and 2017 92
Figure 4.5 Percentage of farms, sales, government payments, and farms receiving government support by farm size (hectares) in 2017 93
Figure 4.6 Average government subsidy per farm by farm size in hectares, 2012 and 2017 94
Figure 6.1 Stages of Change model 159

LIST OF TABLES

Table 2.1 Crop production, USDA predictions in million metric tons (December prediction 2018-2019) 11
Table 2.2 Consumption of meat, fish and seafood, milk, and eggs (2013, kg/person/year) 15
Table 2.3 Establishments dedicated to the production, processing and sale of agricultural products, food, and equipment in the US, 2012 20
Table 2.4 Rank in descending order of states' government payments as a percentage of net cash farm income 22
Table 3.1 18th and 19th century food and beverage brands 47
Table 3.2 Food brands introduced in the US between 1900 and 1979 48
Table 3.3 Top food and beverage companies, 2018 earnings (billion US$) 52
Table 3.4 US household food expenditures by quintile, as a percentage of total expenditures 61
Table 4.1 Definition of a farm for the US agricultural census 88

ABBREVIATIONS

2,4-D	2,4-dichlorophenoxyacetic acid, a herbicide
ABC	Attitude, Behavior, Context theory
ADHD	attention deficit hyperactivity disorder
AL	Alabama
AQUASTAT	FAO's global information system on water and agriculture
AR	Arkansas
ARC	Agriculture Risk Coverage, a US Farm Bill farm subsidy program
BE	Belgium
BLS	Bureau of Labor Statistics of the US
BMI	body mass index
CA	California
CAFO	concentrated animal feeding operation
CDC	Centers for Disease Control and Prevention of the US
CEO	chief executive officer
CFBAI	Children's Food and Beverage Advertising Initiative
CO	Colorado
CO2	carbon dioxide
CO2e	carbon dioxide equivalent
COVID-19	corona virus disease 2019
CPI	consumer price index
CRP	Conservation Reserve Program of the USDA
CRS	Congressional Research Service of the US
CSA	community supported agriculture
CSP	Conservation Stewardship Program of the USDA
CVD	cardiovascular disease
DDT	dichlorodiphenyltrichloroethane
DHHS	Department of Health and Human Services of the US
e. coli	escherichia coli, a common bacteria in the intestines of humans and animals
ELM	Elaboration Likelihood Model
EPA	Environmental Protection Agency of the US
EQIP	Environmental Quality Incentives Program of the USDA
ERS	Economic Research Service of the USDA
EU	European Union

EURO	Regional office of WHO for Europe
FAO	Food and Agriculture Organization of the United Nations
FAOSTAT	FAO food and agriculture data
FAS	Foreign Agriculture Service of the USDA
FAV	fruits and vegetables
FDA	Food and Drug Administration of the US
FMI	Food Marketing Institute
FNS	Food and Nutrition Service of the USDA
FQPA	1996 Food Quality Protection Act of the US
FY	fiscal year
g	grams
GA	Georgia
GBD	Global Burden of Diseases collaborative group
GBP	glyphosate based product
GDP	gross domestic product
GHG	greenhouse gases
GNI	gross national income
H1N1	influenza A virus (1918 flu and 2009 swine flu pandemics)
H2-A	visa for temporary agricultural workers in the US
H5N1	influenza A virus, avian influenza
ha	hectare
HFCS	high fructose corn syrup
HMO	health maintenance organization
IA	Iowa
IARC	International Agency for Research on Cancer of WHO
ICE	Immigration and Customs Enforcement of the US
ID	Idaho
IL	Illinois
IN	Indiana
IOM	Institute of Medicine of the US
IPBES	Intergovernmental Science-Policy Platform on Biodiversity and Ecosystem Services
IQ	intelligence quotient
IRS	Internal Revenue Service of the US
K-12	kindergarten through 12th grade; US elementary and secondary education
kg	kilograms
km	kilometers
km^2	kilometers squared
km^3	kilometers cubed
KS	Kansas

KY	Kentucky
LA	Louisiana
MA	Massachusetts
MERS	Middle Eastern Respiratory Syndrome (viral infection)
MI	Michigan
MMT	million metric tons
MN	Minnesota
MO	Missouri
MS	Mississippi
MT	metric tons
MT	Montana, Figure 2.4 only
MyPlate	US nutrition guidelines
NASA	National Aeronautics and Space Administration of the US
NASS	National Agriculture Statistics Service of the USDA
NC	North Carolina
NCFH	National Center for Farmworker Health
n.d.	no date
ND	North Dakota
NE	Nebraska
NHL	non-Hodgkin lymphoma
NJ	New Jersey
NY	New York
OECD	Organisation for Economic Cooperation
OH	Ohio
OK	Oklahoma
PA	Pennsylvania
PLC	Price Loss Coverage, a US Farm Bill farm subsidy program
POP	persistent organic pollutant
pppd	per person per day
R&D	research and development
RMA	Risk Management Agency of the USDA
SD	South Dakota
SDG17	WHO's 17 sustainable development goals for 2030
SDT	Self Determination Theory
SNAP	Supplemental Nutritional Assistance Program, program that provides money for food assistance to poor Americans
TX	Texas
UK	United Kingdom
UNEP	UN Environment Programme
US	United States of America
USDA	United States Department of Agriculture

WA	Washington State
WHO	World Health Organization
WI	Wisconsin
WIC	Women, Infants, and Children nutrition program of USDA
WWI	World War I
WWII	World War II

CHAPTER ONE

BAD CHOICES

The simple act of eating reflects our choices, policy, and culture. It also affects our health, economy, environment, and society in ways we often do not understand.

Introduction

We live in a time when we have the most knowledge about nutrition that we have ever had. Yet diet is implicated in one in five deaths worldwide (GBD2017 Diet Collaborators, 2019) and diet-related illnesses are the leading cause of death in the US (The US Burden of Disease Collaborators, 2018). How is it that we have the most knowledge and yet the worst diets?

Many people claim that it is because nutrition information is confusing, contradictory, or too complex. The food industry has been behind research that has tried to muddy the waters and it has lobbied to make nutritional information less transparent (Nestle, 2002, 2006). However, despite this, the core advice has been consistent for decades: limit overall calories, sugar, and fats; obtain a greater portion of our diet from fruits, vegetables, and whole grains; and get regular exercise. This sensible advice has been drowned out by the advertising of unhealthy foods, cooking shows, the media, and fad diets. It is easy to ignore the rational, consistent voice of reason against the hype of "miracle diets" and the promotion of "food porn." Everyone wants an easy solution.

The truth is more complicated. Indeed, blaming diet exclusively for our food-related health problems is simplistic. Other factors include lack of exercise; being too sedentary; too much or too little sleep; too much screen time; gut flora; and genetics. However, this book focuses on dietary choices and the role the food system has had in shaping those choices because we are presented with more temptations every day. Restaurants advertise new variations of food that add even more bacon or cheese. Food manufacturers advertise new junk foods and beverages, and variations of existing ones.

Cooking shows, blogs, and books promote new foods and ingredients. Social media addicts post their meals. Across all platforms, what the foods seem to have in common are empty calories. The sheer noise, prevalence, and attention given to unhealthy foods reinforce unhealthy eating habits.

Yet when we fail to lose weight or get our blood sugar under control, we are told it is our fault; we lack sufficient self-control. Is it possible that everyone lacks self-control? Unhealthy diets occur in all countries and across all income levels. Globally, we eat too much sodium, sugar, processed meat, and red meat, and too few nuts, seeds, fruits, and whole grains (GBD 2017 Diet Collaborators, 2019). This points to a systemic problem in the composition and quality of our diets. Why is this so?

In part, the sheer abundance and availability of food contribute to overeating. It is predictable that if food is cheap, we will eat more of it. In many parts of the world, people spend a significant amount on food, but despite this, obesity is now a global problem. However, nowhere is food so relatively cheap as in the US; in 2018, food eaten at home made up only 7.3% of household expenditure (US BLS, 2019). We spent more on healthcare: 8.1% of household expenditure.

In theory, our demand for food should be relatively inelastic because our stomachs have a limited capacity. A closer look at our food might explain why we are ingesting and absorbing more calories—our food is increasingly refined, digestible, and high in calorie density. Despite this, we may not feel fuller, even though our foods and beverages are packed with fat, sugar, alcohol, and salt. Processing, cooking, refining, juicing, and grinding our foods increase the digestibility and availability of those calories for our bodies. The processes may also make foods easier and quicker to eat, so that we eat too much before feeling full. Add to that the distraction of screens when eating, and we may simply not notice that we are full until we have eaten more than we intended. The result is not only that we eat more, but our bodies may also have to work less to absorb more calories, due to foods being highly processed. Also, we may be too sedentary and lack adequate exercise. We also consume large amounts of beverages, full of sugars and alcohol. While they are full of empty calories, they are easy to consume, do not make us full, and may even stimulate our appetites.

In addition, food is all around us, and has found its way into places where it never used to exist. Food can be purchased online and delivered, any time of day, in virtually any place. Mealtimes are moot, eating at a table is passé, and eating with others means looking at one's phone or a screen. We may rarely eat with others in our homes; table manners and the accompanying implicit restraints and pacing of food consumption now constitute a lost art. We do not eat meals, rather, we eat continuously. There are no limits to when or where we eat. We eat in cars, on public transport, during work time, in bed, and while exercising. It would appear that going an hour without eating is impossible. We are distracted when eating, oblivious to what we consume while looking at our phones or other media.

Unsurprisingly, the continuous eating of calorie-dense foods and beverages, the lack of exercise, and the fact we are sedentary result in weight problems, obesity, hypertension, heart disease, type 2 diabetes, strokes, and cancers. The individual is blamed for these diet-related problems and assumed to have the self-control of a two-year-old. Doctors prescribe pills, insulin pumps, and surgery, believing patients are incapable of changing their behavior. People turn to technology, like phone apps and Fitbits, to remind them to achieve their steps, tell them what and when to eat, or help them to sleep. These approaches digitize the well-known principles of behavior change: monitoring, accountability, and support. Anyone familiar with 12-step programs knows how effective real people are in promoting behavior change using these principles, without technology, and at no cost. However, there is money to be made by selling us technology and apps to accomplish what people and culture used to do. There is not just the initial purchase price of the technology, but all the information about our behaviors is collected and sold to third-party companies to target advertising.

While personal choice is often blamed as the cause of our diet-related problems, unlike alcohol or other addictions, one cannot break a food addiction by living in a food-free environment. We need to eat. We must be around food. Our diets may be associated with many health complaints: we are overweight, we feel bloated, we cannot sleep, we are constipated or gassy, we experience pain, and we may find it difficult to simply move. There is an industry who claims to have the perfect diet to lose weight or feel better. This involves fad foods, fad diets, superfoods, fad food preparation, etc. The sad truth is boring by contrast: avoid processed foods; eat regular meals; control portion size; exercise; spend less time sitting and in front of screens; and repeat as long as you wish to live. Diets do not work because they are temporary. However, telling people they need to change what they eat and how they live forever runs counter to the desire for an easy, miracle cure. This is the irony of blaming personal choice; we simultaneously tell people they can "cure" their food-related problems by a short-term change or by adding a fad food. Essentially, we give them tools of personal choice that cannot work.

In addition, we fail to acknowledge how our food choices, sedentary behavior, and lack of activity are influenced by external factors. Much has been written about "food deserts" as a cause of poor eating habits. While many non-profits, healthcare providers, and policymakers assume that the lack of grocery stores causes poor eating habits, reviews of the research do not provide conclusive evidence to support this (Caspi, Sorensen, Subramanian, and Kawachi, 2012; Feng, Glass, Curriero, Stewart, and Schwartz, 2010).

The placement of grocery stores may be as segregated as housing in the US, and even stores in the same chain may carry different items in different neighborhoods. However, while some stores have more and better produce, more than half of all produce harvested in the US is wasted and 45% of all produce harvested globally is wasted (FAO, 2011). In the US, shoppers spend less than 1% of their household budget on fresh produce; US households spend about the same amount on prescriptions, and they spend nearly twice as much on cell phone services (US BLS, 2019). What people do spend their money on is food away from home: 44% of US household food purchases relate to food eaten away from home. It would appear that it is not just people who live in food deserts who make bad choices; everyone is making bad choices.

Looking at grocery stores, it is not hard to see why people make bad choices. There are over 38,000 grocery stores in the US; they average over 41,000 square feet and carry over 33,000 items (Food Marketing Institute, 2019). Most of these items are highly processed (Toops, 2017). In a study of ten countries, 41% of all shelf space was dedicated to soda and junk food, and the greater the shelf space devoted to unhealthy foods, the higher the national BMI (Norman, Hoffman, and Cheskin, 2014). In the US, processed foods account for over three-quarters of calorie intake (Poti et al., 2015). We consume processed food because that is what is available.

If you walk through a typical grocery store, you will see the space devoted to processed foods. In the US, there are entire aisles devoted to frozen pizzas, ice cream, sodas, chips, or cookies. One side of the store wall is usually covered with meats, another with dairy products. Fruits and vegetables are usually placed near the entrance, so one walks through them, conveying a sense of healthiness. At the checkouts, shoppers pile up their purchases of frozen pizzas, soda, ice cream, cookies, and salty snacks. For the convenience of customers too large to walk, stores now provide electric carts to transport shoppers.

To identify what people do buy, one need only look at the shelf space devoted to processed foods. Sales are calculated in terms of floor space or shelf space (Hudson, 2018). Stores charge brands for the space and location of their products. These "slotting fees" make up 2% of grocery store sales (Achrol, 2012). Brands must pay to ensure that their products are not only in stores, but visible, with higher charges for products at eye level. Slotting fees are an important component of grocery retail profitability since their profit margins are so low: only 1.2% after taxes (FMI, 2019).

Somehow, the grocery shopper is supposed to overcome the fact that they are faced with bad choices because nutritional advice tells us what we should eat. However, you have to understand the jargon and the way the information is presented to use the information correctly. The food pyramid tried to present recommended servings of different food groups without being clear about what a serving was. Ironically, in the US, at a time when hardly anyone eats off a plate, MyPlate has been proposed as a means to convey serving size. While the food pyramid recommended moderation in consuming fatty or sugary foods and beverages, MyPlate obfuscates the issue by omitting any mention of junk foods. The omission leaves the eater thinking, "If I eat what MyPlate recommends, I will be healthy, regardless of what I eat in addition." This may simply encourage more overeating because junk foods are invisible and hence not counted.

The prevalence of eating out and the consumption of processed foods further confuse consumers. We assume items are sold in serving sizes. Nothing could be further from the truth; when you read the labels of processed foods, you may be surprised that a product has 2.3 servings, or that a serving size is 1.5 cookies. Restaurants routinely serve twice or more the recommended serving size of meat and never seem to come close to the recommendations for fruits and vegetables or whole grains. If we are never offered a healthy diet, how can we choose it? How are we even to recognize it?

So, are shoppers unable to choose healthy foods? Are they misinformed? Are they being manipulated? Or are they merely being rational by choosing the cheapest foods? The answer is yes to all of these and that is why food-related illnesses continue to rise. It is not simply a matter of personal choice, or even of policy; it is these factors interacting with culture that is at the heart of the current crisis. We have worked very, very hard and very, very long to get to where we are. This book explores the paths that have led to our current crisis and identifies how we might be able to find a new path.

Food-related illnesses, the environment, and societal problems are tied to the policies and culture that influence consumers' food choices. The individual makes food choices within this context, but our choices are both influenced by and reinforce the status quo. To change food choices, we need to examine the co-dependency between food and agricultural policy and consumers' choices and health impacts. This is done by drawing from empirical data and findings on the health, environmental, and societal impacts of food and agriculture; consumer theory; the history of agricultural policy; cultural trends; and current policies.

One limitation of this book is the focus on the US. This is in part because the US has been a leader in industrializing its agricultural and food systems, and is also leading the way in food-related illnesses, but mostly because a writer should write about what they know. For those desiring a more global perspective, either take the US example as a warning or invite me to see how things function in your country.

The intention of this book is to provide a resource, both to inform the individual and to use in the classroom. Data and sources are used to ensure the findings are evidence-based and transparent. The content can be summarized as follows. Chapter Two describes our food system: the resources it uses, its role in our economy, and the impacts it has on our health and environment. Chapter Three examines how we got here, with a focus on US agricultural policy and the rise of the international agro-food industry. Chapter Four examines the health, environmental, and social costs of our global food system. Chapter Five examines social, cultural, and economic trends in food and agriculture. Chapter Six identifies economic, psychological, marketing, and sociological theories that explain why we choose the foods we do. Chapter Seven looks at the role of non-profits in creating a healthier, more environmentally sustainable, and socially just food system. Chapter Eight examines the role of government policies in creating a food system that is aligned with health and environmental objectives. Chapter Nine, the Epilogue, looks at why we blame the individual and why we avoid examining policy solutions. The purpose of this book is to provide information about our current food system: what it is; how it came to be; how it influences what we eat and our health; and what we can do about it.

Exercise: Honor a home cook

Rather than looking to strangers and paid professionals as your heroes, honor someone who has cooked a healthy meal for you, despite the food system we are in. Maybe that person is you. Reflect a minute on why our food heroes are strangers who profit from us rather than the people who feed and love us.

References

Achrol, R. S. 2012. Slotting allowances: a time series analysis of aggregate effects over three decades. Journal of the Academy of Marketing Science, 40(5), 673–694. doi:10.1007/s11747-011-0260-7.

Caspi, C. E., Sorensen, G., Subramanian, S. V., and Kawachi, I. 2012. The local food environment and diet: A systematic review. Health & Place, 18: 1172–1187. http://dx.doi.org/10.1016/j.healthplace.2012.05.006, accessed May 20, 2016.

FAO. 2011. Global Food Losses and Food Waste. http://www.fao.org/3/a-i2697e.pdf, accessed November 15, 2019.

Feng, J., Glass, T. A., Curriero, F. C., Stewart, W. F., and Schwartz, B. S. 2010. The built environment and obesity: A systematic review of the epidemiologic evidence. Health & Place, 16: 175–190. doi:10.1016/j.healthplace.2009.09.008.

Food Marketing Institute. 2019. Supermarket Facts. https://www.fmi.org/our-research/supermarket-facts, accessed November 25, 2019.

GBD 2017 Diet Collaborators. 2019. Health effects of dietary risks in 195 countries, 1990-2017: a systematic analysis for the Global Burden of Disease Study 2017. The Lancet, 393, May 11, https://www.thelancet.com/gbd, accessed November 14, 2019.

Hudson, M. 2018. 8 ways to measure retail performance and productivity. The Balance. https://www.thebalancesmb.com/measuring-retail-performance-and-productivity-2890277, accessed November 25, 2019.

Nestle, M. 2002. Food Politics: How the Food Industry Influences Nutrition and Health. Berkeley, CA: The University of California Press.

Nestle, M. 2006. What to Eat. New York: North Point Press.

Norman, M., Hoffman, J. and Cheskin, L. J. 2014. Shelf space devoted to nutritious foods correlates with BMI. American Journal of Food and Nutrition, 2(2), 18-22. doi:10.12691/ajfn-2-2-1.

Poti, J. M., M. A. Mendez, S. W. Ng, and B. M. Popkin. 2015. Is the degree of food processing and convenience linked with the nutritional quality of foods purchased by US households? American Journal of Clinical Nutrition, 101(6), 1251–62.

Toops, D. 2017. Chapter 2: How did the food industry get (from there) to here? Accelerating New Food Product Design and Development, Second Edition. Edited by J. H. Beckley, L. J. Herzog, and M. M. Foley. Hoboken, NJ: John Wiley & Sons Ltd and the Institute of Food Technologists. http://www.ift.org/~/media/Knowledge%20Center/Publications/Books/Samples/IFTPressBook_ANFPDD_Chapter1.pdf, accessed November 15, 2019.

The US Burden of Disease Collaborators. 2018. The state of US health, 1990-2016: Burden of diseases, injuries, and risk factors among US states. Journal of the American Medical Association, 319(14), 1444–1472. doi:10.1001/jama.2018.0158.

US BLS (Bureau of Labor Statistics). 2019. Consumer Expenditure Survey. Table 1101. Quintiles of income before taxes: Annual expenditure means, shares, standard errors, and coefficients of variation. Consumer Expenditure Survey, 2018. https://www.bls.gov/cex/2018/aggregate/quintile.pdf, accessed November 15, 2019.

CHAPTER TWO

WHAT IS OUR FOOD SYSTEM LIKE?

There is a lot of talk about our food system, but what exactly is it? This chapter examines how much land and water are used by agriculture and what crops and animals we raise. What do we actually eat? How much does our food system contribute to our economy? How much do we spend on food?

Let's start with some basic information about our food system and land use. Roser and Ritchie (2018) estimate that of the 149 million square kilometers of land on Earth, 71% is habitable, and the rest is barren or covered with glaciers. Of the habitable land, 50% is used for agriculture and the rest is covered in forest (37%), shrubs (11%), manmade structures (1%), or freshwater (1%). That means 5.1 billion hectares of land are used for agriculture. Of this, 4 billion hectares are used for livestock and their feed, while only 1.1 billion hectares are used for crops for human use globally. Thus, crops for human consumption use only 23% of the total agricultural land, yet they provide 83% of global caloric intake and 67% of global protein intake.

While much of the agricultural land used for animals is only suitable for pasture or animal production, one-third of all cropland is used to produce animal feeds (FAO, 2012). Almost all the pastureland is used by ruminants like cattle and sheep, yet the largest source of meat globally by weight is from pigs, followed by chickens (FAO, 2019). Pigs and chickens are largely raised in confinement on feeds, while ruminants are kept largely for milk production and for fattening prior to slaughter for meat.

Globally, there is less than one hectare of agricultural land per person (Roser and Ritchie, 2018). Most of that land (77%) is devoted to livestock and their feed; therefore, arable land for crops for human consumption is about 0.2 hectares per person. While that may sound like very little, it is worth noting how productive agricultural land is. The average yields for maize (corn) are 5.8 metric tons per hectare (FAS, 2018), implying 0.2 hectares of maize would produce 3.2 kilos of maize (almost 7 pounds) per person per day (pppd) or almost 2.5 kilos of rice (5.4 pounds) pppd, far more than a person could eat. Given this productivity, the OECD and the FAO predict demand for commodities to be stable over the next decade (OECD, 2018), despite population growth. They also predict that the real prices for most foods will fall. That is largely because agricultural productivity is expected to continue to rise, albeit more slowly.

What does our global agricultural landscape look like? Cereals comprise 65% of all cropland (Roser and Ritchie, 2018). Four crops make up almost half of the cereal cropland (FAOSTAT, 2018): wheat, maize, rice, and soybeans (Figure 2.1). The crop that uses the most land is wheat: 216 million hectares globally, an area the size of Greenland. Maize or corn is second, 188 million hectares globally, somewhat smaller than the entire area of Mexico. Rice is third, at 163 million hectares, somewhat bigger than the size of Mongolia. The global area planted with soybeans is roughly the size of Peru: 128 million hectares.

Given the yield differences per hectare between maize and wheat, the global production of maize is much larger than that of wheat (Table 2.1). The US and China together produce 57% of the world's maize; Brazil is a distant third with less than 9%. Wheat production is much less concentrated because it is widely distributed across many countries. The country with the largest wheat production is China—at 132.5 million metric tons (MMT) in the 2018-19 growing season, it produced 18% of the world's wheat (USDA FAS, 2018). India was the second-largest wheat-producing nation, with almost 100 MMT, followed by Russia at 70 MMT. The 28 nations of the European Union (EU) together produced 137 MMT of wheat. The US is estimated to produce about 7% of global wheat production at 51.3 MMT.

The third-largest crop worldwide in terms of area and yield is rice, with China and India producing 51% of global production by weight. The US produces less than 1.5% of global rice production. Two-thirds of the world's soy, the fourth largest crop, is produced in the US and Brazil. China is a small player, producing only 16 MMT.

Figure 2.1 Global plantings of the top 12 crops, 2016 (million hectares).

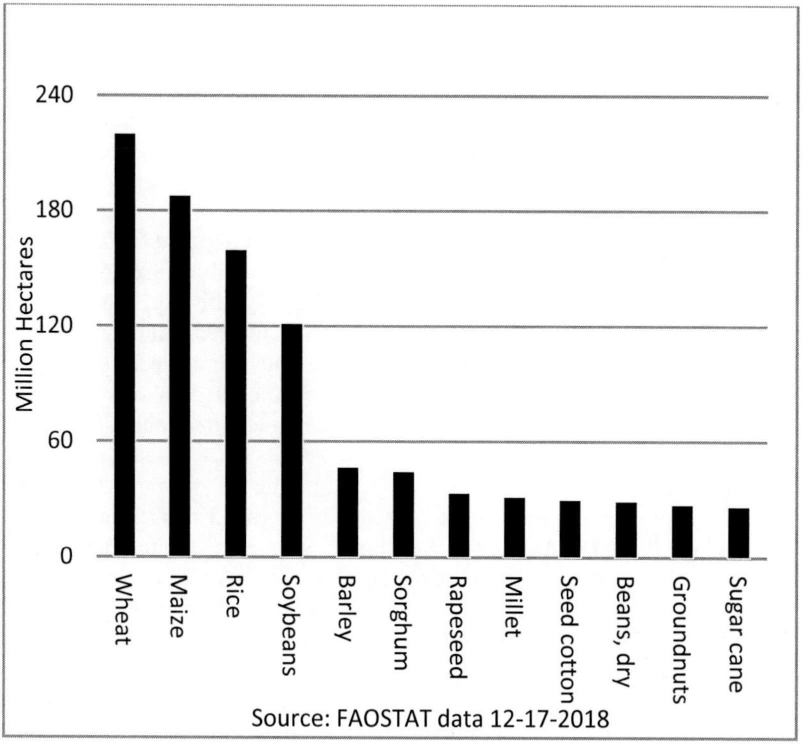

Table 2.1 Crop production, USDA predictions in million metric tons (December prediction 2018-2019).

	World	US	China	Next Largest
Wheat	733.4	51.3	132.5	99.7 India
		7%	18%	13.6%
Maize	1100	371.5	256	94.5 Brazil
		34%	23%	8.6%
Rice	491.4	6.9	143.6	111 India
		1.4%	29%	22.6%
Soybeans	369.2	125.2	16	122 Brazil
		34%	4.3%	33%

Source: USDA FAS, 2018.

All fruits make up 4.7% of global cropland, and all vegetables 4.1% (FAOSTAT, 2018). So, fruits and vegetables (FAV), excluding tubers, comprise 8.8% of cropland, about the same area as is planted with soybeans. Putting this in perspective, US dietary recommendations (MyPlate) suggest that 50% of one's food intake should be FAV. Yet the land used to produce FAV makes up less than 9% of global cropland and less than 3% of all agricultural land. What would our landscapes look like if agriculture followed nutritional guidelines?

In addition to land, agriculture is water intensive. It uses the most water of any human activity. Estimates for 2010 indicate agriculture used 69% of all water withdrawals (FAO AQUASTAT, 2016), while the World Bank estimates that agriculture uses 70% of global freshwater (Khokhar, 2017). It is estimated that animal production, including animal feed, comprises 29% of total water usage (Mekonnen and Hoekstra, 2012). Water usage for animal production comes largely from producing crops for animal feeds.

Agricultural production is expected to continue to increase, but more slowly, driven by improvements in productivity, rather than the expansion of land use (OECD/FAO, 2018). Real prices are expected to fall for cereals, oilseeds, dairy, and meat over the next decade. Trade volumes are expected to slow down and exports will continue to be concentrated in a few countries, with five countries selling more than 70% of all exports for 18 of the 19 top commodities.

What is striking about agriculture is the amount of food waste. It is estimated that globally, one-third of all food produced is wasted: 58% of fruits and vegetables, 40% of fish and seafood, 37% of cereals, 23% of meat, and 18% of milk (FAO, 2011). In the US, estimated food waste is even higher at 40%, which is equivalent to US$ 165 billion per year or 20 pounds (9 kilos) of food per person per month (Gunders, 2012). In Europe and North America, over a third of this waste occurs after consumers purchase the food, while in developing countries, much of the waste occurs between production and retail sale (FAO, 2011).

Food waste has massive environmental consequences. The carbon footprint of global food waste is estimated at 3.3 gigatons, a larger CO2 equivalent than any country except China or the US (FAO, 2011). The blue water footprint (surface and groundwater) used to produce global food waste exceeds the amount of water used by any single country, and the amount of land needed to produce global food waste exceeds the territory of any single country except Russia (FAO, 2011). This means that the land and water used to produce wasted food contributes to deforestation, habitat loss, and species extinction, and all for nothing because the food produced is not eaten.

So, when we think about our food system, think about how agriculture is incredibly productive, and also massively wasteful; a third of production globally is wasted, while 40% of the food produced in the US is wasted. Our food system also dominates land and water use. Globally, our food system uses half of the habitable land, and most of the world's water, with animal production using over three-quarters of that land and about a fifth of the global water footprint.

What foods do we produce with our food system?

It is estimated that there were 7.7 billion people in the world in November 2018. The population is expected to continue to rise to about 11 billion by the end of the 21st century (Roser and Ortiz-Ospina, 2017), with population growth slowing and leveling off. The OECD and the FAO (2018) predict food demand will grow from 1.6 billion MT in 2015-17 to 1.9 billion MT in 2027, with 30% of the additional demand for food due to China. The OECD/FAO predict a 2% increase in per capita cereal demand over ten years; 3% for meat and fish; and the strongest growth for poultry at 5.5%. Demand for sugar will be driven by developing countries because consumption is already very high in OECD countries (over 30 kg per capita per year). The OECD and the FAO identify population as the main cause for increased food demand, even though population growth is slowing.

While wheat and rice are largely used for human consumption, much of the worlds' maize, soy, and coarse grains are used for animal feed. In the US, estimates for the conversion of maize weight to beef weight gain vary considerably: from 5:1 to 9:1, with a target of 6:1 (CSU, n.d.). Using data from Peters et al. (2014), the ratio of maize to edible meat (rather than weight gain) is 5.3:1 for beef, 3.9:1 for pork, and 2.8:1 for chicken. The conversion rate of feed to meat is the reason that it takes so much more land to produce the same amount of protein or calories from meat than from plants. Plants are much more efficient at producing calories and protein than animals are.

The FAO estimated the number of animals globally in 2016 as 23 billion chickens, 1.5 billion cattle, 1.2 billion ducks, 1.2 billion sheep, 1 billion goats, 982 million pigs, plus assorted turkeys, geese, rabbits, buffaloes, etc. (FAOSTAT, 2018a). This is equivalent to three chickens per person, one cow for every five people, one sheep and one duck for every six people, a goose, guinea fowl, turkey, rabbit or hare for every seven people, and one pig and one goat for every eight people. This gives the impression of ample meat available per person globally. The average person consumed about 43 kilos of meat (beef, chicken, pork, lamb, etc.) in 2014, more than twice as much as in 1961 (Ritchie and Roser, 2017).

However, meat consumption is distributed unequally. Industrialized countries account for 15% of the world's population, but 40% of the world's milk consumption and 37% of the world's meat consumption (FAO, 2003). To illustrate the unequal distribution of meat (beef, pork, chicken, etc.) consumption, in 2013, Australians were the biggest meat eaters, consuming 116 kilos (256 pounds) per person per year (Table 2.2), while in India, the average amount of meat eaten was four kilos (less than nine pounds) per person per year (Ritchie and Roser, 2017). Fish and seafood consumption ranged from five kilos (11 pounds) per person per year in India to 35 kilos (77 pounds) per person per year in China. Milk consumption varied from 15 kilos (33 pounds) per person per year in Indonesia to 255 kilos (562 pounds) per person per year in the US. Egg consumption varied from three kilos (less than seven pounds) per person per year in India to 19 kilos (almost 42 pounds) per person per year in China.

Using a boneless meat equivalent, the USDA ERS (2018a) estimates that in 2016, Americans ate a total of 191.6 pounds (86.9 kilos) per capita of meat, poultry, fish, and shellfish. In terms of composition, chicken was the most prevalent at 63.1 pounds (28.6 kilos), followed by 52.9 pounds (24 kilos) of beef, 46.6 pounds (21.1 kilos) of pork, 14.9 pounds (6.8 kilos) of fish and shellfish, and 13.1 pounds (5.9 kilos) of turkey. Compare the 191.6 pounds (86.9 kilos) of boneless flesh eaten to the weight of the average American adult male, 197.9 pounds (89.8 kilos), and the average American adult female who weighed 170.6 pounds (77.4 kilos) in 2015-16 (Fryar et al., 2018). This means that, on average, Americans ate more than their weight in animal flesh in 2016. This equals in excess of a half-pound (227 grams) of meat per person per day. For the average adult woman or man, that is 70% more protein than the recommended daily allowance (MyPlate, 2018), without taking into account other sources of protein, such as dairy or plant-based proteins.

Table 2.2 Consumption of meat, fish and seafood, milk, and eggs (2013, kg/person/year).

	Meat	Fish/Seafood	Milk	Eggs
Australia	116	26	234	9
USA	115	22	255	15
European Union	81	22	236	12
China	62	35	33	19
Indonesia	14	28	15	5
India	4	5	85	3

Source: Ritchie and Roser, 2017.

What does our food system mean for our health?

Every country in the world is affected by malnutrition (World Hunger, 2018). Malnutrition is responsible for 45% of the deaths of children under five years old worldwide. Hunger and food insecurity adversely affect children because their bodies are developing. The result is that 22% of children worldwide are stunted, while 2% of children worldwide are both stunted and overweight, and 3.7% are stunted and wasted (Development Initiatives, 2018).

The logic that increasing production will somehow eradicate hunger belies both theory and empirical analysis. Increasing the production of a commodity with inelastic demand disproportionately decreases the total revenues for those who produce it. In other words, policies that focus on increasing commodity food production will impoverish farmers, sending more people to cities to earn incomes to buy food. The real cause of hunger is not too little food, but too little money; poverty prevents people from being able to buy food (World Food Programme, 2013; World Hunger, 2018). Conflict, war, and violence make it difficult for people affected to access food, while climate, through floods and drought, and food wastage, affect the food supply. Conflict and weather shocks are the main causes of hunger in the Middle East and North Africa (OECD/FAO, 2018). Rather than policies that increase production, hunger can be directly addressed through policies that promote peace and economic stability, and increase incomes, as well as direct access to food.

The affordability and availability of food are not only affected by the use of food as animal feed, but also as fuel. Many nations have policies that encourage or mandate the use of biofuels. The biggest risk factor for grain prices is these biofuel policies because they divert grains from food to fuel. For example, China has put in a mandate for ethanol (OECD/FAO, 2018). However, most countries that have mandates have reached their mandatory blend level, so growth in demand for biofuels will likely level off. This still means that a significant portion of agricultural production is used for biofuels rather than food, making food prices unaffordable for the poor.

Globally, being overweight and obesity are more widespread problems than hunger, affecting two billion adults or 38.9% of adults (Development Initiatives, 2018). Being overweight or obese contributes to 7% of deaths globally. This equates to 120 million healthy years lost, and US$ 3.5 trillion in direct and indirect costs (Development Initiatives, 2018).

Half of all deaths worldwide are attributable to four risk factors: high blood pressure, smoking, high blood glucose, and high body mass index (Horton, 2018). Three of these are related to diet. No country in the world is on track to meet its obesity target, which is simply that obesity must not increase. Nor is any country on track to meet their anemia target, which is also diet-related; worldwide, one-third of females 15 to 49 years old are anemic and the prevalence is increasing. Of the nine global nutrition indicators,[1] not one of the 194 countries committed to these goals is on target to meet more than four goals. Only five countries will meet just four of the goals: Armenia, Belize, Kenya, Sao Tome and Principe, and Swaziland. One hundred countries are on track to meet **zero** of the nine nutrition goals; among these are the US, the UK, Russia, and India.

Globally, adults at all income levels, in all countries, exceed their daily intake of sugary drinks and salt, and consume too little fruit, vegetables, whole grains, nuts, seeds, and milk (Development Initiatives, 2018). School-age children and adolescents eat too many refined grains and sugar, and not enough fruits, vegetables, and whole grains. As an example, among school-age children and adolescents in Latin America and the Caribbean, 33% do not eat any fruit daily, while 59% drink soda daily.

So, while we have plenty of food to feed everyone (World Food Programme, 2013), we know more about nutrition than we ever have, and

---

[1] The nine nutrition goals include targets for: overweight children, child wasting, child stunting, exclusive breastfeeding, diabetes among women, diabetes among men, anemia in women of reproductive age, obesity among women, and obesity among men.

we have more data, poor diets are a leading cause of death worldwide. This has led to the political will to create some policies to promote healthy eating. For example, 59 countries have implemented some form of sugar tax on beverages after the WHO revised sugar intake recommendations in 2015 (Development Initiative, 2018). However, changing agricultural policies to promote healthy food availability, in essence, changing our agricultural landscape, is not on the table. One of the reasons for this is the food system's contribution to the global economy.

What is the contribution of our food system to the global economy?

Global GDP in 2017 was estimated at US$ 80.74 trillion (World Bank, 2019a). Agriculture, fisheries, and forestry contribute just 3.5% of global GDP, or US$ 2.8 trillion (World Bank, 2019b). FAOSTAT (2018b) estimates that over 97% of agriculture's global value is food and that 66% of that food is for crops and 34% for livestock. However, agricultural production is only part of the contribution of the food system to the global economy. The global value of food and beverages in 2017 was estimated at US$ 5.65 trillion (PR Newswire, 2018), about 7% of the global economy. Global spending on eating out was valued at a further US$ 3.3 trillion[2] (Cushman and Wakefield, 2017). The US spends the most on eating out: 22% of global spending, followed by China at 8%, India at 5%, and Spain, Japan, and the UK at 4% each.

The US economy represents nearly one-quarter of total global output. However, agriculture is a much smaller proportion of US output at only 1% (World Bank, 2017). Yet US agriculture represents 9.1% of the global value of agricultural, 7.6% of global crop production, and 11.2% of global animal production (FAOSTAT, 2018b). Unnevehr (2017) estimated that the entire US food industry in 2014 was worth US$ 1.4 trillion, about 5% of US GDP, 10% of employment, and 10% of consumer expenditures.

---

[2] The 2016 global spending on eating out was US$ 3.3 trillion. This is inferred by the US$ 1.174 trillion in spending by Americans being 36% of global spending (Cushman and Wakefield, 2017).

Looking at the US food system: what do we produce and subsidize?

Animal production dominates the US landscape. Looking at the land area in the lower 48 states, where most of US agriculture is located, of the 765 million hectares, 35% of the land is used for rangeland and grassland pasture, while 21% is used for crops (Bigelow and Borders, 2017). However, 76.9% of the cropland planted was used to grow animal feeds, while only 19.8% of the cropland was planted for food crops for humans, with cotton making up most of the rest of the other crops planted. This means 51% of the land in the lower 48 states is used for animal production and 4% is used to grow crops for human consumption.

The area allocated to urban development is also about 4% of the area of the lower 48 states (Bigelow and Borders, 2017). Thus, the US allocates the same area to grow food for human consumption as it dedicates to its cities and towns, while the land allocated for animal production is nearly 13 times as large.

Of the food crops, wheat comprises 80% of the planted area in the US, with rice at 4%, and sunflowers, dry edible beans, and peanuts just under 3% each (Bigelow and Borders, 2017). Of the feed crops, 40% is planted to maize (corn), 32% to soy, and 24% to hay.

Let us compare US nutritional recommendations to how it uses its land. Nearly 93% of US agricultural land in the lower 48 states is allocated to the production of animal foods, and about 6% to wheat and rice, whereas recommendations are that animal and plant protein make up less than one-quarter of the plate, and grains slightly more than one-quarter. The remaining 1% of agricultural land includes not only FAV, but also pulses, beans, oils, and sugars for human consumption. MyPlate recommendations are that FAV should make up half of one's plate, whereas they comprise less than 1% of US agricultural land. Imagine what the American landscape would look like if plantings were to follow MyPlate recommendations (Figure 2.2).

Furthermore, over one-third of US agricultural products were exported in 2017, valued at $US 138.4 billion (US FAS, 2018b). Three-quarters of the cotton produced in the US was exported, along with about half of the soybean and wheat crops, a fifth of the corn and pork, and an eighth of poultry and dairy production. Canada is the largest purchaser, buying US$

20.5 billion or about 15% of US agricultural exports, with China in second place at US$ 19.6 billion, and Mexico in third with US$ 18.6 billion. Japan, the EU, and South Korea were also key purchasers of US agricultural products.

In 2018, US agriculture generated US$ 374.8 billion in cash receipts to farmers (USDA ERS, 2018b). Of this amount, 62.3% were for animal products or animal feeds. Oilseeds generated 11.4%, but most of this was soy and much of the protein cake from soy was fed to animals. Fruits, vegetables, and pulses generated 13% of agricultural cash receipts, food grains 3.1%, cotton 2.1%, sugar beets and sugarcane 0.7%, tobacco 0.3%, and all other agricultural products 7.1%. This means that nearly two-thirds of the revenues from US agricultural production were from animal products and animal feed. The implication is that the US food system is essentially designed to produce animal products.

Figure 2.2 Comparison of nutritional versus agricultural land use allocation.

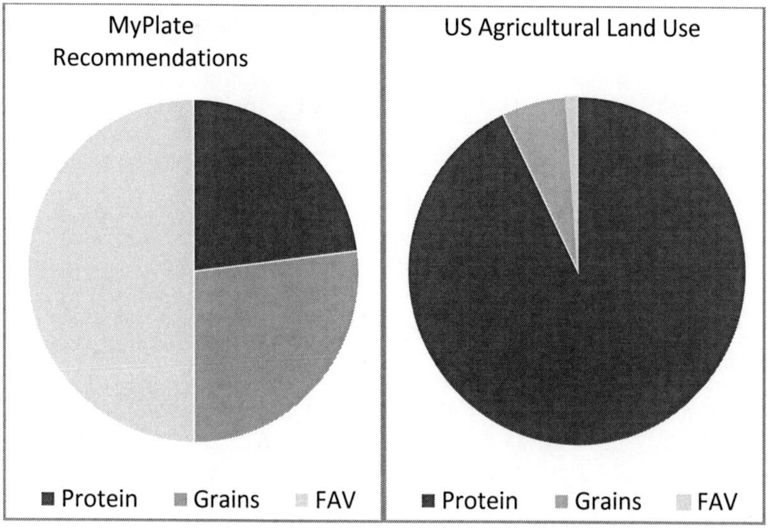

However, agriculture is but a small part of our food system. The revenues from agricultural production make up less than 10% of the value of the US food system (US Census, 2018a).

The latest US industry census found that there were over 921,000 establishments dedicated to the production, processing, and sale of agricultural products, food, and equipment in 2012 (Table 2.3). They had sales of US$ 3.9 trillion, and 16.5 million employees, who were paid US$ 355 billion. Almost two-thirds of the total establishments were dedicated to food or drink; these also employed over 60% of the workers, but generated only 13% of the value of sales and had 41% of the total payroll. Food and beverage stores accounted for 16% of the establishments, with nearly 16% of the sales, and over 17% of the employees and payroll. Grocery wholesalers were less than 4% of the establishments and under 5% of the employees, but their value of sales was over 20%, and their contribution to the total payroll was over 15%. Food manufacturers made up fewer than 3% of all the establishments in this sector, yet had 8.5% of the employees, 19% of the value of sales, and over 15% of the total payroll value.

Table 2.3 Establishments dedicated to the production, processing, and sale of agricultural products, food, and equipment in the US, 2012.

	Establishments	Sales (million $)	Employees	Payroll (million $)
Total	921,621	3,912,461	16,459,991	354,843
Food Manufacturing	25,619 2.8%	739,272 18.9%	1,401,968 8.5%	54,657 15.4%
Grocery wholesalers	33,892 3.7%	807,627 20.6%	769,183 4.7%	37,936 10.7%
Food and beverage stores	147,579 16.0%	620,024 15.9%	2,864,650 17.4%	60,539 17.1%
Food and drinking places	598,656 65.0%	512,280 13.1%	10,057,608 61.1%	145,983 41.1%

Source: US Census Bureau, 2018a. Data from 2012 economic census, all sectors, economy-wide key statistics.

Grocery wholesale sales fell to US$ 635 billion in 2018 (US Census Bureau, 2019). In contrast, food and beverage store sales in 2018 climbed to US$ 730 billion, and food and drink service sales increased to US$ 715 billion (US Census Bureau, 2018b). At US$ 374.8 billion (USDA ERS, 2018b), US farmers earned about half that of each of the major food industries in the US. Clearly, the money to be made in the food system is NOT in the production, but in the processing and distribution of food.

A closer look at farmers in the US indicates that, while their on-farm earnings are low, farmers' net worth is not. There are fewer than two million farms in the US (USDA ERS, 2018c). There are about 130 million households in the US (US BLS, 2018), making farm households about 1.5% of all households. The average income of farm households in 2018 from farming was estimated at US$ 18,637 and the median at US$ -1,548 (USDA ERS, 2018c). While the revenue from agriculture is low, the median US farmer is far from poor in terms of income or wealth. The median farm household income was 24% higher than the US median income due to off-farm income, unearned income, and government payments. Comparing US household net worth to farm net worth in 2016, median household net worth was US$ 97,300 (Federal Reserve, 2017), while farm household median net worth was US$ 896,811 (USDA ERS, 2018c). This means the median net worth of a farm household was 9.2 times that of the median net worth of a US household.

Government payments to farmers are an important component of their incomes. In 2018, US government payments to farmers constituted 17% of their net cash income (Figure 2.3). However, the payments are not distributed equitably. Most payments go to producers of a few crops. Hence, some states fared much better than others in terms of government payments as a proportion of farm receipts. In 2018, government payments made up 1% of California farmers' US$ 18.6 billion in net cash income, while they constituted 134% of Massachusetts farmers' net cash income, as government payments to farmers were more than they earned (USDA ERS, 2018d). New York, Pennsylvania, Wisconsin, North Carolina, Delaware, Vermont, New Jersey, Florida, and Arizona, along with California, were the biggest losers in terms of government payments as a percentage of net cash income (Table 2.4). Alaska, Massachusetts, Nevada, Montana, and Wyoming were the biggest winners in terms of government payments as a percentage of net cash income.

However, some of these states, like Alaska and Massachusetts, had a high percentage of government payments to cash income simply because their farm receipts were very small. The total government payments to farmers in 2018 were US$ 13.6 billion, 3.6% of all farm commodity receipts, and 14.6% of farmers' net cash income (USDA ERS, 2018d). Texas farmers received the most government payments of any state—nearly a billion dollars. This was followed by Nebraska, Iowa, Arkansas, and Kansas (Figure 2.4). While California was 50th in terms of government payments as a percentage of net cash income, it was 22nd in terms of the total value of all payments to farmers.

Figure 2.3 Increase in net cash income of farms due to US government payments (percentage).

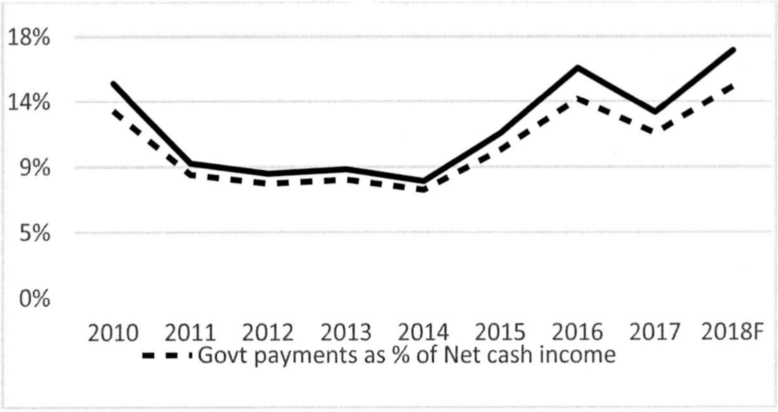

Source: USDA ERS. 2018d.

Table 2.4 Rank in descending order of states' government payments as a percentage of net cash farm income.

>30%	Alaska, Massachusetts, Nevada, Montana, Wyoming
20-30%	Arkansas, Louisiana, North Dakota, Kansas, Colorado, Nebraska, South Dakota
15-20%	South Carolina, Ohio, Missouri, Mississippi, New Hampshire, West Virginia, Tennessee, Illinois, Rhode Island
10-15%	Oklahoma, Michigan, Texas, Indiana, Georgia, Oregon, Hawaii, New Mexico, Iowa, Minnesota, Alabama, Idaho, Utah, Virginia
5-10%	Kentucky, Maryland, Maine, Washington, Connecticut
<5%	New York, Pennsylvania, Wisconsin, North Carolina, Delaware, Vermont, New Jersey, Florida, Arizona, California

Figure 2.4 Top 25 government payments to farmers by state, 2017

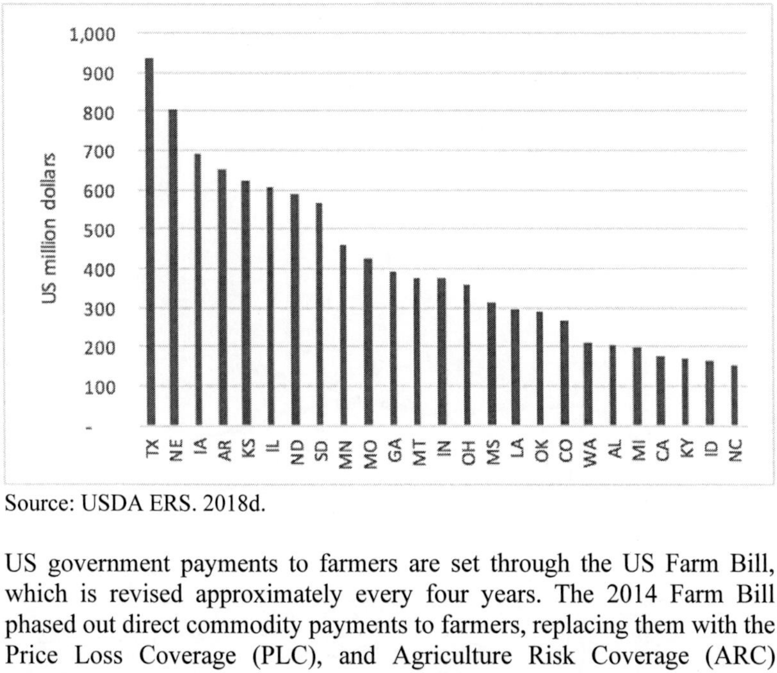

Source: USDA ERS. 2018d.

US government payments to farmers are set through the US Farm Bill, which is revised approximately every four years. The 2014 Farm Bill phased out direct commodity payments to farmers, replacing them with the Price Loss Coverage (PLC), and Agriculture Risk Coverage (ARC) programs. Under the 2014 Farm Bill, farmers chose which program to participate in. The PLC program compensates farmers for selected commodities if prices fall below a reference price. The ARC program compensates farmers for revenue losses based on historical plantings. The subsidized crops include corn (maize), soybeans, wheat, rice, cotton, peanuts, oats, barley, sorghum, and oilseeds. In FY 2016, the cost of PLC and ARC payments was US$ 6.9 billion with 71% of the payments going to corn (43.3%) and wheat (27.7%) (Angadjivand, 2018). Since a lot of US corn and wheat is exported, the programs function as export subsidies, and since corn is mostly fed to animals, the corn payments are essentially a subsidy for animal production, both in the US and the countries it exports to.

Subsidies for farmers in the form of crop insurance, commodity programs (e.g., PLC and ARC), and conservation programs make up 23% of the costs of the 2018 Farm Bill, while 1% is allocated to promote trade, research, and all other programs (Farm Bureau, 2018). Some notable changes in the 2018 Farm Bill are that it expands conservation acreage from 24 (9.7) to 27 (10.9) million acres (hectares), allows farmers to choose annually between the ARC and PLC programs (starting in 2021), and expands government payments to first cousins, nephews, and nieces of farm operators (Abbott, 2018). Figure 2.5 illustrates that while conservation program payments have remained relatively stable, disaster assistance has varied greatly, and miscellaneous programs have been growing.

Figure 2.5 Percentage of US government payments by commodity program.

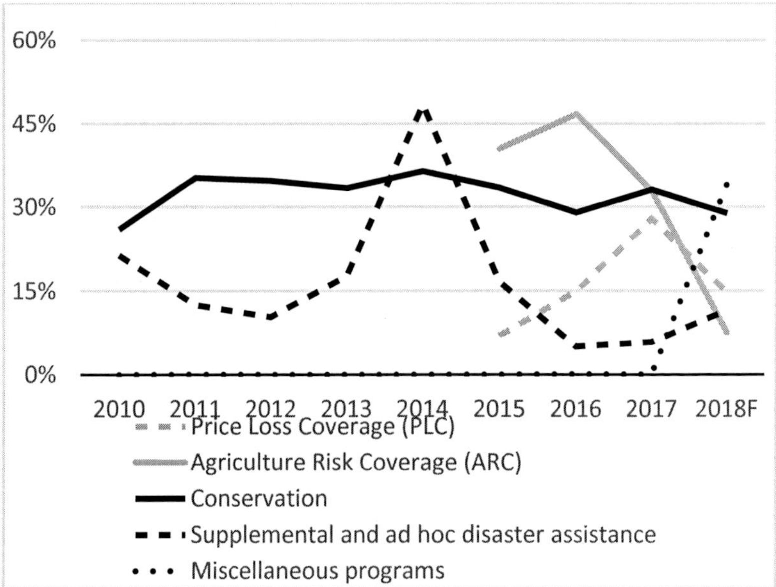

Source: UDSA ERS. 2018d.

The 2018 Farm Bill is estimated to cost US$ 428 billion from 2019-23 or US$ 85.6 billion per year (Farm Bureau, 2018). The Supplemental Nutritional Assistance Program (SNAP) and other nutrition programs, which provide poor Americans with food assistance, are the largest component of the bill, costing US$ 326 billion or 76%. In 2018, over 40 million Americans, or about 12% of the US population, received SNAP benefits averaging US$ 125 a month (USDA FNS, 2018). Feeding America (2018) estimates that about the same percentage of Americans struggle with food insecurity. While some Americans who are food insecure receive SNAP benefits, many more would be food insecure without them; the benefits significantly reduce the proportion of the population that is food insecure.

The US Farm Bill creates strange bedfellows. Since nutrition programs make up the bulk of the Farm Bill, they are often targets for cuts in eligibility and benefits. Yet nutrition programs provide cover for subsidies to farmers who have higher total incomes and far more net worth than the average American, let alone nutrition program recipients. Including nutrition programs in the Farm Bill also creates broad support for legislation that provides farm subsidies which disproportionately benefit a few states, such as Texas, Nebraska, and Iowa. In turn, tying nutrition programs to commodity subsidies builds support for nutrition programs among states who receive the farming subsidies.

Overall, the effect of the commodity programs of the Farm Bill is to encourage the production of subsidized crops, mostly corn (maize) and wheat. Without these programs, farmers would plant fewer acres, the output of these crops would be lower, and presumably, this would raise farm prices. Since the demand for commodities is inelastic, farm revenues would rise if farm prices increased. Meat and dairy prices would likely increase at farm and retail level if subsidies for animal feeds like corn were removed. However, removing wheat subsidies would have little impact on retail prices since wheat comprises only a small proportion of the cost of food products; for example, wheat is only 7% of the retail price of bread (Farm Policy Facts, 2008).

US consumers' expenditures on food

Given that Americans have a food system that is highly productive, subsidized, and dedicated to producing animal feed and wheat, how do they spend their money on food? For one thing, they spend proportionally less on food than other people around the world. The average US household spends proportionally the least of its income on food eaten at home (6.4%) of any country in the world (Gray, 2016). Singapore, the UK, Switzerland, Canada, Ireland, Australia, and Austria are all under 10%, but Nigerians spend 56% of their income on food.

Americans not only spend proportionally less on food than other nations, but they also spend proportionally less on food than they ever have historically. In 1901, the first comprehensive survey found that American households spent 43% of their income on food; this percentage fell steadily over the twentieth century (US Department of Labor, 2006). By 2017, housing made up one-third of US household expenditures, transportation was 15.9%, and 12.9% was spent on all food (US BLS, 2018). However, if you take away the US$ 3,365 spent on food away from home, households only spent US$ 4,363 per year on food at home, on average, or 7.3% of all household expenditure. This is less than the average annual household expenditure on pensions/social security (US$ 6,353) or on healthcare (US$ 4,928).

Looking at how Americans spend their food budget, 61% of the calories from food eaten at home were from highly processed products (e.g., ready-to-eat foods, soda, candy) and 16% were from moderately processed foods (e.g., sweetened fruit juice, potato chips, cheese) according to Unnevehr, (2017). In 2017, Americans spent US$ 588 on fresh FAV, compared to US$ 558 on alcohol, US$ 332 on tobacco, US$ 710 on pets, and US$ 1,118 on cell phone services (US BLS, 2018).

As a share of their expenses, the poor spent more on food at home. The poorest 20% of US households spent 9.9% of their total expenditure on food at home, whereas the richest 20% only 5.7% (US BLS, 2018). It is worth noting that the poor, who are often SNAP recipients, spend differently than the rich. Although often accused of making bad decisions, the poorest 20% of US households actually spent a greater proportion on fresh FAV than the richest 20% of households: 1.3% versus 0.8%. In addition, the poor spent a lower proportion on alcohol than the rich, 0.6% versus 1%, but about the same proportion on food away from home, 5.7% versus 5.5%.

On average, Americans spend less on food as a percentage of their income than people in any other country and at any other time in history. The proportion spent on food away from home has been rising relative to food eaten at home across all income levels, and much of the food eaten at home and away is highly processed. While the direct cost of food has fallen, the indirect costs in terms of food-related health problems have risen. US households now spend more on healthcare than on food eaten at home (US BLS, 2018). Furthermore, the US is on track to meet none of its global nutrition targets (Horton, 2018).

What is your food system like?

Americans spend proportionally the least in the world on food eaten at home, and part of the reason is that they spend the most on food eaten away from home. In either case, Americans are not getting the recommended amounts of whole grains or FAV. They are eating more processed foods, meat, sugar, salt, saturated fat, and alcohol than the recommended amounts (US DHHS and USDA, 2015). They are also not getting the recommended level of exercise and are too sedentary. As a consequence, it is not surprising that two-thirds of American adults and one-third of American children are overweight or obese.

However, when asked, most people say their diet is healthy (Zepeda and Deal, 2008). That is because diet-related illnesses occur over time, and in the meantime, one is healthy, therefore, people conclude that their diet must be healthy. By the time a diet-related illness (heart disease, stroke, type 2 diabetes, or certain types of cancers) is diagnosed, it may be too late to reverse the effects of years of bad eating habits, and changing eating habits is certainly difficult. The word diet refers to what one eats. That is why temporary changes in one's diet have, at best, temporary effects. To have a permanent effect, one needs to change one's diet permanently, as well as exercise, cut screen time, and not remain sedentary.

The first step in making a change in what one eats is to examine one's personal food system. What exactly are you eating? What are you eating too little of? What are you consuming too much of? You may think you know what you are eating, but the chances are, you have no idea. To find out, take a picture of everything that you consume over a 24-hour period, including pictures of all the beverages you drink as well. Then, look at the images.

How many servings of actual fruits and vegetables did you eat in 24 hours? Do not count beverages that are highly processed and are full of salt or sugar. For a 2,000 calorie diet, you should be eating about two to three pieces of fruit, and about five servings of vegetables a day. A serving is approximately the size of your palm, and double that for leafy, raw greens.

How many servings of whole grains did you eat? For a 2,000 calorie diet, you should eat six ounces (170 grams) of grains, at least half of which should be whole grains. An example of six servings is: two slices of bread, a cup (237 milliliters) of cooked rice or pasta, and two ounces (57 grams) of ready-to-eat cereal.

Dairy recommendations for 2,000 calories are three servings; a serving is eight ounces of milk (237 milliliters), six ounces (177 milliliters) of yoghurt, or 1.5 ounces (43 grams) of cheese. For protein, five ounces is the daily recommendation. That is equivalent to any one of the following: one hamburger patty; five medium eggs; five tablespoons (177 milliliters) of peanut butter; 2.5 ounces (71 grams) of nuts or seeds; or 1.25 cups (296 milliliters) of cooked beans or pulses.

Using nutritional recommendations can be tricky. MyPlate recommends eating half a plate of FAV and filling the other half with grains and protein, as well as drinking a glass of milk. The recommendations raise several questions: how big is the plate, how big is the glass, how many meals are eaten per day, and what happens if one does not use a plate, or eats from communal dishes?

To get a sense of what MyPlate recommendations are for 2,000 calories, it may be helpful to illustrate what three meals a day might look like:

> Breakfast: banana, 2 oz (57g) of whole grain cereal with 1.2 oz (34 g) of nuts, 1 cup (237 ml) of milk, and coffee or tea
>
> Lunch: 2 slices of whole grain bread, 1 tablespoon (15 ml) of peanut butter, apple, and 1 cup (237 ml) of milk
>
> Dinner: 1 cup (237 ml) of cooked collards, 1 cup (237 ml) of cooked brown rice, ¾ cup (177 ml) of cooked beans/lentils, 2 cups (473 ml) of lettuce, ½ cup (118 ml) of tomato, 6 oz (177 ml) of plain yoghurt, and an orange

If one added salad dressing (73 calories for one tablespoon or 15 milliliters) to the salad and oil to cook the collards (120 calories for one tablespoon or 15 milliliters), these meals would be 1780 calories. Replacing the beans/lentils with four ounces (113 grams) of meat, the calories would increase to 1880. That would allow one to have one serving of wine (five ounces or 148 milliliters) at 123 calories. If instead of wine, one chose a small piece of pie (300 calories) or one four-inch (10 centimeter) diameter chocolate chip cookie (200 calories), one would be over 2,000 calories.

The chances are that your diet looks nothing like this. If you are like 80% of Americans, it is unlikely you eat enough FAV (US DHHS and USDA, 2015). It is also likely that you eat many times the recommended servings of meat. You are truly exceptional if you do not exceed the maximum recommendations for salt and sugar. Furthermore, it is unlikely that you eat three meals a day. You probably snack. Taking a photo every time you eat or drink will make you conscious of just how often you are eating. Indeed, it will likely alter your eating decisions because taking a picture will make you conscious of when you are eating and drinking (Zepeda and Deal, 2008).

When observing others' behaviors, it is clear that Americans do not often eat meals … because they are eating constantly. Eating in America, for many people, used to mean three meals a day, sitting at a table, eating with others, at specific mealtimes. Rather than serving food already plated, people sat at a table with empty plates. Food was often served family-style from serving dishes passed around the table. Table manners involved the use of "please" and "thank you," not taking more than one's share of food, pacing oneself so as not to finish before everyone else, eating with utensils rather than pushing food onto utensils with fingers, and conversing with others at the table, without food in one's mouth. Whether one was religious or not, there was an explicit sense of gratitude about food. Meals were when one ate, and one ate only during meals, therefore, one was generally hungry at mealtimes.

Now there are no boundaries for when or where one eats. Rather than eating at a table with others at specific mealtimes, Americans eat in their cars, they eat at their desks at work, they eat on couches or beds, and they even eat in public bathrooms. Americans eat while distracted: while they drive, while they work, while they look at their phones, or while they are watching entertainment. These behaviors are the norm and they obfuscate how often and what we consume. Without the rituals of meals, we have lost many of the social cues about when, how, how much, and how fast to eat. Instead, we get our cues about serving size, how to eat, and what to eat from businesses making a profit from selling us those foods. They routinely give us twice or more than an actual serving size; for example, a double patty burger is twice the meat recommended per day and will cause one to exceed a 2,000 calorie diet. This resetting of boundaries and social cues when eating has encouraged us to consume more food, more often, and in more places. Add to that the lack of exercise and is it any wonder that Americans are overweight?

After you have completed a 24-hour photo food diary, reflect on what you ate. Why is it that you ate what you did? Frequently, the answer is habit, but how do habits form and how do they change? Habits are simply repetitious behaviors that become familiar and automatic. We do not realize we are creating habits as we form them. Indeed, we are so unaware of our habits that we view others who have different habits as "strange."

Changing our habits requires much the same actions as creating them in the first place: repeat new behaviors until they are familiar and automatic. However, the difference is that if we want to change our habits, we must be conscious of what we are doing and take deliberate action to form new habits. It requires, first, being aware of one's behavior and wanting to change it; second, identifying the steps to take to change one's behavior; third, actually changing one's behavior and monitoring that one is doing so; and fourth, doing the new behaviors long enough that they become automatic and, hence, habits. All of this, of course, is rather difficult to do.

Addiction can teach us something about how to facilitate behavior change. One has to want to change and that usually is precipitated by some sort of consequence or crisis. With food, the motivation might be being overweight, or the associated health consequences, which can be life-threatening. To break an addiction, it helps to remove oneself from the environment that facilitates the addiction and surround oneself with a support group to reinforce behavior change. The problem is, while one can remove oneself from an environment of heroin or alcohol use, one can never remove oneself from food; we need to eat.

However, we can manipulate our food environment to encourage healthier eating. If we do not want to eat certain foods, do not have them around. It is unreasonable for parents to demand that their children do not drink soda or eat sugary cereals if these products are in the home. It is unreasonable to keep candy on one's desk "for others" and expect that you will not eat it. If you do not want to eat something or do not want your children to eat it, do not keep it in the house, do not have it at work, and do not order it when you are out. Whether your support network is your family, co-workers, or friends, for this strategy to work, they must know about it and agree to support it. Thus, having parents with different attitudes to healthy eating is likely to encourage children to be manipulative, pitting one parent against another. What parent has not been outsmarted by their preschooler's devious strategy of divide and conquer?

A more complicated aspect of the food environment is where we get our food. In the US, most of us get our food from grocery stores. If we live in a food desert, we may have few options. Certainly, grocery stores provide better options than convenience stores, but simply because they offer FAV, does not mean they offer fewer unhealthy food options than convenience stores. Walking into a US grocery store, the entrance often takes one through the produce section. The operative word is "through." The produce section is largely decorative. Much of the produce will never be sold; it will be thrown away (FAO, 2011). However, the produce section provides a halo effect; it exudes healthiness, so everything else in the store must be healthy, right? Tellingly, the produce section is a well-lit open space; anyone can see the shoppers as they pick these healthy foods. This section also tends to have wide aisles for easy movement, so one can move quickly to the less well-lit and narrower aisles filled with processed foods. There, one has more privacy to pick out cookies, sodas, and chips. The meats and dairy tend to be at the back, forcing shoppers through the store aisles of processed foods. The checkout line exposes one's purchases to the scrutiny of other shoppers, but that is being replaced by the more private and cost-reducing self-checkout.

The sheer availability and proportion of processed foods in grocery stores mean that it is unlikely that shoppers buy only healthy foods. Access to Nutrition Foundation (2018) analyzed 23,000 packaged products in nine countries; they found 69% had low nutritional quality and only 14% met the WHO EURO nutritional requirements for children. To ensure we buy healthy foods, we need to avoid or buy fewer processed foods. So, let's suppose we manage to fill our refrigerators and cupboards with only healthy foods, creating a healthy food environment in our homes. We still need to prepare these foods. We need a place and the utensils to cook. If we do not have access to a kitchen or do not have the pots and other things to cook with, how can we prepare food? We also need time and skills. Without basic cooking skills, preparing food can seem very time-consuming and daunting. These factors mean that many people buy processed, prepared and take-out foods, and eat out. The sellers of these foods increase their profits by telling us how busy we are, how we deserve a break, and how unreasonable it is for us to cook. However, to control our food environment and to ensure we eat healthy foods, we can save money, save time, and save our lives by cooking.

Exercise: Questions to ask yourself about your 24-hour photo food diary

How much processed food did you eat? How many FAV? How many whole grains, nuts, and seeds? How many servings of sugary drinks, juice, or alcohol did you have? Did you change what you were going to eat because you did not want to photograph it?

Extra credit: Look at your photos again. Are there any clues as to where the foods were from or how they were produced? What land and water resources were embedded in your food? What kind of energy was used to produce, process, transport, and cook your food? What labor was used, and what were their working conditions and pay?

References

Abbott, C. 2018. 10 things to know about the 2018 Farm Bill. Successful Farming, December 27. https://www.agriculture.com/news/business/10-things-to-know-about-the-2018-farm-bill, accessed February 11, 2019.

Access to Nutrition Foundation. 2018. Access to Nutrition Index, 2018. Global Index 2018. www.accesstonutrition.org/index/global.2018, accessed February 14, 2018.

Angadjivand, S. 2018. U.S. Farm Commodity Support: An Overview of Selected Programs. CRS Report, April 17. Congressional Research Service. https://fas.org/sgp/crs/misc/R45165.pdf, accessed February 11, 2019.

Bigelow, D. P. and Borders, A. 2017. Major Uses of Land in the United States, 2012. USDA ERS, Economic Information Bulletin Number 178, August 2017. https://www.ers.usda.gov/webdocs/publications/84880/eib-178.pdf?v=0, accessed February 8, 2019.

Colorado State University. Cooperative Extension and Animal Science. (n.d.) Feeding Market Beef. https://extension.unh.edu/resources/files/Resource002288_Rep3366.pdf, accessed January 31, 2019.

Cushman & Wakefield. 2017. The Global Food & Beverage Market, Summer. http://www.upa.it/static/upload/cw_/cw_global-food-and-beverage-report.pdf, accessed February 4, 2019.

Development Initiatives. 2018. 2018 Global Nutrition Report: Shining a light to spur action on nutrition. Bristol, UK: Development Initiatives. https://globalnutritionreport.org/reports/global-nutrition-report-2018/, accessed February 4, 2019.

FAO. 2003. Livestock commodities. In World Agriculture: towards 2015/2030. http://www.fao.org/docrep/005/y4252e/y4252e05b.htm, accessed January 28, 2019.

FAO. 2011. Global food losses and food waste—Extent, causes and prevention. Rome: Food and Agriculture Organization.

FAO. 2012. Livestock and landscapes. http://www.fao.org/docrep/018/ar591e/ar591e.pdf, accessed January 28, 2019.

FAO. 2019. Animal Production. http://www.fao.org/animal-production/en/, accessed January 28, 2019.

FAO AQUASTAT. 2016. Water withdrawal by sector, around 2010. November. http://www.fao.org/nr/water/aquastat/tables/WorldData-Withdrawal_eng.pdf, accessed February 4, 2019.

FAOSTAT. 2018a. Animal production, 2016. http://www.fao.org/faostat/en/#data/QA), accessed January 28, 2019.

FAOSTAT. 2018b. Value of agricultural production, 2016. Gross production value agriculture, crops, livestock and non-food. http://www.fao.org/faostat/en/#data/QV, accessed February 4, 2019.

Farm Bureau. 2018. Reviewing the 2018 Farm Bill Baseline. December 17. https://www.fb.org/market-intel/reviewing-the-2018-farm-bill-baseline,accessed February 11, 2019.

Farm Policy Facts. 2008. Farmers don't get much bread for that loaf. March 21. https://www.farmpolicyfacts.org/2008/03/farmers-dont-get-much-bread-for-that-loaf/, accessed February 12, 2019

Federal Reserve. 2017. Survey of consumer finances. Table 4. Family net worth, by selected characteristics of families, 1989–2016 surveys (in nominal dollars). October 31. https://www.federalreserve.gov/econres/scfindex.htm, accessed February 6, 2019.

Feeding America. 2018. Facts about poverty and hunger in America. https://www.feedingamerica.org/hunger-in-america/facts, accessed February 12, 2019.

Fryar, C. D., Kruszon-Moran, D., Gu, Q, and Ogden, C. L. 2018. Mean body weight, height, waist circumference, and Body Mass Index among adults: United States, 1999–2000 through 2015–2016. National Health Statistics Reports, Number 122, December 20.
https://www.cdc.gov/nchs/data/nhsr/nhsr122-508.pdf, accessed January 31, 2018.

Gray, A. 2016. Which countries spend the most on food? This map will show you. World Economic Forum. December 7.
https://www.weforum.org/agenda/2016/12/this-map-shows-how-much-each-country-spends-on-food/, accessed February 12, 2019.

Horton, R. 2018. GBD 2017: a fragile world. Lancet, 392(10159), 1683.
https://doi.org/10.1016/S0140-6736(18)32858-7, accessed November 10, 2018.

Khokhar, T. 2017. Chart: Globally, 70% of Freshwater is Used for Agriculture. The World Bank, March 22.
https://blogs.worldbank.org/opendata/chart-globally-70-freshwater-used-agriculture, accessed February 4, 2019.

Mekonnen, M. M. and Hoekstra, A. Y. 2012. A global assessment of the water footprint of farm animal products. Ecosystems, 15, 401–415. doi: 10.1007/s10021-011-9517-8.
https://waterfootprint.org/media/downloads/Mekonnen-Hoekstra-2012-WaterFootprintFarmAnimalProducts_1.pdf, accessed February 4, 2019.

OECD/FAO. 2018. OECD-FAO Agricultural Outlook 2018-2027. Paris: OECD Publishing and Rome: Food and Agriculture Organization. doi: 10.1787/agr_outlook-2018-en.

Peters, C. J., Picardy, J. A., Darrouzet-Nardi, A., and Griffin, T. S. 2014. Feed conversions, ration compositions, and land use efficiencies of major livestock products in US agricultural systems. Agricultural Systems, 130, 35–43.

PR Newswire. 2018. Food and Beverages, Global Market Report 2018, February 22. https://www.prnewswire.com/news-releases/food-and-beverages-global-market-report-2018-300602932.html,
accessed February 4, 2019.

Ritchie, H. and Roser, M. 2017. Meat and seafood production and consumption. https://ourworldindata.org/meat-and-seafood-production-consumption, accessed February 4, 2019.

Roser, M. and Ritchie, H. 2018. Yields and land use in agriculture. https://ourworldindata.org/yields-and-land-use-in-agriculture, accessed February 4, 2019.

Unnevehr, L. 2017. Economic contribution of the food and beverage industry. Committee for Economic Development of The Conference Board. https://www.ced.org/pdf/Economic_Contribution_of_the_Food_and_Beverage_Industry.pdf, accessed February 4, 2019.

US BLS. 2018. Table 1101. Quintiles of income before taxes: Annual expenditure means, shares, standard errors, and coefficients of variation, Consumer Expenditure Survey, 2017. September. https://www.bls.gov/cex/2017/combined/quintile.pdf, accessed February 6, 2019.

US Census Bureau. 2018a. American Fact Finder. 2012 Economic census, all sectors, economy wide key statistics. Released April 19. https://factfinder.census.gov/faces/nav/jsf/pages/download_center.xhtml, accessed February 7, 2019.

US Census Bureau. 2018b. Advance monthly sales for retail and food services, November 2018. https://www.census.gov/retail/marts/www/marts_current.pdf, accessed February 7, 2019.

US Census Bureau. 2019. Business and industry. Monthly wholesale trade: Sales and inventories. 4244: Grocery and related products: US total not seasonally adjusted sales. February 1. https://www.census.gov/econ/currentdata/dbsearch?program=MWTS&startYear=2018&endYear=2019&categories%5B%5D=4244&dataType=SM&geoLevel=US&adjusted=1&notAdjusted=1&submit=GET+DATA&releaseScheduleId=, accessed February 13, 2019.

USDA. 2018. Choose MyPlate.gov. August 10. https://www.choosemyplate.gov/protein-foods, accessed February 12, 2019.

USDA ERS. 2018a. Food availability (per capita) data system. Red meat, poultry, and fish October 29. https://www.ers.usda.gov/data-products/food-availability-per-capita-data-system/, accessed January 31, 2019.

USDA ERS. 2018b. Cash receipts by commodity, 2010-2018F. Nominal (current dollars). https://data.ers.usda.gov/reports.aspx?ID=17845, accessed February 4, 2019.

USDA ERS 2018c. Principal farm operator household finances, 2013-18F. November 30. https://www.ers.usda.gov/data-products/farm-household-income-and-characteristics/, accessed February 6, 2019.

USDA ERS. 2018d. Farm income and wealth statistics, net cash income. November 30. https://data.ers.usda.gov/reports.aspx?ID=17831, accessed February 8, 2019.

USDA FAS. 2018. World Agricultural ProductionWAP12-18. December, pp 15, 17, 22, 24.
https://apps.fas.usda.gov/psdonline/circulars/production.pdf, accessed December 18, 2018.

USDA FAS. 2018b. US agricultural exports 2017.
https://www.fas.usda.gov/data/top-us-agricultural-exports-2017, accessed February 12, 2019.

USDA FNS. 2018. Supplemental Nutrition Assistance Program (SNAP). Participation and costs. December 7.
https://fns-prod.azureedge.net/sites/default/files/pd/SNAPsummary.pdf, accessed February 12, 2019.

US Department of Health and Human Services and US Department of Agriculture. 2015. 2015–2020 Dietary Guidelines for Americans. 8th Edition. December. http://health.gov/dietaryguidelines/2015/guidelines/, accessed February 13, 2019.

US Department of Labor. 2006. 100 years of US consumer spending. Report 991. May. https://www.bls.gov/opub/100-years-of-u-s-consumer-spending.pdf, accessed February 12, 2019.

World Bank. 2017. Table 4.2 World development indicators: Structure of output. http://wdi.worldbank.org/table/4.2, accessed February 4, 2019.

World Bank. 2019a. GDP (current US $).
https://data.worldbank.org/indicator/NY.GDP.MKTP.CD,
accessed February 4, 2019.

World Bank. 2019b. Agriculture, forestry, and fishing, value added (% of GDP). https://data.worldbank.org/indicator/NV.AGR.TOTL.ZS, accessed February 4, 2019.

World Food Programme. 2013. What causes hunger? November 5. https://www.wfp.org/stories/what-causes-hunger, accessed February 4, 2019.

World Hunger. 2018. 2018 World hunger and poverty facts and statistics. Hunger note. https://www.worldhunger.org/world-hunger-and-poverty-facts-and-statistics/#produce1, accessed February 4, 2019.

Zepeda, L. and Deal, D. 2008. Think before you eat: photographic food diaries as intervention tools to change dietary decision-making and attitudes. International Journal of Consumer Studies, 32, 692–698.

CHAPTER THREE

HOW DID WE GET HERE?

A brief history of US agricultural policy

To understand our current food system, it is useful to examine the policies that created it. US agricultural policy has its roots in colonial policies that were based on an abundance of land, a shortage of labor, wealth transfers to the rich, and export crops. Britain hoped to find gold and silver in the American colonies. However, the only resource it found in abundance to compensate investors in the Virginia Company was agricultural land to grow tobacco for export (Grymes, 2018). Tobacco was the main export crop of the American colonies during the 17th and 18th centuries, and after independence (Spielmaker, 2018).

The chronic shortage of labor influenced legislation and contracts to secure indentured servants and slaves in the Southern colonies (Grymes, 2018). Attempts to subjugate the indigenous peoples as slaves failed. Instead, the northern colonies secured labor through contracts with Europeans that granted skilled laborers land and restricted their ability to work for others, and through wage legislation that attempted to limit wages (US Labor Bureau, 1934). During the 17th century, the shortage of labor to cultivate land was so acute that, 50, then 100 acres (20, then 40 hectares) were granted to landowners for each person they brought to the colonies, whether an indentured servant or slave (Grymes, 2018). However, land was not granted to those working the land unless they were able to pay their own passage to the colonies. Some indentured servants who had completed their servitude were granted small parcels of three acres to encourage them to stay in the colonies.

During the War of Independence, the Continental Congress, strapped for cash and unable to pay soldiers, granted land for service in the Continental Army (Spielmaker, 2018). After independence, the Land Ordinance of 1785 standardized land surveys and the sale of public lands was viewed as a way for the US government to raise money (US National Archives and Records

Administration, 2016). However, the minimum sale size of 640 acres (259 hectares) at US$ 2 an acre (Spielmaker, 2018) was too costly and required too much labor for a typical American. For example, the highest wage for agricultural laborers in 1785 was 46 cents a day (Wright, 1889) and laborers were often paid in kind with lodging and food, making it impossible for a laborer to accumulate the cash to purchase these land tracts. The sizes of the tracts for sale were enormous by the standards of the day. As a point of comparison, in England, even though farm size increased dramatically in the 18th and 19th centuries, 71% of farms in1885 were under 50 acres (20 hectares) (Beckett, 1983). Labor during the 18th and early 19th centuries was largely unskilled and unaided by machinery, with only crude tools (Wright, 1889). Thus, 640 acres (259 hectares) was absolutely impossible for a family to farm by itself; it could only be farmed if one had additional labor. Since indentured servitude largely ended in America with the American Revolution (Guasco, 2011), and hired labor was considered costly (Morris, 1976), this meant these tracts of land were either meant for speculation and sale, or if farmed, were intended to be done so using slaves. Hence, the Land Ordinance of 1785 was a means for the wealthy to become wealthier and to encourage the use of slave labor.

Looking at how agricultural land was used, in the late 18th century, New England largely consisted of small family farms dedicated to subsistence agriculture (Morris, 1976). Cash crops were grown in the southern states, where landholdings were large, and slave labor dominated. In 1790, tobacco was the most important export crop, valued at over US$ 4 million, comprising 44% of US exports (Spielmaker, 2018). Tobacco and cotton were grown almost exclusively for export; three-quarters of the tobacco crop was exported in 1810 and 80% of the cotton crop was exported in the 1830s (Lipsey, 1993). By 1803, the value of cotton exports surpassed tobacco, but the value of cotton and tobacco as a proportion of US exports increased throughout the 19th century until 1860, when they were almost 60% of the value of all US exports (Lipsey, 1994). Thus, the economy of the nascent US was oriented to creating large agricultural holdings to grow cash crops for export.

Despite independence, one of America's largest trading partners continued to be Britain. Trade between the US and Britain increased after the abolition of the Corn Laws in the UK in 1846. The results of the Corn Laws were that Britain's production of wheat, barley, and wool fell by half, five million hectares of farmland were converted to pasture and heath, farm incomes fell by one-third, agricultural wages fell, and rural areas lost their population

(Mazoyer and Roudart, 2006). As a result, Britain became increasingly dependent on food imports and remains so today. During the latter half of the 19th century, about half of all US exports went to the UK (Lipsey, 1994), with the proportion of grains and meat increasing vis-à-vis cotton. Taking a different approach than Britain to the availability of cheap grain, Denmark and the Netherlands used imported grain as feed to specialize in producing higher-value meat and dairy products for export (Mazoyer and Roudart, 2006).

Back in the US, the role of the federal government in distributing land to the wealthy was codified in the 1796 Public Land Act; it authorized federal government sales of a minimum size of 640 acres (259 hectares) of public land at US$ 2 per acre (less than US$ 5 per hectare) (Spielmaker, 2018). Clearly, the size of the minimum sale excluded all but the very wealthy from purchasing public land because only the very wealthy had US$ 1,280 to purchase even the minimum land allotment. It created a class of wealthy landowners in need of agricultural labor to work these vast lands. Thus, early US policies did much to foster slavery, and expansionist policies acquired land from indigenous peoples to further benefit the wealthy. These land sales were used to raise money for the federal government to fund such activities as armies to take land from the indigenous peoples or other nations so that it could be sold to wealthy people who had cash.

Faced with a surplus of public land and a need for cash, in 1800, the federal government halved the minimum land sale to 320 acres (129 hectares) at US$ 1.25 per acre, payable in four installments; these conditions remained in effect until 1854 (US National Archives and Records Administration, 2016). A free laborer made an average of 42 cents a day in 1800, climbing to between US$ 0.75 to US$ 1 a day in 1835 (Wright, 1889). However, given that in 1833, a household of three people spent 46% of their income on food (Cummings, 1940), four installments of US$ 100 were far more than an average worker could afford. The wealthy and speculators could afford to buy the best land, leaving marginal lands unsold. Therefore, in 1854, the federal government reduced the price of land, unsold for at least 30 years, to 12.5 cents per acre (less than 31 US cents per hectare) (US National Archives and Records Administration, 2016).

After the war with Mexico (1846-48), which resulted in the acquisition of 525,000 square miles (about 1.36 million square kilometers) of new territory (History.com editors, 2019), there was pressure to open up the acquired lands to homesteading (US National Archives and Records

Administration, 2016) to populate them with US citizens, and to displace the native peoples and Mexicans living there. The House of Representatives passed homesteading legislation in 1852, 1854, and 1859, but each time it was defeated by the Senate. Eastern Senators opposed homesteading as they feared that they would lose scarce labor because their workers would move to the new territories, making wages rise. Southern Senators opposed homesteading as they feared that small farmers in the new territories would compete with slave plantations, thus cutting into their profits. Finally, in 1860, both the House and Senate passed homesteading legislation, but it was vetoed by President Buchanan. The Homestead Act finally passed in 1862 during the Civil War, under President Lincoln.

The Homestead Act of 1862 granted 160 acres (64.7 hectares) of public land to a head of household, a 21-year-old person, or a US veteran, who was a US citizen or intended to become a US citizen, and had never fought against the US (USDA, National Agricultural Library, 1862). The Act required the homesteader to register their claim, pay US$ 10, and state they would cultivate the land for themselves and not others. To protect homesteaders from opportunists who might target them for unscrupulous loans, the claims could not be used to secure loans. Homesteaders received the title to their land only after five years of continuous residence, during which time they were obliged to cultivate crops. They had the option of purchasing the land at US$ 1.25 per acre (about US$ 3 a hectare) after six months of residence.

While the intent of the Homestead Act was to grant land to the average American household, few could afford the cost of the tools, seed, animals, travel, and also the living expenses until the first crop could be sold. In many cases, land needed to be cleared before one could even plant. Of the 500 million acres (202 million hectares) of land dispersed by 1904, 84% went to speculators, railways, cattlemen, miners, and lumbermen (Our Documents, n.d.). Only 80 million acres (32.4 million hectares) went to homesteaders by 1900 (Library of Congress, 2018). So, while the Homestead Act did increase access to land and the number of farmers in the US, it did much more to enhance the wealth of the already wealthy during the 19th century.

Contrary to popular belief about pioneers in the US, more than twice as much land went to individuals under the Homestead Act after 1900 as before; an additional 190 million acres (almost 77 million hectares) was granted by 1934. The Homestead Act was not repealed in the lower 48 states until 1976 and in Alaska until 1986, under the 1976 Federal Land Policy and Management Act (US National Archives and Records Administration, 2016).

During the 19th century, agricultural products continued to dominate US exports. In 1800, agricultural exports made up 75% of all US exports; they were valued at US$ 23 million (Spielmaker, 2018). By 1810, they were valued at US$ 40 million and made up 87% of the value of all US exports. By 1810, cotton had replaced tobacco as the most important export. By the start of the Civil War in 1860, agricultural exports were US$ 189 million, or 81% of all US exports, and cotton alone made up 54% of all US exports. Slaves were used to produce cotton in the South prior to the Civil War. When slavery was abolished, sharecropping replaced slavery in the South. The conditions of sharecropping kept African Americans in abject poverty and also kept agricultural exports flowing. Agriculture continued to dominate America's exports; by the end of the 19th century, it represented US$ 703 million per year or 71% of all exports. Agricultural exports continued to climb in value throughout the 20th century to US$ 48 billion a year, but fell proportionately to 9.5% of all exports.

Three other key pieces of legislation had important impacts on US agriculture by providing the resources and funding to support agricultural education, research, and extension. In 1862, the Morrill Act granted public lands to agricultural colleges (Spielmaker, 2018). It permitted the sale of millions of acres of public land to fund higher education and led to the founding of 69 universities in the US (Peshek, 2018). A second Morrill Act provided land grants to African American colleges in 1890 (Spielmaker, 2018). The 1887 Hatch Act established experiment stations to conduct agricultural research at these 1862 (and later 1890) institutions. Taken together, this legislation was instrumental in creating the US public higher education, research, and extension system that exists today. These public universities and experiment stations developed new technologies, new seeds and breeds, new production systems, and introduced management systems that increased the productivity and yield of American agriculture. In response to continued labor shortages, they focused on ways to mechanize agriculture. This included developing breeds of crops and animals suitable for mechanization, and practices to intensify production that favored chemical inputs, monocultures, and larger farms.

In the early 20th century, American farmers benefitted from high commodity prices due to WWI (Heiligenstein, 2014). Cotton was still a quarter of the value of US exports, but tobacco had fallen to 2%, while meat and grains/flour had climbed to about a quarter of all exports (Lipsey, 1993). However, commodity prices fell during the 1920s and hit rock bottom in 1932 during the Depression (Heiligenstein, 2014). This led to the demand for a policy response to aid farmers.

Thus, the first US Farm Bill was passed in 1933 to assist American farmers by raising commodity prices and setting production limits. Essentially, before 1934, the federal government subsidized agricultural production through granting land; with the first Farm Bill in 1933, it subsidized agriculture directly by paying farmers for specific crops (Farm Policy Facts, 2018). In addition, between 1939 and 1943, the Department of Agriculture stimulated demand to keep commodity prices up by implementing a food stamp program; the program also rid the government of surplus food by giving it to hungry Americans (Heiligenstein, 2014). This idea was revived in the 1960s and codified in the 1964 Food Stamp Act. However, it was not until the 1977 Food and Agriculture Act that food stamps became part of the US Farm Bill.

From the 1960s through the 1980s, an important component of the US Farm Bills was using surplus commodities for the poor in the US, as aid to developing countries, and as an in-kind incentive to promote trade to develop markets. To address the huge agricultural commodity surpluses and low commodity prices, the 1985 Farm Bill introduced payments to farmers to not grow crops under the guise of conservation with the Conservation Reserve Program and the Wetlands Reserve Program (Farm Policy Facts, 2018). The 1996 Farm Bill attempted to remove subsidies paid to farmers, but a drop in commodity prices led to legislation (1998-99) for emergency assistance to farmers (Spielmaker, 2018). Subsequent Farm Bills continue to pay farmers to not grow crops on marginal lands through conservation programs. They also provide farmers with crop insurance, and provide subsidies for corn (maize), soybeans, wheat, rice, cotton, peanuts, oats, barley, sorghum, and oilseeds.

In FY 2016, 71% of the US$ 6.9 billion cost of the two commodity support programs went on subsidizing corn (43.3%) and wheat (27.7%) (Angadjivand, 2018). Corn is largely used as an animal feed, while wheat is eaten by humans. However, a large portion of both crops is exported. Hence, the US farm programs subsidize agricultural exports. In addition, government subsidies to farmers make up an important part of their income. In 2018, US government payments to farmers represented 17% of all farm income (USDA ERS, 2018).

The incorporation of the food stamp program into the Farm Bill in 1977 ensured that there was support from members of Congress across the US. While a handful of states received most of the farm subsidies, every state had hungry people. Over time, the size of the food stamp program grew as a proportion of the Farm Bill. In 2002, the Farm Bill expanded the food stamp program dramatically (Heiligenstein, 2014). This filled a vital gap in addressing poverty because there had been severe cuts in the welfare system in the 1990s. The war on poverty in the 1960s turned into a war on the poor in the 1990s. Providing money to the poor was politically unpopular, but providing money that could only be spent on food to bolster demand for agricultural products was politically desirable. It provided cover for farm subsidies.

As a result of changes to the 2002 Farm Bill, spending on these nutrition programs went from US$ 17 billion in 2000 to US$ 38 billion in 2008, and recipients rose to 28 million people. The financial crisis of 2008 led to even more recipients of government food assistance: 45 million in 2011 and costs rose to US$ 80 billion in 2013 (Heiligenstein, 2014). Despite a financial recovery, in 2018 there were still 40 million food assistance recipients, or about 12% of the population, averaging payments of US$ 125 a month (USDA FNS, 2018). Nutrition programs were estimated to cost just over US$ 65 billion per year making up 76% of the costs of the 2018 Farm Bill (Farm Bureau, 2018). However, costs are expected to be higher because of the pandemic; by April 2020, SNAP recipients surged to nearly 43 million (USDA FNS, 2020).

The sheer size of the nutrition programs does much to dwarf the costs of farm subsidies and to divert attention from farmers to food assistance recipients. As such, those wishing to reduce the costs of the Farm Bill focus on restricting access or reducing benefits to nutrition programs. Yet even though food has never been more plentiful or cheaper than it is currently in the US, one in eight Americans relies on federal nutrition programs. So, while agricultural policy has fostered the production of cheap food and promoted food aid for the poor, it has not addressed the problem of poverty. With the numbers of people eligible for nutrition programs in the US rising during the 21st century, the cost of the Farm Bill will become increasingly more expensive. This focuses attention on cutting benefits or eligibility for nutrition program recipients rather than the agricultural programs that have subsidized a food system that leaves many Americans hungry and unhealthy.

The rise of the international agro-food industry in the 19th century

Prior to the rise of the agro-food industry, US diets were largely based on wheat and salted, cured meats. Produce was only available seasonally. People did not live long enough to experience many of the food-related illnesses we encounter today because life expectancy was low. Data from Massachusetts, the only state that apparently kept statistics during this period, indicated that life expectancy in 1789 for men was 34.5 years and 36.5 years for women (US Bureau of Census, 1949). Life expectancy in Massachusetts increased by about ten years over the 19th century, reaching 44.1 years for men and 46.6 years for women by 1893-97.

The 19th-century diet was limited because there were few means of preserving foods. Historically, processing food is as ancient as cooking, fermentation, and preservation methods like drying and salting. Processed foods produced high-value products from perishable commodities, making food palatable, digestible, and storable. Processed foods, like oil, wine, and garum, as well as grains, have been traded locally and extensively for millennia, but it was not until the 19th century that industrial food processing began.

The agro-food industry was stimulated by new technologies in the 19th century to preserve foods. Both canning and refrigeration allowed diets in the US to include more varied and fresh foods all year round. Canning was developed in response to Napoleon Bonaparte's offer of 12,000 francs in 1795 for food preservation ideas to feed his army. Nicolas Appert won the prize in 1810 for inventing canning (Everts, 2013). In Britain, Peter Durand obtained a patent by modifying Appert's approach; he used tin cans rather than glass jars sealed with corks.

As canning became widespread during the 19th century, so did food poisoning. To allay consumers' fears, branding became a way to assure quality (Toops, 2017). Brands had been used for beverage products, like tea, chocolate, and whiskey, as well as flour in the 18th century for quality assurance and product differentiation (Table 3.1). Branding of canned goods took off in the 1850s in the US and was used to sell canned condensed milk, condiments and vegetables, and later meats and ground coffee. Concerns about food poisoning led some brands to take extreme measures to assure their customers that their food was safe; the Heinz company advertised that it required its workers to have weekly manicures, regular showers, and to change their underwear, as measures to reduce contamination of food (Everts, 2013).

Along with canning, refrigeration assisted in the development of the agro-food industry during the 19th century. While ice had been used for centuries, it started being used widely to transport fresh food in the US in 1830 (Krasner-Khait, 2000). Initially, natural ice was harvested to cool shipments of fresh foods in ships and later rail cars. Ice-cooled rail cars were used widely to transport dairy products, starting in the 1840s. Beer brands emerged in the US in the mid-19th century (Table 3.1). The sheer demand for natural ice led to the use of contaminated ice and a search for a way to find a cheaper and cleaner alternative. Mechanical refrigeration was introduced commercially in brewing in the 1870s and in meatpacking in the 1880s in the US. The high cost of mechanical refrigeration equipment fostered the concentration of both meatpacking and brewing, causing large brands to dominate both industries in the US. The first mechanically refrigerated ship, the SS Dunedin, transported meat and dairy products from New Zealand in 1882 (Hueston and McLeod, 2012). Refrigeration facilitated exports of meat to Europe, creating new markets for distant farmers. Also, during the 1880s, household iceboxes started being used in homes in US cities (Krasner-Khait, 2000), allowing Americans to diversify their diet with fresh foods.

Both canning and refrigeration facilitated branding as well as the concentration of food companies. The cost of mechanical refrigeration was a barrier to small companies, resulting in branded refrigerated products with large market shares. Branding of canned foods helped with quality assurance, allowing companies to increase their market share. In the late 19th century, emerging food brands included meats, beverages, snacks, and sweets. As a result, over the 19th century, American diets transformed from a few commodities, often self-provisioned, to a diet that included many branded, highly processed foods.

Table 3.1 18th- and 19th-century food and beverage brands.

Year	Brand	Where	Product(s)
1706	Twinings	London, UK	tea
1764	Baker's Chocolate	Dorcester, MA	imported cacao for chocolate
1780	Laird's & Co.	Scobeyville, NJ	distillery for apple jack
1790	Arthur's Flour	Boston, MA	imported English flour
1795	Jim Beam	Kentucky	bourbon whiskey
1824	Cadbury	Birmingham, UK	tea, coffee, chocolate, candy
1844	Pabst	Milwaukee, WI	beer
1852	Anheuser-Busch	St. Louis, MO	beer
1853	Keebler	Philadelphia, PA	bakery, biscuits, cookies
1857	Borden	Connecticut	condensed milk
1859	Heinz	Pittsburg, PA	condiments, sauerkraut
1867	Armour	Chicago, IL	meatpacking
1868	Tabasco	Avery Island, LA	hot sauce
1869	Campbell's	Camden, NJ	vegetable, condiments, soup, jellies, meats
1872	Pillsbury	Minneapolis, MN	flour
1872	Folgers	San Francisco, CA	coffee
1875	Swift	Chicago, IL	meatpacking
1877	Quaker oats	Akron, OH	breakfast cereal
1883	Oscar Meyer	Chicago, IL	cured meat, sausages
1886	Coca-Cola	Atlanta, GA	cocaine-laced beverages
1886	Hershey's	Philadelphia, PA	caramels, chocolate
1887	Cudahy	Omaha, NE	meatpacking
1889	Aunt Jemima	St. Louis, MO	pancake mix
1897	Jell-O	Leroy, NY	gelatin desserts
1898	Nabisco	Chicago, IL	biscuits, cookies, crackers
1898	Pepsi-Cola	New Bern, NC	beverages

Sources: Anheuser-Busch, 2016; Borden, 2019; Chicago Historical Society, 2005; Halloran, 2013; Jitchotvisut, 2018; Leffler, 2018; Myers, 2015; Quaker Oats Company, 2019; The Pepsi Store, n.d.; Yehia, 2014.

Brands in the 20th century

While brands existed during the 19th century, they grew to dominate the food people ate during the 20th century. New products and brands were developed, and food companies began consolidating. At the beginning of the 20th century, Kellogg's and Post marketed breakfast cereals as healthy alternatives to the typical meat-laden breakfasts of the day (Toops, 2017). Meanwhile, J. L. Kraft started selling cheese in Chicago in 1903, and by 1916, had patented a way to re-pasteurize cheddar cheese scraps, selling canned processed cheese (Clark, 2009). By 1930, Kraft sold 40% of the cheese Americans ate. Gone were the days of homemade or locally made cheese.

Refrigerated rail cars also started being used to transport produce from around the US. In 1910, refrigerated rail cars were used to transport iceberg lettuce from California to the East Coast, not because iceberg lettuce was tasty, but because it traveled well (Everts, 2013). Iceberg lettuce replaced local butter and leaf lettuce that were only available on the East coast during spring. Frozen fruits and vegetables were also marketed, but they tended to be mushy and unappetizing. Flash freezing, which preserved the flavor and texture of foods, was not invented until the 1920s. Refrigerators began to appear in homes in the US. However, frozen food sales did not expand until after World War II, when freezers became common in American grocery stores and homes (Schlosser, 2002).

By 1920, ethnic food brands emerged in the US: Italian pasta and Mexican and Chinese food brands (Table 3.2). During the 1920s, homes in the US began to have refrigerators and gas or electric stoves. Techniques like flash freezing made frozen foods available and cellophane was used to pre-package meat. Commercial baby food and pre-sliced bread were introduced (Toops, 2017). The 1920s saw processed foods take off, as well as national branding for commodities like butter. The products were varied and brands tended to be upscale, appealing to households with growing incomes. In contrast, during the Depression, candy, snacks, and quick meals like canned soup dominated the new brands.

Table 3.2 Food brands introduced in the US between 1900 and 1979.

1900s	Kellogg's corn flakes, Post Toasties, Wesson oil, Karo corn syrup, French's mustard, Dr. Pepper, Ovaltine, Canada Dry ginger ale, Barnum's animal crackers, Planter's nuts, Hershey's kisses
1910s	Crisco shortening, Mazola corn oil, Domino sugar, Ocean Spray cranberry sauce, Hellmann's mayonnaise, Whitman sampler chocolate candies, Del Monte canned fruits and vegetables, Ronzoni pasta, Old El Paso Mexican foods, Oreo cookies

1920s	La Choy Chinese foods, Eskimo Pies, Wonder Bread, Baby Ruth, Betty Crocker mixes, Land O'Lakes butter, Girl Scout cookies, Wheaties, Lifesavers, Gummi bears, Welch's grape jelly, Reese's Peanut Butter Cups, Birdseye frozen food, Gerber baby food, Rice Krispies, Peter Pan peanut butter, Progresso canned foods, Kool-aid drink powder, Oscar Meier wieners, Twizzlers licorice
1930s	Hostess Twinkies, Mott's apple sauce, Snickers, Kit Kat bars, Bisquick baking mix, Fritos, Skippy peanut butter, Nestle Toll House chocolate chips, Campbell's chicken noodle soup, Kraft Miracle Whip, Ritz crackers, Goya foods, Kraft Macaroni & Cheese, Ragu spaghetti sauce, Lay's potato chips, Spam, Nescafe
1940s	M&Ms candies, Cheerios cereal, Chiquita bananas, Reddi-Whip, Nestle Quik chocolate powder, V-8 vegetable juice, Kraft sliced American cheese, Sara Lee cheesecake
1950s	Sugar Pops, Minute Rice, Ore-Ida frozen potato products, Cheeze Whiz, Tropicana frozen juice, Sugar Frosted Flakes, Mrs. Paul's Fish Sticks, Sugar Smacks, Swanson's TV Dinners, Pepperidge Farm cookies, Eggo frozen waffles, Trix, Stouffer's frozen meals, Butterball Turkeys, Marshmallow Peeps, TreeSweet juices, Pam cooking spray, Tang breakfast drink, Rice-A-Roni, Cocoa Puffs
1960s	Total cereal, Green Giant frozen peas, Pop-Tarts, Carnation Instant Breakfast, Lucky Charms, Shake 'n Bake meat coating, Cool Whip, Apple Jacks, SpaghettiOs, Diet Pepsi, Doritos, Frosted Mini-Wheats, Pringles chips
1970s	Hamburger Helper, Celestial Seasonings tea, Stove Top stuffing, Cup of Noodles, Miller Lite beer, Country Time lemonade, Pop Rocks, Twix candy, Ben & Jerry's ice cream, Reese's Pieces

Source: Olver, 2000.

Between 1942 and 1947, the US rationed food to divert it to the military (Olver, 2000). While civilians were asked to cut back on their food purchases and grow Victory gardens, food processors focused their attention on lucrative military food contracts. Meatpacking companies, Armour and Swift, had contracts with the US military to develop food rations for soldiers that incorporated their products, while Kraft worked with the military to develop a spread made of butter and hydrogenated oil, and later butter and cheese (Risch, 1995). The US military also purchased large amounts of canned, frozen, and dehydrated foods. Approximately one billion rations costing about US$ 675 million were purchased by the US military during WWII (Koehler, 1958). Companies like Heinz, Nescafe, Wrigley's, and Dentyne had contracts to supply the ingredients for the US military rations (Beranty, 2018). In 1944, 90% of Hormel's canned foods, including the iconic Spam, was purchased by the US government (Hormel Foods, 2019), while billionaire, J. R. Simplot, began his potato empire by selling dehydrated potatoes to the military (Schlosser, 2002).

WWII also gave us aluminum foil and the accidental discovery of cooking with microwaves by the military contractor, Raytheon (Toops 2017). Through food ration contracts with agro-industrial companies, the US military did much to develop and finance the technology that transformed the American diet. With an eye to getting lightweight foods to soldiers, the military bought dehydrated potatoes, converted rice, canned meats like Spam, and frozen foods where possible, to replace cans that used the metal needed for armaments. Food companies built a huge manufacturing and supply chain capacity to supply the US military, and after WWII, they turned their attention to civilian consumers. They marketed the foods they had developed for the military. Thus, consumers were inundated with dehydrated, frozen, instant, and boil-in-a-bag foods during the 1950s (Table 3.2). Innovative food packaging was also a product of the military's efforts to feed soldiers. So, after WWII, there was also an increase in the amount and variety of food packaging. The dehydrated, instant, and frozen foods all required packaging. In addition, new packaging was used for familiar products; aluminum cans were introduced to replace metal and glass, and disposable plastic was used for milk instead of reusable glass (Toops, 2017). With the cessation of rationing after WWII, meat and dairy consumption in the US took off, along with the consumption of baked goods. Television became increasingly central to the American home; two-thirds of American families watched TV during dinner (Toops, 2017). TV dinners and other heat-and-eat foods were developed. Meals became something you did while watching TV, and shows were used to market the very brands people ate while watching TV. New brands of sugary cereals were developed and advertised during children's shows. Most of the cereal brands launched during the 1950s aimed at children had names that bragged about their main ingredient: Sugar Pops, Sugar Frosted Flakes, Sugar Smacks, Trix, and Cocoa Puffs (Table 3.2).

Sugary cereals aimed at children continued to be launched during the 1960s: Lucky Charms, Captain Crunch, Apple Jacks, and Frosted Mini-Wheats

(Table 3.2). Companies also developed and promoted sugary breakfast alternatives to cereal: Pop-Tarts and Carnation instant breakfast. Savory snacks and convenience foods also dominated the food offerings in the 1960s. The 1970s saw the beginning of an era of divergent new food offerings as a glimmer of consciousness seemed to arise about the need for healthier foods. On the one hand, natural brands began to emerge, as well as generic brands to address the economic crisis, and low-calorie beer and other foods to address weight gain. On the other hand, convenience foods to create meals, and a new wave of candy bars were also prominent (Olver, 2000).

The 1980s also gave us contrasting choices: Nouvelle Cuisine, Jell-O pudding pops, Boboli pizza crusts, Healthy Choice frozen dinners, and salad in a bag (Olver, 2000). By the 1990s, the American public began to take note that people were getting fatter. So, brands tried to convince us that we could eat healthier versions of junk food: fat-free Snackwell cookies, Turkey bacon, Lay's baked potato chips, and fat-free Pringles.

By the 2000s, an obesity crisis was declared. The response has been a variety of "miracle" diets, the media insisting that we did not know why people were getting fatter, and a continued rise in obesity and being overweight. Meanwhile, US grocery stores stock over 40,000 different items, almost all of which are highly processed, even though individual shoppers buy no more than 150 items. Over 10,000 new products were being introduced each year in the US during the 2000s, and 90% failed (Toops, 2017). Among the new innovations were utensil-less foods, like yoghurt in a tube. The introduction of foods to speed up eating by dispensing with utensils seems like a strategy that at best could be viewed as being tone-deaf to the obesity crisis.

The consolidation of food and beverage companies

The money to be made through the successful branding of processed foods was reflected in the consolidation of food companies. Throughout the 20th and 21st centuries, food companies merged and successful brands were acquired to create larger and larger companies. Currently, the largest food corporation in the world is Nestle, with annual sales in excess of US$ 90 billion a year (Table 3.3). Nestle has grown continuously through mergers and acquisitions since it was founded in 1867 by Henri Nestle in Switzerland to create formulas for infants (Nestle, n.d.). In 1905, Nestle merged with the Anglo-Swiss Condensed Milk Company. In the 1920s,

Nestle started making chocolates and powdered drinks, and in the 1930s, Nescafe and Nestea. After WWII, Nestle began to diversify into a wide variety of food products. It started by merging with the Swiss soup and flavoring company, Alimentana S. A., which owned the Maggi brand. In 1960, Nestle acquired the British food company, Cross & Blackwell, the Swedish Findus frozen foods company in 1962, American canned foods company, Libby's, in 1970, and American dairy products company, Carnation, in 1980. After 1990, Nestle acquired San Pellegrino water, the British Spillers pet foods, American pet food company, Ralston Purina, and several ice cream and frozen food brands. Nestle brands include numerous candy brands, e.g., Baby Ruth, Kit Kat, Butter Finger, Sweet Tarts, Laffy Taffy and Nerds, as well as baby formula and baby food brands like Gerber, pet foods, ice cream brands like Dreyer's, premium water like Perrier, coffee brands like Taster's Choice, and meal and snack brands like Nesquik, Power Bars, Hot Pockets, DiGiorno, Stouffers, and Jenny Craig. Most consumers are unaware that many of the brands they buy are in fact Nestle brands.

Table 3.3 Top food and beverage companies, 2018 earnings (billion US$).

Parent Company	US$	Selected Brands, Commodities
Nestle (Swiss)	91.4	candies, coffees, Gerber, Hot Pockets, Perrier, Stouffer's
PepsiCo (US)	64.7	sodas, Quaker Oats, Cheetos, Tropicana, Aunt Jemima
ADM (US)	64.3	Flours, grains, beans, oils, sweeteners, feed, ethanol
Unilever (UK, Dutch)	62.7	Lipton, Hellman's, Skippy, margarine, Ben & Jerry's
Anheuser-Busch InBev (BE)	55	Becks, Budweiser, Michelob, Rolling Rock, 100+ other
JBS (Brazil)	51.5	Swift, Cargill Pork, Tyson in Brazil and Mexico, Moy Park
Tyson (US)	40.1	Jimmy Dean, Ball Park, Hillshire Farms, IBP, pizza
Mars (US)	35	candies, Wrigley, Uncle Ben's rice
Coca-Cola (US)	31.9	sodas, bottled teas, bottled waters
Heineken (Dutch)	30.4	Amstel, Red Stripe, Lagunitas, Tecate, Sol, Moretti, Tiger
Danone (France)	27.9	Yoplait, other yoghurts, bottled waters

Mondelez (US)	25.9	Cadbury, Heinz, Kraft, Nabisco, Tang,
WH Group (China)	23.6	Pork, Smithfield, Armour
Assoc. British Foods (UK)	20.4	Twinings, Karo syrup, Mazola oil
Ashai (Japan)	19.2	Ashai, Tsingtao, Molson, Grolsch, Miller, Peroni, Coors
Kirin (Japan)	17.4	beverages Japan, US, Asia, Australia, Brazil, New Zealand
Diageo (UK)	15.9	Guinness, Baileys', Johnny Walker, Tanqueray, Smirnoff,
General Mills (US)	15.7	cereals, Hamburger Helper, Haagen-Daz, Betty Crocker, Pillsbury, Old El Paso, Green Giant
Kellogg's (US)	13.5	cereals, Eggo, Pringles, Pop-Tarts

Sources: Anheuser-Busch, 2018; Ashai, 2019; Associated British Foods, 2019; Coca-Cola, 2019; Danone, 2019; Diageo, 2019; General Mills, 2018; Heineken, 2019; JBS, 2018; Kellogg's, 2019; Kirin, 2019; Marketwatch, 2019; Mars, 2019; Mondelez, 2019; Nestle, 2019; Oxfam, 2013; PepsiCo, 2019; Reuters, 2019; Taylor, 2016; Tyson, 2018; Unilever, 2018, 2019.

Nestle, like the other companies listed in Table 3.3, reflects the acquisition and merger of companies begun in the 19th century and the early part of the 20th century. The history of Nabisco offers an excellent example of consolidation and acquisitions that occurred in the US to create one of the world's largest food and beverage companies. Nabisco was formed in 1898 as the National Biscuit Company when the New York Biscuit company and the American Biscuit company merged over 100 bakeries that they had purchased (Bellis, 2019). The New York Biscuit Company and American Biscuit Company each had begun through acquisitions of bakeries in 1889 and 1890, respectively. They were formed by investors with little or no baking experience who were simply searching for investments where they could park their excess wealth. While some food empires, like Heinz or Anheuser-Busch, were built on the expansion of existing businesses, Nabisco was created by businessmen with cash and a plan to generate profits through the acquisition of small companies, with the objective of monopolizing markets.

In order to increase its market share, Nabisco became a leader in the use of advertising to solidify its customer base. They allocated US$ 1 million in 1904 to advertising. They were also a leader in product development; Nabisco sold over 500 kinds of cookies, crackers, breads, and cakes by 1940

(Modelez, n.d.). They also sought lucrative military contracts during both WWI and WWII to supply soldiers' rations.

Nabisco went global after WWII, expanding to Africa, the Persian Gulf, and Latin American. By 1958, Nabisco was selling in 82 countries. Not only did Nabisco sell its brands abroad, but it also acquired foreign brands. For example, it purchased Mexican Fabricas Modernas S. A. in 1953, acquired Frears Ltd. of the UK in 1962, and acquired British biscuit company, Huntley and Palmer Foods in 1982, with businesses in Canada, France, Germany, Ireland, India, and the Far East (Bellis, 2019; Modelez, n.d.). It also continued to acquire American brands like Lifesavers and Standard Brands. In 1985, Nabisco itself was acquired by the tobacco company, R. J. Reynolds, which added brands like Grey Poupon, A.1., Del Monte, and others to the Nabisco company (Mondelez, n.d.). Nabisco continued to expand its brands and international presence. It formed a joint venture with the Yili Food Corporation in China and started producing Ritz, Premium, Escort, and Maria brands in Beijing in 1988.

Nabisco's strategy of acquisitions and global expansion changed in the late 1980s to a financialization strategy that involved mergers, reorganizations, and the trade of assets. Rather than focusing on product sales, buying and selling assets became the best way to generate profits. In 1988, Nabisco was part of the largest leveraged buyout to date; Kohlberg Kravis Roberts & Co, bought R. J. Reynolds Nabisco for US$ 26 billion, making it a private company (Mondelez, n.d.). Assets in Europe and South Africa worth US$ 5 billion were sold to pay off part of the purchase debt.

Nabisco was again publicly traded in 1990 as R. J. R. Nabisco Foods Group. Then it began a series of reorganizations. In 1992, Nabisco was reorganized so that its international companies were separated from Nabisco Foods Group and both were under R. J. R. Nabisco Holdings Corporation. The following year, among other things, Nabisco sold its cold cereals to Kraft General Foods and reorganized again as a single company, with the international companies as part of Nabisco Foods Group. In 1995, Nabisco acquired the assets of Kraft Foods' US and Canadian margarine businesses. Three years later, it sold its margarines, brands like Fleischmann's, Blue Bonnet, Parkay, Chiffon, and others, to ConAgra.

In the mid-1990s, Nabisco returned to its strategy of acquiring foreign companies: Venezuelan Galletera Tejerias, S. A. in 1995 and Lucky Enterprises Corporation Limited, the largest biscuit company in Taiwan, in

1996 (Modelez, n.d.). By the end of the 1990s, Nabisco had combined the strategies of global acquisitions and financialization into a global financialization strategy. Nabisco was reorganized again in 1999 and Nabisco Holdings Corporation acquired the candy companies, Favorite Brand International Inc. and Trolli Inc., Sather Trucking Corporation, and secured partial ownership of United Biscuits. In turn, United Biscuits purchased Nabisco's businesses in Spain, Portugal, the Middle East, and Africa, while Nabisco got United Biscuits' operations in China, Hong Kong, and Taiwan.

Nabisco lost its independent identity as a company in the 21st century, becoming a target for the very acquisition and financialization strategies it used to grow as a company in the 20th century. It was acquired by the tobacco company, Philip Morris, in 2000 and merged with Kraft Foods in 2001 (Bellis, 2019) making Nabisco a subsidiary of Kraft. The parent company, Philip Morris, changed its name to Altria in 2003 (Mondelez, n.d.). Kraft pursued a policy of global acquisition; it acquired Russian, Polish, and Turkish snack businesses in 2002; Egyptian companies in 2003; and Croatian and Slovenian companies in 2005. In 2007 it purchased Danone's biscuit brands; it purchased Cadbury in 2010; and it bought Ukrainian bakeries in 2011. Kraft also pursued a strategy of financialization. In 2007, Kraft spun off from Altria and in 2012, it split into two separate companies: Mondelez (global snacks) and Kraft Foods (North American grocery products). Nabisco became part of Mondelez. Kraft Foods later merged with Heinz to become Kraft Heinz. Mondelez continues a strategy of buying assets; in 2016 it attempted and failed to buy Hershey.

After all these complicated machinations, Nabisco is no longer a company—it is a brand that is part of Mondelez. Of course, the objective of its founders was never about making food, Nabisco began as an investment strategy, to acquire existing bakeries and monopolize markets. After more than a century operating as a company, Nabisco has become a "billion-dollar brand" (Mondelez, n.d.). Its products, like Oreos, Ritz, Triscuits, and Fig Newtons, are produced and sold around the world under the Nabisco brand or local brands, such as Christie in Canada. It grew by eliminating the competition by buying it out. In a sense, Nabisco has come full circle; it began as an investment strategy through acquisition and was so profitable it was acquired.

Nabisco's history offers an excellent example of the trends in the food and beverage industry. Food companies grew through mergers and acquisitions until the end of the 20th century (Toop, 2017). Food companies have become oligopolies, eliminating competition to increase their profits (Caiazza and Volpe, 2012). Few consumers are aware that the foods they buy come from a few companies, let alone who makes what. Indeed, the Nabisco example shows how frequent sales and reorganizations of assets among the companies make it difficult to follow who owns what. The vast array of brands masks a food and beverage industry that is highly concentrated, giving consumers "an illusion of choice" (Howard, 2017). The five largest food companies own two out of three global food brands (Ramsey, 2003). So, any branded food you buy is likely from just five global companies.

The concentration of companies masks who really owns the products we consume. Budweiser is owned by a Belgium company, Anheuser-Busch InBev, which also produces over 100 other brands of beer, some of which are touted as craft beers, like 10 Barrel Brewing. Not only is a Belgian company selling American beer, but much of the beef in the US is slaughtered by the Brazilian company, JBS, while a Chinese company, WH Group, slaughters most of the pork eaten by Americans. Four companies control 85% of the beef slaughtered in the US, 66% of pork slaughtered, and 51% of chicken slaughtered (Hendrickson, Howard and Constance, 2017). Anglo-Dutch company, Unilever, owns that little Vermont company, Ben & Jerry's ice cream. In 2014, the Mexican company, Grupo Bimbo, sold 64% of the packaged bread in the US and 62% in Canada (Grupo Bimbo, 2016). Grupo Bimbo owns over 40 brands of bread in the US, including Ball Park, Boboli, Thomas' English muffins, Orowheat, and Sara Lee (Grupo Bimbo, n.d.). These large companies are able to acquire and create brands to appeal to new tastes. For example, Flowers Foods, the maker of Wonder bread, acquired Dave's Killer organic breads and Canyon Bakehouse gluten-free breads (Flowers Foods, 2019).

Where will this lead? Food brands dominated the food system during the 20th century, but food retailers will dominate the food system during the 21st. Ramsey (2003) argues that during the 21st century, food manufacturers will scale back the number of brands they sell because they are currently trying to maintain too many. Also, consumers will be less interested in brands because they will eat more food in restaurants and institutions, and global retailers will promote global private labels, making food manufacturers increasingly dependent upon food retailers. He predicts that food manufacturers will increase their production of products for retailers and the food service industry, whose global food brands will gain in importance. Ramsey's predictions are based on the assessment that the technology requirements to produce foods are low, technological breakthroughs in food manufacturing are rare, and anyone can easily copy a recipe. Toops (2017) concurs—less money is being spent on R&D in food manufacturing and there is a greater emphasis on private labels. Therefore, competition between food brands is focused on marketing, not actual differences in products or quality.

Is this what consumers wanted?

Looking at the list of the largest food companies and the products they make (Table 3.3), it should be no surprise that obesity and other diet-related problems plague contemporary society. These companies dictate the products offered to consumers, selling highly processed foods and beverages. No nutritional guidelines recommend that one eat candies, sodas, snacks, beer, sweeteners, processed meats, or processed foods. None of these foods are needed as part of one's diet. They are, at best, treats that should be consumed in moderation, if our diets can permit empty calories. Yet these foods dominate what is available in the global economy, our supermarkets, and as such, what we eat. These foods are not eaten as treats, but are our core diet. Processed foods accounted for over three-quarters of calorie intake in the US in 2012 (Poti et al., 2015). So, is it any wonder that weight problems, obesity, diabetes, heart disease, strokes, and diet-related cancers are rising when our food system is dominated by foods that cause these problems? Is it any wonder that people "choose" these foods when these foods dominate their food environment: where they shop, eat, or view media?

US farmers also face a lack of choice when it comes to buying their inputs and selling their products. Four companies control over half of the seed market, over 60% of the agrochemical market, and two-thirds of swine genetics (Hendrickson, Howard and Constance, 2017). Three companies control 95% of broiler genetics, and only two companies control 94% of laying hen genetics. Farmers simply have very little choice in what seeds, chemicals, or genetics they can use to produce foods. They also have very little choice whom to sell to. For example, a joint venture between Cargill, ConAgra, and CHS, called Ardent Mills, controls one-third of the wheat flour market, while four companies in the US control 85% of beef slaughter (Hendrickson, Howard and Constance, 2017).

The illusion of choice permeates consumers' shopping options as well. The first supermarket chain in the US, Piggly Wiggly, began in the 1910s (Toops, 2017). A century later, supermarket chains dominate where Americans get their food and there are very few chains to choose from. Currently, the top five food retailers in the US are Wal-Mart, Kroger, Albertson's, Costco, and Ahold Delhaize USA, a Dutch subsidiary that owns Food Lion, Giant, Stop & Shop, and Peapod, among others (Costco, 2018; Dudlicek, 2018). Between them, in 2017 they sold US$ 403 billion in groceries. That same year, total US grocery sales in supermarkets and clubs were estimated at US$ 839 billion (Dudlicek et al., 2018), meaning these five companies sold 48% of the groceries in the US. Convenience store sales in the US are not included in these sales figures; they represent another US$ 450 billion in sales. One company, 7-Eleven, makes about 25% of all convenience store sales (Hendrickson, Howard and Constance, 2017). Just a handful of retailers sell most food in the US.

Notice that US retail food sales dwarf global sales by food brands (Table 3.3). Just as Ramsey (2003) predicted, the concentration of brands that dominated the 20th century has been supplanted by the concentration and economic power of food retailing during the 21st century. Indeed, food retailing dominates global retail sales of all goods. Six of the top ten global retailers are primarily food retailers: Wal-Mart, Costco, Kroeger, Schwarz Group (Lidl), Aldi, and Carrefour (Deloitte, 2018). Three others—Walgreens Boots Alliance Inc, Amazon, and CVS Health Corporation—have increased their food sales. The only retail company in the top ten that does not sell food is Home Depot.

Since everyone has to eat, food retailing is a big business and concentration is the strategy used to gain market power, just as food brands did during the 20th century. The largest retailers have the market power to force suppliers to reduce prices if they want to sell to them, require brands to pay premiums for shelf space in stores or virtual space on websites, and as Ramsey (2003) predicted, contract food manufacturers to supply private label products to retailers.

Similar concentration occurs within institutional food and fast food companies. McDonald's, Yum! Brands (KFC, Pizza Hut, Taco Bell), Doctor's Associates Inc. (Subway), and Wendy's sell 40% of the fast food in the US (Hendrickson, Howard and Constance, 2017). Two companies, Sysco and US Foods, sell most of the food to US restaurants, hotels, hospitals, prisons, and other institutions. Consumers are funneling their hard-earned money to just a few food companies that give us an illusion of choice. Yet most of the food available is highly processed, high in calories, and low in nutritional value.

That eating a diet of processed foods should result in weight gain and health problems, especially if one is sedentary and does little exercise, should not surprise anyone. Yet rather than blame the food system, we look for scapegoats. As an example, food deserts are blamed for being the cause of obesity and other food-related diseases, particularly among minority communities and in rural areas. However, this is an assumption, rather than a conclusion based on evidence. Despite a vast number of studies, the weak evidence to support a correlation between food access and obesity has been misconstrued as causality. Meta-analyses of studies on the relationship between store locations and health outcomes include: Caspi et al. (2012) who examined 38 studies; Walker et al. (2010) who examined 31 studies; and Feng et al. (2010) who examined 63 studies. The studies used different methodologies and measurements, and controlled for different factors. Taken together, they provide weak support for a correlation between the food environment and obesity, not causality. LeDoux and Vojnovic (2013) investigated the shopping habits of poor people living in a food desert and offered an explanation of why the evidence of correlation is weak; those living in food deserts simply travel outside their environment to shop. Looking specifically at FAV consumption in England, Pearson et al. (2005) found that FAV prices, poverty, and distance to supermarkets were not factors in FAV consumption. Another issue missed by researchers is the lack of variation in the dependent variable; most Americans and Britons are overweight, so what is the control group?

Despite the weak evidence of correlation, food deserts are widely touted as the cause of obesity, and efforts to bring healthy foods to marginalized communities are viewed as a panacea. The focus on funding and publicity to increase food access misses the point. The problem is much bigger, because no matter where you live, most of the foods available to you in stores are unhealthy. Having access to a grocery store does not create an oasis, because grocery stores are in fact swamps filled with unhealthy foods.

Changes in household food expenditure over time

Let's take a look at US consumers' spending on food over time. Cummings (1940) estimated that a household of three people in 1833 spent 46% of their income on food. Over the course of the 19th century, little changed; by 1901 households spent 43% of their income on food (US Department of Labor). During the 20th century, food expenditure dropped dramatically to less than 13%. As food became relatively cheaper in the US, more food was eaten away from home (Figure 3.1). In 1909, only 3% of food expenditure was on food eaten away from home (Jacobs and Shipp, 1990). This climbed to 44% in 2016 (US BLS, 2018).

In 2017, average household expenditure was $60,060 for a household of 2.5 people with 1.3 earners (US BLS, 2018). The average household spent 7.3% of its expenditure on food at home, and an additional 5.6% on food away from home, or 43% of its total food budget on food away from home. The largest single category of food eaten at home was "other," which represented over 36% of at-home food expenditure and included sugar, sweets, oils, fats, prepared foods, and sodas. Cereal and baked goods represented another 12% of food eaten at home, with meats at 22%, dairy at 10%, and all FAV at 19%.

As a point of comparison, American households spent as much on alcohol in 2017 as they did on cereals and baked goods, and more than they spent on beef and pork combined. They spent more on cell phone services than on FAV or all meats. They spent 4.5 times the amount on housing and more than twice as much on transportation as they did on food at home, and in the age of food-related illnesses, 12% more on medical care than on food eaten at home.

Average expenditures mask some interesting patterns. In 2017, the poorest 20% of households in the US spent an average of US$ 26,000 (US BLS, 2018). These poor households were somewhat older (54 versus 51 years), smaller (1.6 versus 2.5 people), with fewer earners (0.5 versus 1.3), more females (62% versus 53%), more likely to rent (59% versus 37%), and more likely to be African American (20% versus 13%) than average US households. All food purchases of the poor represented 15.6% of expenditure as opposed to 12.9% for the average US household. The dollar amounts spent were much lower than average since their incomes were so low. However, the poor spent about the same proportion on food away from home as the average household (Table 3.4), but spent a higher proportion on food at home, 9.9% versus 7.3%. Contrary to popular belief, the poor spent a higher proportion of their income on FAV than middle-class or rich households. Across all food categories, expenditure proportions decrease with income, except for alcohol, which increases as income rises. The percentage of expenditures on food away from home is lowest among the second quintile of households (5.2% of expenditures), and highest (6.0%) among the middle quintile.

Figure 3.1 Percentage of US household expenditure spent on food away from home, 1909-2017.

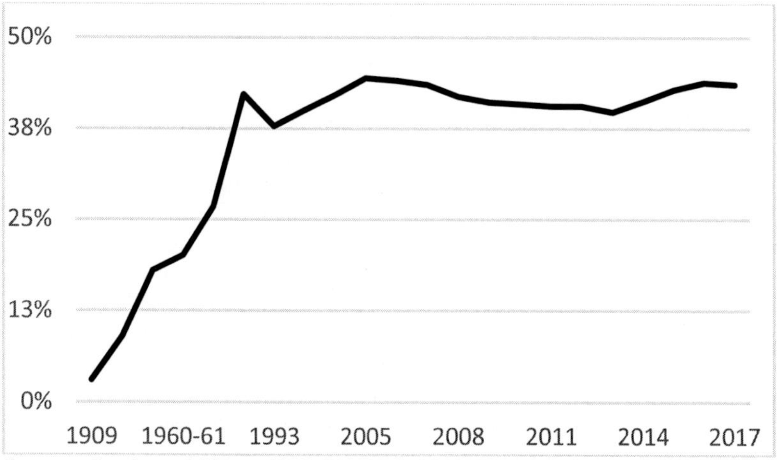

Sources: Jacobs and Shipp, 1990; US BLS, 2014; US BLS, 2018; US Department of Labor, 2006.

Table 3.4 US household food expenditures by quintile, as a percentage of total expenditures.

	Average	Poor	Lower	Middle	Upper	Rich
Alcohol	0.9%	0.6%	0.8%	0.8%	1.0%	1.0%
All Food	12.9%	15.6%	14.4%	14.0%	13.0%	11.2%
Food away from home	5.6%	5.7%	5.2%	6.0%	5.7%	5.5%
Food at home	7.3%	9.9%	9.3%	8.0%	7.2%	5.7%
Cereals	0.9%	1.3%	1.2%	1.1%	0.9%	0.7%
FAV	1.4%	1.9%	1.7%	1.5%	1.4%	1.1%
Dairy	0.7%	1.0%	0.9%	0.8%	0.8%	0.6%
Meats	1.6%	2.2%	2.1%	1.8%	1.5%	1.2%
Other	2.6%	3.5%	3.3%	2.9%	2.6%	2.1%

Source: US BLS, 2018.

These expenditures illustrate how cheap food is in the US. Even poor Americans spend a smaller proportion of their income on food than average consumers in most countries around the world. The average American spends less of their income on food than any people on Earth (Gray, 2016) and at any time in history. So, if food is so cheap in the US, why do we have so many food-related illnesses?

Where are we now?

The US developed its food system to produce cheap commodities for export, using national policies that concentrated access to land and subsidies for the wealthy. The rise of food processing during the 19th century led to brands and strategies of acquisition and consolidation within food manufacturing. These trends continued into the 20th century and went global. Financialization at the end of the 20th century has led to increased concentration, resulting in a few dozen global food and beverage companies that own hundreds of brands, and a handful of retailers that sell us our food.

Our food system produces cheap processed foods which supply over three-quarters of the calories in the US (Poti et al., 2015). Whether we live in a food desert or have multiple grocery stores located nearby, the food choices in our retail environments are predominantly highly processed foods. No matter what choices we make, if we buy branded products, our money goes to a few global agro-food companies, and a handful of food retailers.

As consumers, we are beneficiaries of cheap food, but we are increasingly victims of food-related illnesses, due to eating a diet of highly processed foods and sedentary lifestyles. We choose these foods because that is what we are offered. New brands are sold to us as "healthy" by reducing fat (and increasing sugar) or adding fiber (and sugar, salt, or fat). The fact remains that the majority of foods we eat are highly processed and eating a diet of highly processed food is nutritionally harmful, particularly if we are sedentary and get little exercise. These foods are often calorie-dense, making it easy to consume empty calories. These are not the foods we should eat, but they are the foods that are available, whether we live in a food desert or next door to a supermarket. Asking consumers to sift through 40,000 items in a typical grocery store and only choose foods that contain no sugar, salt, or empty calories is like asking someone not to catch a cold; you can take precautions to protect yourself, but unless you want to isolate yourself completely, the chances are you will succumb.

Exercise: Tally your food expenditures for a week

What did you buy? How much of it was processed food? How much did you spend on FAV? How much did you spend on food eaten away from home? What does this tell you?

References

Angadjivand, S. 2018. US Farm Commodity Support: An Overview of Selected Programs. CRS Report. April 17. Congressional Research Service. https://fas.org/sgp/crs/misc/R45165.pdf, accessed February 11, 2019.

Anheuser-Busch. 2016. For the love of lager: the history of Anheuser-Busch. Anheuser-Busch. December 14. https://www.anheuser-busch.com/about/heritage.html, accessed February 21, 2019.

Arnot, C. 2018. The dangerous disconnect: Food and agriculture trust gaps. Food Processing, January 17.
https://www.foodprocessing.com/articles/2018/power-lunch-food-ag-trust/, accessed February 18, 2019.

Ashai. 2019. Summary report of financial results (Fiscal 2018).
https://www.asahigroup-holdings.com/en/ir/pdf/2018_yend_results.pdf, accessed February 14, 2019.

Associated British Foods. 2019. Financial headlines.
https://www.abf.co.uk/investorrelations/annual_report_2018, accessed February 24, 2019.

Beckett, J. V. 1983. The debate over farm sizes in eighteenth and nineteenth century England. Agricultural History, 57(3 July), 308-325.
https://www.jstor.org/stable/3742457, accessed February 20, 2019.

Bellis, M. 2019. The evolution of the Nabisco brands.
https://www.thoughtco.com/history-of-nabisco-1991760, accessed February 25, 2019.

Beranty, R. 2018. The world's best fed army. Warfare History Network. https://warfarehistorynetwork.com/daily/wwii/the-worlds-best-fed-army/, accessed February 21, 2019.

Borden. 2019. The history of Borden dairy. https://www.bordendairy.com/history/, accessed February 21, 2019.

Braden, C. R. and Tauxe, R. V. 2013. Emerging trends in foodborne diseases. Infectious Diseases Clinic of North America, 27(3), 517–533 http://dx.doi.org/10.1016/j.idc.2013.06.001, accessed February 18, 2019.

Caiazza, R. and Volpe, T. 2012. The global agro-food system from past to future. China-USA Business Review, 11(7), 919–929.

Caspi, C. E., Sorensen, G., Subramanian, S. V., and Kawachi, I. 2012. The local food environment and diet: A systematic review. Health & Place, 18, 1172–1187.

Chicago Historical Society. 2005. The Electronic Encyclopedia of Chicago. Armour & Co.
http://www.encyclopedia.chicagohistory.org/pages/2554.html;
Cudahy Packing Co.
http://www.encyclopedia.chicagohistory.org/pages/2635.html;
Swift & Co. http://www.encyclopedia.chicagohistory.org/pages/2869.html, accessed February 21, 2019.

Clark, D. 2009. A brief history of "American cheese," from colonial cheddar to Kraft singles. Mental Floss. January 7. http://mentalfloss.com/article/20537/brief-history-american-cheese-colonial-cheddar-kraft-singles, accessed February 22, 2019.

Coca-Cola. 2019. Coca-Cola reports strong results for fourth quarter and full year 2018. February 14. https://www.coca-colacompany.com/press-center/press-releases/coca-cola-reports-strong-results-for-fourth-quarter-and-full-year-2018, accessed February 24, 2019.

Costco. 2018. Annual report 2018, fiscal year ended September 2, 2018. http://investor.costco.com/Mobile.view?c=83830&d=10&v=100, accessed February 28, 2019.

Cummings, R. O. 1940. The American and his food. A history of food habits in the United States. Chicago: University of Chicago Press.

Danone. 2019. Solid performance in 2018: Accelerating sales growth and efficiencies. February 19. https://www.danone.com/content/dam/danonecorp/medias/medias-en/2018/corporatepressreleases/pr_fy_2018_en.PDF, accessed February 24, 2019.

Deloitte. 2018. Global powers of retailing 2018. https://www2.deloitte.com/content/dam/Deloitte/at/Documents/about-deloitte/global-powers-of-retailing-2018.pdf, accessed February 28, 2019.

Diageo. 2019. Annual report 2018. https://www.diageo.com/PR1346/aws/media/6212/b0000391_diageo_ar-2018_interactive.pdf, accessed February 24, 2019.

Dudlicek, J. 2018. Top 50 grocers: Amazon in 8th place while rest of industry restrategizes, reshuffles. The Progressive Grocer, May 7. https://progressivegrocer.com/top-50-grocers-2018-ranked, accessed February 28, 2019.

Dudlicek, J., Goldschmidt, B., Hofbauer, R., and Martin, K. 2018. 85th annual report of the grocery industry. Progressive Grocer, 97(4), 26-30. http://www.nxtbook.com/nxtbooks/ensembleiq/pg_201804/index.php#/30, accessed February 28, 2019.

Everts, S. 2013. Processed: Food science and the modern meal. Distillations, Fall. https://www.sciencehistory.org/distillationsfall-2013 winter-2014, accessed February 18, 2019.

Farm Bureau. 2018. Reviewing the 2018 Farm Bill baseline. December 17. https://www.fb.org/market-intel/reviewing-the-2018-farm-bill-baseline, accessed February 11, 2019.

Farm Policy Facts. 2018. Farm Bill: a short history and summary. https://www.farmpolicyfacts.org/farm-policy-history/, accessed February 15, 2019.

Feng, J., Glass, T. A., Curriero, F. C., Stewart, W .F., and Schwartz, B. S. 2010. The built environment and obesity: A systematic review of the epidemiologic evidence. Health & Place, 16, 175–190.

Flowers Foods. 2019. Our family of brands. https://www.flowersfoods.com/brands, accessed February 27, 2019.

General Mills. 2018. General Mills reports fourth-quarter and full year fiscal-year 2018 results; provides 2019 outlook. June 27. https://s22.q4cdn.com/584207745/files/doc_financials/2018/q4/General-Mills-Fiscal-2018-Fourth-Quarter-Earnings-Press-Release.pdf, accessed February 24, 2019.

Gray, A. 2016. Which countries spend the most on food? This map will show you. World Economic Forum, December 7. https://www.weforum.org/agenda/2016/12/this-map-shows-how-much-each-country-spends-on-food/, accessed February 12, 2019.

Grupo Bimbo. 2016. Investor presentation, 2015 results. https://grupobimbo.com/sites/default/files/BIMBO_Presentacio_%20inversionistas_4Q15_1.pdf, accessed February 28, 2019.

Grupo Bimbo. n.d. Our brands. https://grupobimbo.com/en/our-brands, accessed February 27, 2019.

Grymes, C. A. 2018. How colonists acquired title to land in Virginia. Virginia Places. http://www.virginiaplaces.org/settleland/headright.html accessed February 14, 2019.

Guasco, M. 2011. Indentured servitude. In Atlantic History, T. Bernard, ed. http://www.oxfordbibliographies.com/view/document/obo-9780199730414/obo-9780199730414-0113.xml, accessed February 20, 2019.

Halloran, A. 2013. The history of Aunt Jemima's mill: Branding an American wheat product. Lancaster Farming. November 9. https://www.lancasterfarming.com/news/main_edition/the-history-of-aunt-jemima-s-mill-branding-an-american/article_26fc99b9-d1b8-5bc1-b036-d2e4cacbfc35.html, accessed February 21, 2019.

Heineken. 2019. Heineken N. V. 2018 full year earnings release. February 13. https://www.theheinekencompany.com/Investors/Reports-and-Presentations?Skip=0&Take=10&SubjectFilters=429AD32AD8504E8991602AB8A3CF5C36, accessed February 24, 2019.

Hendrickson, M. K., Howard, P. H., and Constance, D. H. 2017. Power, food and agriculture. Implications for farmers, consumers and communities.

University of Missouri, College of Agriculture, Food & Natural Resources Division of Applied Social Sciences Working Paper. https://philhowardnet.files.wordpress.com/2017/11/hendrickson-howard-constance-2017-final-working-paper-nov-1.pdf, accessed February 28, 2019.

Hieligenstein, M. X. 2014. A brief history of the Farm Bill. The Saturday Evening Post, April 17. https://www.saturdayeveningpost.com/2014/04/a-brief-history-of-the-farm-bill/, accessed February 15, 2019.

History.com editors. 2019. Treaty of Guadalupe Hidalgo. A&E Television Networks. February 6. https://www.history.com/topics/mexican-american-war/treaty-of-guadalupe-hidalgo, accessed February 20, 2019.

Hormel Foods. 2019. History with US military. https://www.hormelfoods.com/careers/military-recruitment/history-u-s-military/, accessed February 21, 2019.

Howard, P. H. 2017. Decoding diversity in the food system: Wheat and bread in North America. https://philhoward.net/2017/05/11/decoding-diversity-in-the-food-system-wheat-and-bread-in-north-america/, accessed February 28, 2019.

Hueston, W. and McLeod, A. 2012. Overview of the global food system: Changes over time/space and lessons for future food safety. Improving Food Safety through One Health Approach. Eds Institute of Medicine. Washington DC: The National Academies Press.

Jacobs, E. and Shipp, S. 1990. How family spending has changed in the US. Monthly Labor Review, March 20-27. https://www.bls.gov/opub/mlr/1990/03/art3full.pdf, accessed March 4, 2019.

JBS. 2018. 2017 Results. http://jbss.infoinvest.com.br/enu/4523/4Q17%20Earnings%20Release%20%28Final%29.pdf, accessed February 24, 2019.

Jitchotvisut, J. 2018. The fascinating origin stories behind 20 of America's favorite foods. Insider, February 5. https://www.thisisinsider.com/how-iconic-food-brands-came-to-be-2018-2, accessed February 21, 2019.

Kellogg. 2019. Kellogg Company reports 2018 results and issues 2019 guidance. February 7.
https://investor.kelloggs.com/Cache/1001248225.PDF?O=PDF&T=&Y=&D=&FID=1001248225&iid=4133514, accessed February 24, 2019.

Kirin. 2019. Summary of consolidated financial results for the year ended December 31, 2018 (unaudited). February 14.
https://pdf.irpocket.com/C2503/drYi/T7JE/FJaV.pdf, accessed February 24, 2019.

Koehler, F. A. 1958. Special rations for the armed forces, 1946-53, QMC Historical Studies, Series II, No. 6, Historical Branch. Washington DC: Office of the Quartermaster General.
http://old.qmfound.com/army_rations_historical_background.htm#Operational%20Rations%20in%20World%20War%20II, accessed February 21, 2019.

Krasner-Khait, B. 2000. The impact of refrigeration. The History Magazine, February/March. https://www.history-magazine.com/refrig.html, accessed February 20, 2019.

LeDoux, T. F. and Vojnovic, I. 2013. Going outside the neighborhood: The shopping patterns and adaptations of disadvantaged consumers living in the lower eastside neighborhoods of Detroit, Michigan. Health & Place, 19, 1–14.

Leffler, S. 2018. 12 famous brands that are over 100 years old. Eat This, Not That! May 4. https://www.eatthis.com/oldest-food-brands-in-america/, accessed February 21, 2019.

Library of Congress. 2018. Homestead Act.
https://www.loc.gov/rr/program/bib/ourdocs/homestead.html,
accessed February 15, 2019.

Lipsey, R. E. 1994. US foreign trade and the balance of payments, 1800-1913. NBER working paper series, no. 4710, April. Cambridge, MA: National Bureau of Economic Research.
https://www.nber.org/papers/w4710.pdf, accessed February 20, 2019.

macrotrends. 2018. Anheuser-Busch Revenue 2007-2018. https://www.macrotrends.net/stocks/charts/BUD/anheuser-busch/revenue, accessed February 24, 2019.

Marketwatch. 2019. Annual financials for Archer Daniels Midland Co. https://www.marketwatch.com/investing/stock/adm/financials, accessed February 24, 2019.

Mars. 2019. About Mars. https://marspresscenter.com, accessed February 24, 2019.

Mazoyer, M. and Roudart, L. 2006. A History of World Agriculture: From the Neolithic Age to the Current Crisis. London: Earthscan.

Mondelez. 2019. Mondelez International reports 2018 results. January 30. https://ir.mondelezinternational.com/node/22571/pdf, accessed February 24, 2019.

Mondelez. n.d. Our corporate timelines. https://www.mondelezinternational.com/about-us/our-corporate-timelines, accessed February 25, 2019.

Morris, R. B. 1976. Chapter 1. The emergence of American labor in bicentennial history of the American worker. R. B. Morris, ed. Washington DC: US Department of Labor. https://www.dol.gov/general/aboutdol/history/chapter1, accessed February 20, 2019.

Myers, D. 2015. America's 10 oldest food and drink companies. The Daily Meal, September 17. https://www.thedailymeal.com/eat/america-s-10-oldest-food-and-drink-companies-0, accessed February 21, 2019.

Nestle. 2019. Nestle reports full year results for 2018. February 14. https://www.nestle.com/media/pressreleases/allpressreleases/full-year-results-2018, accessed February 24, 2019.

Nestle n.d. History. https://www.nestle-ea.com/en/aboutus/history/ history _detailed, accessed February 24, 2019.

Olver, L. 2000. Food Timeline.
http://www.foodtimeline.org/fooddecades.html, accessed February 21, 2019.

Our Documents n.d. Homestead Act (1862).
https://www.ourdocuments.gov/doc.php?flash=false&doc=31, accessed February 15, 2019.

Oxfam. 2013. Behind the brands illusion of choice.
https://www.oxfamamerica.org/static/media/files/Behind-the-brands-illusion-of-choice-graphic-2048x1351.jpg, accessed February 21, 2019.

Pearson, T., Russell, J., Campbell, M. J. and Barker, M. E. 2005. Do 'food deserts' influence fruit and vegetable consumption? A cross-sectional study. Appetite, 45, 195–197.

PepsiCo. 2019. PepsiCo reports fourth-quarter and full-year 2018 results; Provides 2019 financial outlook.
https://www.pepsico.com/docs/album/investors/q4-2018/q4-2018-earnings-release_jxwwalwh2hhtz213.pdf, accessed February 24, 2019.

The Pepsi Store. n.d. History of the birthplace.
https://www.pepsistore.com/history.asp, accessed February 21, 2019.

Peshek, S. 2018. The Morrill Act, explained. Texas A&M Today, July 1.
https://today.tamu.edu/2018/07/01/the-morrill-act-explained/, accessed February15, 2019.

Poti, J. M., Mendez, M. A., Ng, S. W., and Popkin, B. M. 2015. Is the degree of food processing and convenience linked with the nutritional quality of foods purchased by US households? American Journal of Clinical Nutrition, 101(6), 1251–62.

Quaker Oats Company. 2019. Our oats origins.
https://www.quakeroats.com/about-quaker-oats/content/quaker-history.aspx, accessed February 21, 2019.

Ramsey, J. 2003. Whither global branding? The case of food manufacturing. Journal of Brand Management, 11(1), 9–21.

Reuters. 2019. WH Group Ltd financials. https://www.reuters.com/finance/stocks/financial-highlights/0288.HK, accessed February 24, 2019.

Risch, E. 1995. The Quartermaster Corps: Organization, supply and services, vol I. Washington DC: US Army, Center for Military History. https://history.army.mil/html/books/010/10-12/CMH_Pub_10-12-1.pdf, accessed February 21, 2019.

Schlosser, E. 2002. Fast Food Nation. New York: Perennial.

Spielmaker, D. M. 2018. Growing a nation. Historical timeline, March 21. https://www.agclassroom.org/gan/timeline/index.htm, accessed February 15, 2019.

Taylor, K. 2016. These ten companies control everything you buy. Business Insider, September 28. https://www.businessinsider.com/10-companies-control-the-food-industry-2016-9, accessed February 21, 2019.

Toops, D. 2017. Chapter 2: How did the food industry get (from there) to here? Accelerating New Food Product Design and Development, Second Edition. Edited by J. H. Beckley, L. J. Herzog, and M. M. Foley. Hoboken, NJ: John Wiley & Sons Ltd and the Institute of Food Technologists. http://www.ift.org/~/media/Knowledge%20Center/Publications/Books/Samples/IFTPressBook_ANFPDD_Chapter1.pdf, accessed February 4, 2019.

Tyson. 2018. Tyson foods produces solid fourth quarter, fiscal 2018 earnings. November 13. https://ir.tyson.com/news/news-details/2018/Tyson-Foods-Produces-Solid-Fourth-Quarter-Fiscal-2018-Earnings/default.aspx, accessed February 24, 2018.

Unilever. 2018. Making sustainable living commonplace. Charts 2017. https://www.unilever.com/Images/unilever-charts-2017_tcm244-516457_en.pdf, accessed February 24, 2019.

Unilever. 2019. Full-year results show continued profitable growth in volatile markets. January 31. https://www.unilever.com/news/press-releases/2019/full-year-results-show-continued-profitable-growth-in-volatile-markets.html, accessed February 24, 2019.

US BLS. 2014. Consumer Expenditure Survey. Data from 1960-2011. https://www.bls.gov/cex/csxstnd.htm#196061, accessed March 4, 2019.

US BLS 2018. Consumer Expenditure Survey, 2017. Table 1101. Quintiles of income before taxes: Annual expenditure means, shares, standard errors, and coefficients of variation. September. https://www.bls.gov/cex/2017/combined/quintile.pdf, accessed February 6, 2019.

US Bureau of Census. 1949. Historical statistics of the United States 1789-1945. A supplement to the Statistical Abstract of the United States. Washington DC: US Government Printing Office. https://www2.census.gov/prod2/statcomp/documents/HistoricalStatisticsoftheUnitedStates1789-1945.pdf, accessed March 11, 2019.

USDA National Agricultural Library. 1862. Homestead Act. https://www.nal.usda.gov/homestead-act accessed February 15, 2019.

USDA ERS. 2018. Farm income and wealth statistics, net cash income. November 30. https://data.ers.usda.gov/reports.aspx?ID=17831, accessed February 8, 2019.

USDA FNS. 2018. Supplemental Nutrition Assistance Program (SNAP). Participation and costs. December 7. https://fns-prod.azureedge.net/sites/default/files/pd/SNAPsummary.pdf, accessed February 24, 2019.

USDA FNS. 2020. Featured reports: Summary of major programs for latest available month. Program Data Overview, August 21. https://www.fns.usda.gov/pd/overview, accessed October 26, 2020.

US National Archives and Records Administration. 2016. The Homestead Act of 1862. https://www.archives.gov/education/lessons/homestead-act, accessed February 15, 2019.

US Department of Labor. 1934. History of wages in the United States from colonial times to 1928. Revision of bulletin 499. https://babel.hathitrust.org/cgi/pt?id=uc1.32106007458745;view=1up;seq=8, accessed February 12, 2019.

US Department of Labor. 2006. 100 years of US consumer spending. Report 991, May. https://www.bls.gov/opub/100-years-of-u-s-consumer-spending.pdf, accessed February 12, 2019.

Walker, R. E., Keane, C. R., and Burke, J. G. 2010. Disparities and access to healthy food in the United States: A review of food deserts literature. Health & Place, 16, 876–884.

Wright, C. 1889. Comparative wages, prices, and cost of living. Boston: Wright and Potter Printing Company.
https://babel.hathitrust.org/cgi/pt?id=wu.89071501472;view=1up;seq=9, accessed February 15, 2019.

Yehia, A. 2014. Britain's 8 oldest iconic brands. Real Business, March 20.
https://realbusiness.co.uk/britains-8-oldest-iconic-brands/,
accessed February 21, 2019.

CHAPTER FOUR

THE OTHER COSTS OF OUR CHOICES

Our food "choices" have many consequences. We can, however, only choose what is available, and given that the overwhelming offerings in our stores are processed foods, that is what we "choose" to buy. The food offerings are dominated by processed foods because they are profitable to multinationals. They are profitable because a few food companies and a few retailers provide most of our choices. As oligopolies, they can extract higher profits than firms who have to face open competition. The tens of thousands of brands and dozens of food retailers give us the appearance of choice and the illusion of competition, but in the US, nearly all the food we eat is made by and purchased from a few large companies.

The consequences of the choices we are given are many. As taxpayers, we pay for the subsidy programs that promote our agricultural production system, most of which in the US goes to large corn and wheat producers. As consumers, we suffer the health impacts of eating a diet that is dominated by processed foods. As shoppers, we are blamed for the social and environmental externalities caused by our current food system. Whether it is food waste, GHG emissions, groundwater contamination, destruction of fisheries due to eutrophication, exploitation of immigrant labor, overgrazing, animal health issues related to their grain-heavy diet, animal welfare concerns due to overcrowding and cruelty, food safety, worker safety, etc., the problems generated by our current food system are costly to those who are made to bear them. This chapter outlines some of the consequences of the foods we eat.

Health impacts of our food system

Cummings (1941) has a dramatic set of photographs of the health impacts of diet. They are pictures of two rats who are twin brothers. One was fed a diet exclusively of meat, potatoes, bread, and butter. His twin had the same diet, but it also included fresh vegetables and milk. At six months, the former weighed 89 grams, was stunted, had unhealthy looking fur, and his bones were frail. In contrast, his brother weighed 194 grams, was robust, not fat, with a larger overall skeleton and bones, and healthy-looking fur. The photos demonstrate not just the unhealthy impacts of the typical American diet of the time—meat, potatoes, bread, and butter—but also the awareness and concern 80 years ago about the prevalence of poor eating habits in the US. In 1940, these foods were termed "nonprotective," whereas fruits, vegetables, and milk were denoted as "protective" (Cummings, 1941). Eighty years later, we are still struggling to encourage people to eat fruit and vegetables, and to get enough calcium. What is different today is that 80 years ago, as the US was drawn into WWII, the concerns about diets lacking in vegetables were stunting and weakness. While globally, stunting is still a problem, the primary concern about diet in the US (and globally) today relates to being overweight or obese, and the associated food-related illnesses.

In 2015-16, 40% of US adults (over 93 million) were obese, and 18.5% of children aged 2-19, or 13.7 million children and adolescents, were obese (CDC, 2017a). Fifteen years earlier, the percentages were 30.5% and 13.9% for adults and children, respectively. Obesity rates were less than 15% of the adult population between 1960 and 1980 (US DHHS, 2013). They have climbed steeply since. The percentage of adults who are either overweight or obese in the US exceeds 71% (Figure 4.1). The CDC (2017b) identifies the causes of obesity as mostly behavioral: diet, lack of exercise, and physical inactivity. They concede that some medicines can exacerbate obesity and that one's food and physical activity environment, education, and skill level, as well as food marketing and promotion, can contribute to obesity. While the CDC (2017b) acknowledges that genetics may be a factor in weight gain for an individual, it rules this out as the cause of the rise in obesity in the US population because "Genetic changes in human populations occur too slowly to be responsible for the obesity epidemic."

To avoid weight gain and obesity, the CDC (2017b) recommends eating whole grains, FAV, lean protein, low-fat and fat-free dairy products, drinking water, 150 minutes of moderate or 75 minutes of vigorous exercise per week, and strength training twice a week. This is reminiscent of Sylvester Graham's (of graham cracker fame) recommendations 190 years ago. In 1830, he recommended that Americans eat less meat and white flour, get more exercise, eat fresh FAV, and use whole wheat flour (Cummings, 1941). At the time, Graham's diet recommendations were not new; he was just more "fearless, independent and clear" than other advocates. That the problem was widely recognized at the time is demonstrated by the 1832

Massachusetts Medical Society's statement that gluttony was a prevalent health problem. It set recommendations about the maximum amount of food one should eat and advocated skipping dinner once a week. Hence, concerns about the health impacts of the quantity and quality of the American diet have been around for 190 years, and the behavioral recommendations have been remarkably consistent: whole grains, FAV, less meat, and more exercise.

Figure 4.1 Prevalence of overweight, obesity, and diabetes, adults and adolescents, 1988-2016 (percentage of the population).

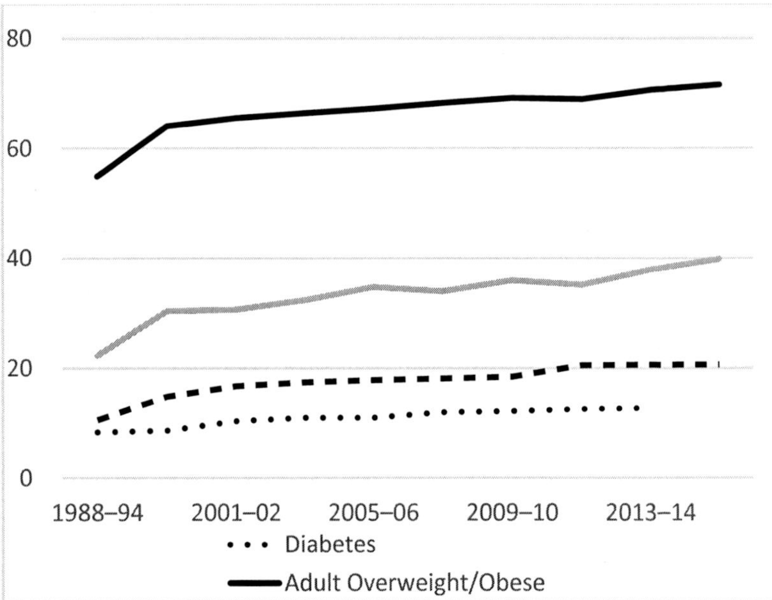

Source: CDC, 2017c.

While the dietary recommendations are similar, the health concerns have changed over the last two centuries. In 1830, the concerns were dyspepsia (indigestion), gout, and lack of strength and vigor. Today, with over 70% of the adult population overweight or obese, being overweight is the rule, not the exception. This has added another danger: normalization. So why are healthcare providers concerned about obesity today? It is not esthetics and it is not fat shaming; the primary concern is that obesity kills. Obesity reduces life expectancy and increases the risk of high blood pressure; type 2 diabetes; coronary heart disease; stroke; osteoarthritis; sleep apnea and breathing problems; endometrial, breast, colon, kidney, gallbladder, and liver cancers; mental illnesses such as depression and anxiety; body pain and difficulties with body functions; and reduces the quality of life (CDC, 2017b). Obesity also costs a lot. The annual medical costs of obesity in the US are estimated at US$ 147 billion and the annual economic loss in the US due to reduced productivity is estimated at between US$ 3 and 6 billion (CDC, 2017b). This is expected to rise because obesity also increases the risk that those who contract COVID-19 will become severely ill and die as it interferes with the immune system (Varney, 2020). A global study has found that obesity makes it twice as likely that those with COVID-19 will end up in the hospital, and 48% more likely that they will die (Boseley, 2020). Furthermore, any COVID-19 vaccine that is developed is likely to be less effective for those who are obese.

Life expectancy in the US went down for the first time in 2017, from 78.7 years to 78.6 years (Murphy et al., 2018). In 2017, 2.8 million people died in the US, almost 70,000 more than died in 2016. Heart disease and cancers account for 43.6% of all deaths in the US. These, along with eight other causes, accounted for 74% of all deaths: unintentional injuries; chronic lower respiratory diseases; stroke; Alzheimer's disease; diabetes; influenza and pneumonia; kidney disease; and suicide. Diabetes deaths alone increased by 2.4% over 2016.

Life expectancy in the US is 5.9 years less than in Hong Kong, which had the longest life expectancy in 2017. The US ranks 45th worldwide in life expectancy behind Japan, all of western Europe, Canada, Australia, New Zealand, South Korea, Israel, Chile, Cyprus, Taiwan, Lebanon, Costa Rica, Cuba, and many other countries (World Population Review, 2017). Heart disease is the leading cause of death, responsible for one-quarter of all deaths in the US (CDC, 2017d). High blood pressure is a major risk factor for heart disease. Research on the relationships between obesity and health conditions found that 81% of high blood pressure and 46% of strokes could be explained by obesity (Akil and Ahmed, 2011). Being overweight or obese increases the risk of stroke directly, and indirectly because excess weight is associated with high blood pressure, sleep apnea, and diabetes, which are all associated with increased risk of stroke (Obesity Action Coalition, n.d.). Both obesity and diabetes are risk factors for heart disease, and obesity also increases the chance of having type 2 diabetes (Barnes and Coulter, 2011).

In addition to heart disease, diabetes, and stroke, obesity increases the risk of hypertension, high cholesterol, gallbladder disease, osteoarthritis, sleep apnea, respiratory problems, and some cancers (US DHHS, 2013). The US DHHS found that weight loss among overweight and obese people reduced their chances of diabetes, reduced symptoms if they had diabetes, improved their cholesterol levels, and reduced blood pressure. The American College of Cardiology (Cardiology Magazine, 2018) states that body fat directly contributes to cardiovascular disease, that metabolically healthy obesity is in fact rare, and recommends that patients reduce body fat through diet, exercise, and surgery, if necessary.

The problem, of course, is that it is very hard to lose weight and one will not lose weight unless one changes what one eats and becomes more active. This means a change in lifestyle, not a temporary change in what one eats. Clearly, the diet that led to weight gain will continue to do so unless changed permanently. There are hundreds of diets purported to help one lose weight. However, the Harvard Medical School (2019) states any diet can help one lose weight as long as it reduces calories below what one uses, but that most diets fail. They recommend that a diet should avoid "bad" foods and make one feel "good." Their food recommendations are similar to Sylvester Graham's in 1830: eat more whole grains and FAV, limit meat consumption, and have a moderate alcohol intake.

The point is that there is no single diet that is a miracle cure-all, but there are guidelines for a diet (and exercise) that would help improve health and reduce weight. These guidelines were outlined nearly 200 years ago, based on observations of their effects on health. More recently, they have been supported by scientific research. What does not seem to be made clear is that current eating patterns are filled with empty calories and that in order for diets to work, eating habits must change permanently. It should not be surprising that one should avoid eating empty calories if one does not want to gain weight or wants to lose weight. What may be difficult to comprehend is that empty calories make up most of what we currently eat; highly processed foods accounted for 61% of all calorie intake in the US and processed foods for over three-quarters of calorie intake (Poti et al., 2015).

This is why it is so difficult to lose weight or to avoid gaining weight. Maintaining a healthy weight means avoiding nearly all the foods we normally eat, nearly all the foods that are sold in supermarkets, and virtually all the foods that are sold in restaurants and institutions. In other words, one would need to avoid our current food system entirely or maneuver it very selectively. No wonder diets fail; it is because our food system has failed us.

The environmental impacts of our food system

Our food system is also failing our planet. Agriculture is the largest user of land and water globally. Over 35% of all land and 50% of all habitable land, or 51 million square kilometers, are devoted to agriculture (Roser and Richie, 2018). Of this, 77% or 40 million km^2 are used to raise livestock, while 23% or 11 million km^2 are used for crops. Agriculture by definition changes the habitat, contributing to species extinction. Loss of tropical forests where biodiversity and species are highest has been driven by conversion to crop and livestock production (NASA, 2007). More recently, industrial agriculture has driven deforestation; five million hectares of forest were lost each year between 2001 and 2015 to industrial commodity agriculture (Stokstad, 2018).

Agriculture is the biggest user of water globally. It uses 69% of all water, or 2,769 km^3 per year, worldwide (FAO, 2016). Asia consumes 75% of the water used for agriculture worldwide. Both Africa and Asia use 81% of all their water consumption for agriculture. Agriculture is responsible for 80% of consumptive water use in the US, and it is 90% in many western states (USDA ERS, 2018b). Less than 8% of all agricultural land is irrigated in the US, but irrigated crops are responsible for half the value of crop sales. Nebraska, followed by California, Arkansas, Texas, and Idaho have the largest areas of irrigated land in the US. Corn (maize) makes up 25% of all irrigated land in the US, hay and forage for animals 18%, soybeans 14%, cotton 7%, and wheat 7%. Since most corn and soy are used for animal feed, that means approximately 57% of the irrigated land in the US is used to feed animals. Mekonnen and Hoekstra (2012) estimate that livestock are responsible for 29% of agriculture's global water footprint, and 98% of livestock's footprint is due to their feed. They calculate that globally, beef cattle contribute 33% of livestock's global water footprint, dairy cattle 19%, pigs 19%, and broilers 11%.

Water scarcity is a growing problem because water usage is increasing at twice the rate of population growth (UN Water, 2018). Yet institutions fail to ensure adequate water supply or infrastructure. The result is that two billion people worldwide are experiencing moderate to high water scarcity all year round (UN Water, 2018) and 4.3 billion are experiencing moderate to high water scarcity at least one month a year (Mekonnen and Hoekstra, 2016).

As the scarcity of water increases, so does the cost of water. Household water rates in the US increased by over 56% between 2010 and 2018 (Circle of Blue, 2018). However, consumers pay much higher rates for water than agricultural producers do. Wholesale untreated water rates for 2019 for municipal and industrial utilities in Southern California were US$ 1,341 per acre-foot (San Diego County Water Authority, 2018). In the Central Valley of California where much of California's irrigated agriculture is located, the 2019 rates for water for agriculture vary from US$ 13 to US$ 95 per acre-foot depending on the month and amount used per acre (Central California Irrigation District, 2019). In other words, the price of untreated water for urban use costs 14 to 103 times more than water for agricultural use.

Agriculture also adversely affects water quality. Nitrates from agriculture are the largest polluter of groundwater globally (FAO, 2017). The nitrates come from fertilizer as well as livestock manure. Mineral fertilizer use increased tenfold between 1960 and 2010. Furthermore, hundreds of millions of liters of manure are stored in lagoons, leaking nitrates, bacteria, viruses, and parasites that cause illnesses (Verberg, 2019). Infants are particularly susceptible to water with elevated nitrates; it can lead to trouble breathing, diarrhea, vomiting, and dehydration (CDC, 2013).

Runoff and soil erosion can also pollute surface water with nutrients and pesticides (FAO, 2017). High levels of nutrients in surface water can cause eutrophication that can kill all life in water, while pesticides find their way into the food web, causing illnesses and reproductive problems in humans and wildlife. It is often difficult to trace the source of pollution to make polluters change their practices or make them pay for the damage they cause. Furthermore, because regulatory efforts to monitor and enforce production methods are costly, little is done to reduce contamination. Hence, the people and the environment downstream pay the costs of pollutants with their health, and at times, their lives.

Livestock produce enormous quantities of waste, which is particularly difficult to dispose of or treat when they are concentrated in feeding operations or dairies (FAO, 2017). Animal waste often finds its way into surface water and contaminants can leach into groundwater. Livestock waste contains pathogens that are responsible for hundreds of thousands of illnesses a year, heavy metals from pesticides and animal feeds, and over

700 emerging pollutants such as antibiotics, vaccines, growth promotors, and hormones used to treat livestock. Aside from the environmental impacts of these contaminants, they pose health risks; standard water treatment methods do not remove them from our tap or bottled water.

Pesticides are another source of contamination. Rachel Carson raised awareness of the dangers of pesticide usage in her best-selling book *Silent Spring* (1962). She documented that residues of pesticides were found all over the globe in the water, soil, and tissues of people and animals for years after the pesticides had been applied. These chemicals result in reproductive problems and death. Indeed, so many birds died that the spring was no longer filled with birdsong, hence the name of the book. These persistent organic pollutants (POPs), like DDT, were responsible for the near extinction of the national symbol, the Bald Eagle, in the lower 48 states of the US. In addition, weed killers were used on tens of millions of hectares. Insecticides and herbicides filled waterways and were sprayed from WWII surplus planes. Chemicals like DDT were found in our food and in mothers' milk. She conveyed research that showed that people who handled insecticides had the same symptoms: aching limbs, joint pain, exhaustion, and irritability. Carson's book raised awareness, eventually leading to the ban on DDT and other POPs in the US (CDC, 2002). Bald eagle and songbird populations began to recover.

We now know that DDT and related chemicals cause cancer in animals and are probable carcinogens in humans (CDC, 2002). DDT and other POPs are stored in body fat and break down very slowly. Despite being banned in 1972 in the US, DDT breaks down so slowly and is so prevalent in the environment, that we continue to ingest it through our food. Nearly all of us have detectable amounts in our blood and babies are born with DDT already in their bodies. DDT is in our food because 614 million kilos of DDT were sprayed in the US over a period of 30 years (Elert, 2010). DDT, along with other POPs, bio-accumulate and accumulate in fat, so they are concentrated in top predators like humans. They are also prevalent in animals high in the food chain, like farmed salmon, which are often fed products made from animal fats.

While DDT has been banned in many countries, it is still widely used in the developing world. In the US and elsewhere, organochlorine insecticides, like DDT, have been replaced with organophosphates, like malathion, because the latter break down faster, and are hence considered safer (Hertz-Picciotto et al., 2018). However, organophosphates originated as biological weapons against humans: nerve gas in the 1930s and 40s. So, it should not be a surprise that the EPA and the WHO consider over 40 commonly used organophosphates as hazardous to human health. While organophosphates have caused deaths, particularly in developing countries, the greatest risk is prenatal exposure. Even low levels of prenatal exposure increase the risk of cognitive and behavioral problems among children, including mental and motor delays, decreased verbal comprehension, lower IQ, ADHD, and autism spectrum disorders.

Autism spectrum disorders in the US have risen by 2,200% since 1980 (Dufault et al., 2012). This dramatic increase has been traced to the ingestion of mercury which weakens the body's ability to break down organophosphates. The US has 11 times the rate of autism spectrum disorder as Italy. However, there are no significant differences in most sources of mercury between the US and Italy: fish consumption, exposure to coal fire plants, food coloring consumption, thimerosal in vaccines (which has not been used in 20 years), and dental fillings. The only source of mercury that differs between Italy and the US is the consumption of high fructose corn syrup (HFCS). Mercury compounds are used in the processing of HFCS (Institute for Agriculture and Trade Policy, 2009). Italians consume almost no HFCS, whereas Americans have consumed over 9.1 kg dry weight of HFCS per year since 1980 when the rise in autism began (Default et al., 2012). Consumption of HFCS in the US climbed to over 27.3 kg dry weight per capita per year from 1998 to 2004. Consumption in 2017 by Americans was 19.4 kg dry weight per capita (USDA ERS, 2018a).[3] HFCS makes up about 10% of all calories consumed by Americans (Institute for Agriculture and Trade Policy, 2009). Thus, HFCS consumption explains the rise in autism spectrum disorders in the US.

Concern about the use of organophosphates themselves resulted in the passage of the 1996 Food Quality Protection Act (FQPA). As a result, between 2000 to 2012, organophosphate insecticide usage in the US decreased from 31.8 million kg per year to 9.1 million kg per year (US EPA, 2017a). More recently, in March 2017, the EPA decided not to ban chlorpyrifos, the most widely used organophosphate in the US, despite a 2016 EPA study that showed that the prevalence of chlorpyrifos in food and water exposed reproductive-aged women, infants, and children to unacceptable levels of chlorpyrifos (Hertz-Picciotto et al., 2018). Chlorpyrifos has been detected in 17.8% of corn samples, 16.7% of wheat,

---

[3] 6,316.4 million kg of HFCS dry weight divided by 325.7 million people.

and 35.5% of almonds (Dufault et al., 2012). In August 2018, the 9th US Circuit Court of Appeals ruled that the EPA had violated federal law by ignoring its own scientists and ordered the EPA to remove chlorpyrifos from sale in the US within 60 days (CBS News, 2018). The Trump administration successfully asked the 9th Circuit Court of Appeals to revisit its decision. The Court gave the EPA 90 days to address concerns by farmworkers and environmental groups about chlorpyrifos before making a final decision on whether to allow or ban it (Davies, 2019). The EPA decided not to ban chlorpyrifos and plans to reassess its decision in 2022 (US EPA, 2019). However, California, New York, and the EU have implemented bans on chlorpyrifos, and its manufacturer plans on halting production by the end of 2020.

One reason it has been difficult to get governments to ban dangerous pesticides is that they generate so much profit. Pesticide usage grew from less than US$ 1 billion in sales in 1970 to over US$ 35 billion per year in 2014 (FAO, 2017). So, just as Carson described nearly 60 years ago, we continue to soak the "green mantle" of the Earth in chemicals, albeit different ones, and expose ourselves and every other species to toxic chemicals that harm our health and the development of our children. It is tragic that anti-vaxxers pursue misplaced, unfounded strategies in the name of "protecting" their children from autism or other health problems, when there is scientific evidence that links autism and many other developmental and cognitive problems with commonly used pesticides and HFCS. While the public is sorely lacking in information about the health impacts of pesticides, the executive branch in the US is doing all it can to protect the interests of pesticide manufacturers.

Herbicides represent two-thirds of all pesticides used in the US (Osteen and Fernandez-Cornejo, 2016). Virtually all conventional corn (maize), soy, and cotton are treated with herbicides, and they are used on 70% of conventional wheat. Corn and soybeans account for 82% or 161.4 million kg per year of herbicide active ingredients in the US. Along with cotton and wheat, these four crops account for 95-97% of US herbicide usage since 1971. Prior to WWII, farmers controlled weeds using mechanical methods and herbicides made from arsenic, sodium, and sulfur. After WWII, synthetic herbicides like 2,4-D were developed, reducing the need for mechanical weed control. Herbicide use in the US increased from 21.8 million kg of active ingredients in 1964 to a peak of 196.8 million kg in 2012. Herbicide usage fell between 1982 and 2002 in the US due to economic and policy factors that influenced which crops were grown, new regulations that limited pesticide usage, new compounds that were applied at lower rates per acre, and the adoption of genetically modified herbicide-tolerant crops in the mid-1990s.

In 1982, glyphosate represented 1% of herbicide usage in the US. It rose to 4% by 1995 as genetically modified (GM) glyphosate-tolerant corn and soy were being introduced, and reached 40% by 2012 (Osteen and Fernandez-Cornejo, 2016). In 2012, 93% of soy, 73% of corn, and 80% of cotton in the US were planted with GM glyphosate-tolerant seed. Since GM glyphosate-tolerant wheat is not available, wheat farmers were slow to adopt glyphosate, but now 80% of conventional durum wheat is treated with glyphosate to dry the wheat so it can be harvested quicker. Glyphosate sales globally were estimated at US$ 8.8 billion for 2019 and are expected to grow (Transparency Market Research, 2018).

Over 1.6 billion kg of glyphosate have been used in the US between 1974 and 2014, and 8.6 billion kg of glyphosate have been used globally between 1994 and 2014 (Benbrook, 2016). Glyphosate is the most widely used herbicide and it is ubiquitous in our environment and in our bodies. Given its heavy use, scientists have already found that weeds intended to be killed by the chemical are developing resistance to glyphosate. There are also human health concerns. We all ingest glyphosate, primarily through food ingredients treated with glyphosate, including baby formulas, and we are also exposed through contaminated soil, water, and air.

The US EPA and the European Union (EU) have ruled that glyphosate does not pose a human health problem, but the WHO's International Agency for Research on Cancer (IARC) has ruled that glyphosate and glyphosate-based products (GBPs) are probable carcinogens (Zimmer, 2018). The difference in risk assessment between these agencies has to do with the methods of analysis used, and that the EPA and the EU have focused on studies of glyphosate, not GBPs, inferring that the evidence is not conclusive (Tarazona et al., 2017). The IARC has taken a more conservative stand on the contradictory findings of glyphosate studies, and has included studies of GBPs; the formulations made with glyphosate for actual use have been found to be much more toxic than pure glyphosate. More recently, Zhang et al. (2019) examined studies of the linkage between non-Hodgkin lymphoma (NHL), a cancer caused by exposure to toxins, and exposure to GBPs; they found that high exposure increased the likelihood of NHL by 41%.

In August 2018, a jury in a California trial found Roundup, a GBP made by Monsanto, contributed to groundskeeper Dwayne Johnson's NHL and awarded him US$ 289 million in compensatory and punitive damages (Yan and Holcombe, 2019). The judge reduced this to US$ 78 million, and Monsanto appealed the case. In March 2019, a jury in a federal trial, also in California, ruled that Roundup contributed to Edwin Hardeman's NHL. The jury awarded him with US$ 80 million (Gonzales, 2019). Many more cases are pending. In the meantime, some local governments, such as Miami, have banned the use of Roundup (Yan and Holcombe, 2019).

In addition to pesticide contamination, agriculture is also a large contributor to climate change. Globally, cultivation of crops, livestock, and deforestation for agriculture are responsible for 24% of greenhouse gas emissions (GHG), while in the US, it is estimated that agriculture contributes to 9% of GHG emissions (US EPA, 2017b; US EPA, 2018). The entire food system, when one includes inputs like fertilizer, as well as processing, packaging, and storage, is estimated to contribute to one-third of all GHG (Gilbert, 2012). Animal products embed higher amounts of GHG because animals require feed. The CO2 equivalents (CO2e) per serving of the following common foods are: beef 3 kg; cheese 1.1 kg; pork 0.8 kg; chicken 0.6 kg; eggs 0.4 kg; milk 0.3 kg; legumes 0.05 kg; and potatoes 0.01 kg (Center for Sustainable Systems, 2018). In other words, a serving of beef has 300 times the carbon footprint as a serving of potato.

Food waste is also an important environmental consequence of our food system. Food is wasted all along the food system, from production, to processing and storage, in retail centers and restaurants, and by households. Globally, it is estimated that one-third of food that is produced is never eaten (FAO, 2011). The blue water footprint of global food waste is estimated at 250 km^3, more than the water used by any single country. The land required to produce food that is wasted is estimated at 1.4 billion hectares, larger than any country except Russia. The carbon footprint of food waste is estimated to be 3.3 trillion kg of CO2e, larger than the emissions of any single country, except for China or the US. Reducing food waste is, therefore, a substantial way to conserve water, reduce deforestation, prevent habitat loss and species extinction, and reduce carbon emissions.

In developing countries, relatively little food is wasted by consumers, and most is lost from production to retail (FAO, 2011). In developed countries, consumers are responsible for about one-third of all wasted food. Overall, perishable foods have high wastage along the entire food chain; over 58%

of FAV and over 40% of fish and seafood harvested are never eaten. However, FAV use relatively little land and water compared to other crops and livestock, and generally have very low carbon footprints. However, the wastage of less perishable foods is surprisingly high; over 36% of cereals are wasted globally. This contrasts with lower rates for high-value products: 23% of meat and 18% of milk are wasted globally.

In the US, the proportion of food waste is estimated at 40% (NRDC, 2017). This is equivalent to US$ 218 billion each year or 1.3% of US GDP. Food waste has increased by 50% since the 1970s. It is now the largest component of landfills, 21% by weight, contributing to the rising cost of solid waste disposal. Reducing food waste conserves land, water, and reduces GHG; US food waste is equivalent to 19% of all US cropland, 21% of all agricultural water use, 18% of all fertilizer use, and 2.6% of all US GHG. Households are responsible for 43% of all food waste in the US, equivalent to 1,250 calories per person per day, and worth US$ 1,800 annually for a household of four. Based on average consumer food expenditure (US BLS, 2018), this is equivalent to wasting more than 40% of their expenditure on food at home.

Overall, we have a food system that is wasteful, and has numerous adverse health and environmental implications. The latter include habitat loss, species extinction, water scarcity, poor water quality, climate change, and toxic chemicals that have detrimental health impacts on humans and other life. Surely, at least farmers are benefiting from our current food system?

Social justice impacts of our food system: US policy and farmers

As it turns out, the US food system is quite profitable, but for the few and the wealthy. Starting with farmers, the US food system is linked with a decline in the number of farms and a rise in very large farms. Historically, the number of farms in the US rose from less than 1.5 million in 1850 to almost 6.5 million in 1920, and has mostly declined since (Figure 4.2). However, part of the changes in farm numbers has to do with changes in how farms have been defined over time (Table 4.1). Prior to 1870, enumerators were not given a definition of a farm (US Department of Commerce, 1954), so each enumerator could decide for themselves. From 1870 to 1890, the definition of a farm was fairly restrictive; operations less than three acres (1.2 ha) could only be counted as farms if they sold at least US$ 500 in agricultural products a year, a rather substantial sum at the time.

The dramatic rise in the number of farms in the 1900 census was due, in part, because the definition of a farm eliminated the minimum acreage and value of production. Any operation could be called a farm, including city dairies, market gardens, or nurseries, as long as at least one person devoted their full time to its care. The definition of a farm for the 1910 and 1920 agricultural censuses changed again, adding acreage and value back in, but was effectively the same as 1900, because it also allowed any operation of any size to be called a farm if at least one person devoted their full time to it (US Department of Commerce, 1928).

Part of the decline in the number of farms since 1920 can be explained because the definition of a farm became more restrictive for the 1925 to 1940 censuses; a farm was any property of three or more acres (1.2 hectares) where there were agricultural operations, or any property less than 3 acres if the value of production for home use and/or sale was worth at least US$ 250 (US Department of Commerce, 1954). The 1950 census excluded home gardens, but the definition of a farm was generally more liberal; farms larger and smaller than 3 acres were required to produce at least US$ 150 for sale and/or home use. The large drop in the number of farms from 5.4 to 4.7 million between 1950 and 1959 was in part due to a much more restrictive definition of a farm starting in 1959. From 1959-1969, a farm was defined as having 10 acres or more with at least US$ 50 in agricultural product sales, or if less than 10 acres (just over four hectares), at least US$ 250 in sales (US Department of Commerce, 1973). Since 1974, the definition of a farm has been any operation that sells or could sell at least US$ 1000 in agricultural products (USDA, 2019; USDA NASS, 2014a).

There are roughly as many farms in the US today as there were in 1860. However, accounting for inflation, the US$ 500 in sales from 1870 that defined a farm would equal US$ 13,856 in 2017 dollars (CPI Inflation calculator, 2019). Since 58% of US farms earned less than US$ 10,000 in 2017, this means that, using the same definition of a farm as in 1870 and adjusting for inflation, the current number of farms would be less than 850,000 (USDA, 2019). Thus, one can see how changing the definition of a farm can change the number of farms counted. Indeed, since the definition of a farm was standardized in 1974, the number of farms has remained fairly constant: between 2.1 and 2.2 million farms.

Figure 4.2 Number of US farms, 1850-2017.

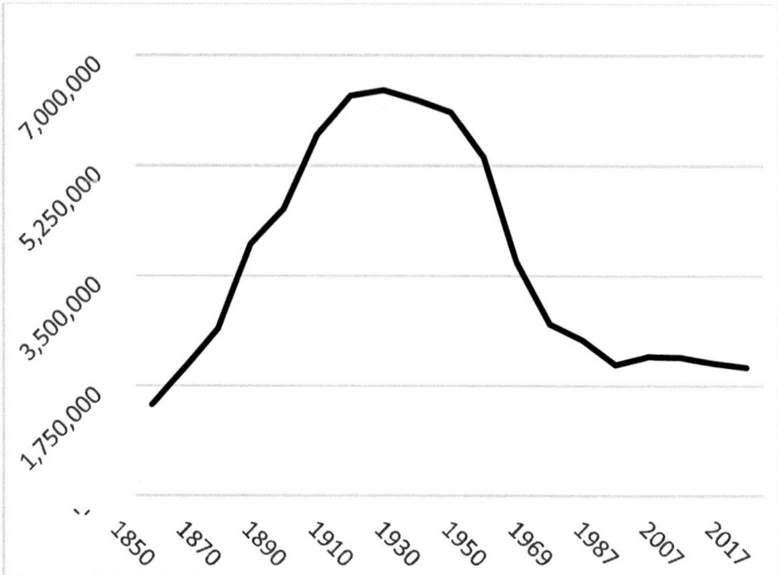

Data sources: USDA, 2019; USDA NASS, 2018; and USDA, n.d.

Table 4.1 Definition of a farm for the US Agricultural Census.

1860	no definition given to enumerators
1870-1890	3+ acres (1.2+ ha); if <3 acres, must sell US$ 500+ in agricultural products
1900	no minimum acreage or value of production, 1+ person full time to its care
1910-1920	any tract of land 3+ acres used for agricultural purposes; if <3 acres, 1+ person devoted full-time to its care or produced at least US$ 250.
1925-1940	3+ acres with agricultural operations, and any property <3 acres if the value of production for home use and/or sale was worth at least US$ 250
1950	home gardens excluded; 3+ acres and produce US$ 150+ for sale and/or home use; properties <3 acres if they produced US$ 150 for sale or home consumption
1959-1969	10+ acres (4+ ha) and sold US$ 50+ in agricultural products; if <10 acres, sold US$ 250 or more
1974-2017	sales of agricultural products of US$ 1000+

Sources: USDA, 2019; USDA NASS, 2014a; US Department of Commerce, 1928; US Department of Commerce, 1954; US Department of Commerce, 1973.

Average farm size in the US has always been large by global standards; in 1850, the average farm size was 82 hectares (Figure 4.3). Farms in the US were large because until 1800, the minimum sale of public land was 259 ha (640 acres) and from 1800 to the Homestead Act in 1862, the minimum was 129 ha (320 acres). Therefore, only the very wealthy could afford to buy public lands, and these properties were too large for a family to farm by themselves. Since hired labor was deemed expensive throughout the 18th and 19th centuries, these public land sales were intended to be farmed using slaves, or re-sold as smaller parcels by speculators.

After the 1846-48 war with Mexico (US National Archives and Records Administration, 2016), which resulted in the acquisition of 525,000 square miles (1.36 million square km) of new territory (History.com editors, 2019), political pressure to make public lands more accessible to more people mounted. The House of Representatives passed homesteading legislation in 1852, 1854, and 1859, only to have the legislation rejected by the Senate. Southern senators were opposed to homesteading because they did not want homestead farmers competing with plantations in their home states. Congress finally passed homesteading legislation in 1860, but it was vetoed by President Buchanan, who despite being a Northerner, sympathized with Southern states and supported slavery in the Kansas territory. During Lincoln's presidency in 1862, in the midst of the Civil War, when secessionists were not allowed to vote in Congress, the Homestead Act finally passed.

The Homestead Act granted almost 65 hectares (160 acres) for a US$ 10 registration fee and gave title after proof of five years of continuous residence cultivating crops (History.com editors, 2019). While it helped many Americans become farmers, the average American still could not afford to homestead because of the costs of travel, tools, and seeds, and living expenses until the first harvest was sold. Thus, it mostly benefited existing farmers in states adjacent to the new territories. Furthermore, the majority of land allocated by the Homestead Act went to speculators, railways, cattlemen, miners, and lumbermen; by 1904, only 16% of the land distributed by the Homestead Act actually went to farmers (Our Documents, n.d.).

Figure 4.3 Average US farm size, 1850-2017 (hectares).

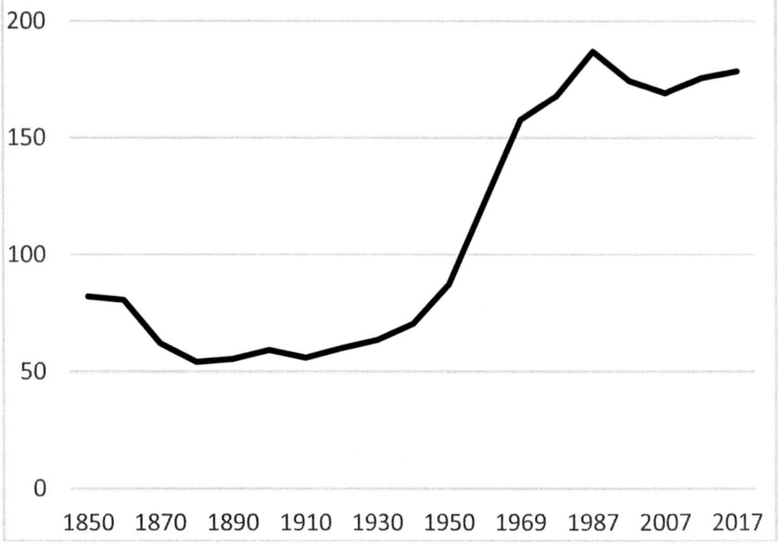

Data sources: USDA NASS, 2019; USDA NASS, 2018 and USDA, n.d.

Average farm size grew from 55.9 ha in 1910 in part because of the way the Agriculture Census defined a farm, and in part as the number of farms decreased and farms consolidated. Average farm size peaked at 187 ha in 1987. Average farm size in the US was 178.5 ha in 2017. Looking at the distribution of farms by size, the number of farms between 50 and 1,999 acres (20 and 809 ha) declined between 1987 and 2017, while the number of farms larger than 2,000 acres (more than 809 ha) has increased (USDA NASS, 2019; USDA NASS, 2018). The number of farms under 50 acres (less than 20 ha), which made up 41.9% of all farms in the US in 2017, has fluctuated from census to census, but increased overall between 1987 and 2017. These farms are often referred to as "hobby" farms because they earn little by way of revenue. Rather, their purpose is often to allow their owners to subsidize their lifestyle because property taxes on agricultural land in the US are a fraction of that for residential land, and owners of these farms can receive subsidies and income tax breaks.

Most revenues from agriculture come from large farms. Farming is highly concentrated: 5.2% of all farms in the US account for 75% of agricultural sales (USDA NASS, 2019). The average size of these large farms is 2,557 acres (1,035 ha). Five products represent 65.5% of all agricultural sales: beef, corn (maize), poultry/eggs, soybeans, and milk (USDA NASS, 2019).

In 2017, only 31.5% of US farms received government payments. These totaled nearly US$ 9 billion in government subsidies, averaging US$ 13,906 per farm (USDA NASS, 2019). Since subsidies are tied to production, the largest subsidies went to the largest farms; 74.1% of government payments went to farms over 202 ha (500 acres) (USDA NASS, 2019). Only 15% of US farms are this large.

Government payments to farms increased from about US$ 8 billion in 2012 to nearly US$ 9 billion in 2017, but those payments have increasingly gone to larger farms (Figure 4.4). Since the US government only subsidizes certain products, such as grains and cotton, only 31.5% of all farms receive subsidies (Figure 4.5). While over 74% of farms over 500 acres received subsidies in 2017, only 19.7% of farms under 220 acres (89 ha) received government support, which averaged US$ 4,298 per farm. Farms larger than 2,000 acres (809 ha) received subsidies averaging US$ 54,343 per farm (Figure 4.4). These government subsidies were nearly equal to the median income per US household in 2017 of US$ 57,652 (US Census Bureau, 2019). Government subsidies were concentrated among a few large farms that already had large incomes: farms over 2,000 acres represented 4.2% of all farms and had an average net farm income of US$ 327,432, while farms under 100 acres (40 ha) represent 56.5% of all farms and their average net farm income in 2017 was US$ 7,995.

Figure 4.4 Government subsidies per farm by farm size (hectares) 2012 and 2017.

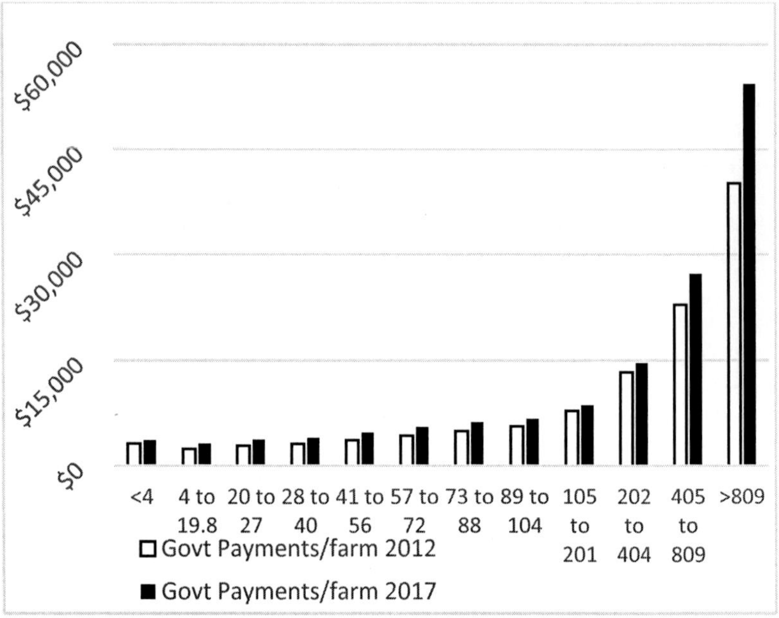

Source of data: USDA NASS, 2014b and 2019.

Figure 4.5 Percentage of farms, sales, government payments, and farms receiving government support by farm size (hectares) in 2017.

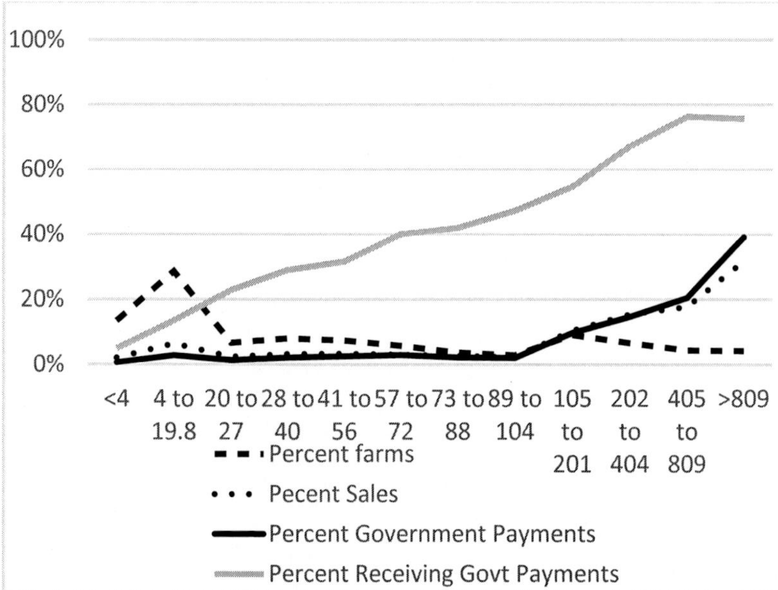

Data source: USDA NASS, 2019.

The largest farms receive the most money because US government agricultural subsidies are tied to production; the more you produce, the more you get. Of course, if all farmers produce more, commodity prices fall, which means farmers need to produce more and/or receive more subsidies to maintain their incomes. Hence, production subsidies incentivize larger and larger farms, simply to maintain farm income. The data on farm size reflect this through growth in the number of the largest category of farms. The overall number of farms declined between 1997 and 2017 by 8%, while during that same period, the number of farms of 2,000 acres (809 ha) or more climbed by 14% (USDA NASS, 2019). The number of farms less than 50 acres (20 ha) has also risen by 51.7% during this period, but given the average net annual income for these farms in 2017 was US$ 4,943, most do not represent economically viable businesses; instead, they are "hobby" farms. The main decline in farm numbers has been among farms in the middle, between 50 and 2,000 acres (20 to 809 ha).

Therefore, the US agricultural system, despite being worth nearly US$ 389 billion in sales annually and receiving almost US$ 9 billion per year in subsidies, is not supporting the majority of farmers. Indeed, the proportion going to the largest farms is increasing (Figure 4.6). The largest farms are reaping the greatest profits and the greatest subsidies. This is not an accident, but the predictable outcome of over two centuries of US land and agricultural policies.

Figure 4.6 Average government subsidy per farm by farm size in hectares, 2012 and 2017.

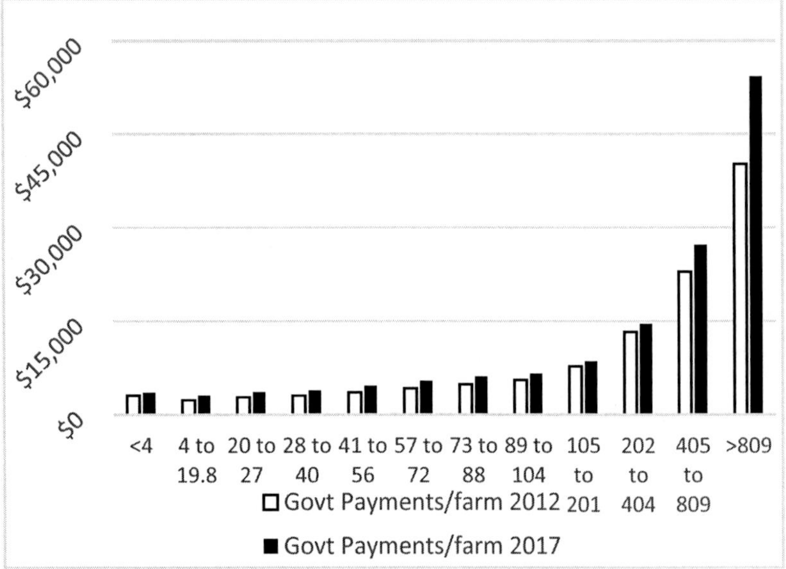

Data sources: USDA NASS, 2014b and 2019.

US agricultural policy has failed most US farmers, with most benefits going to a small number of very large farms. However, remember that farm households, on average, earn more income and have more wealth than the average US household. Looking at who these farmers are reveals even more social injustice. The USDA asks farm operators to designate who is primarily involved in running the farm and to denote one "primary producer" for each farm. Who are these US farmers? The simple answer is that they are old White men: 67.8% of primary producers were White men averaging 58.6 years old (USDA NASS, 2019). About one-quarter of all primary producers were White men 65 years or older. Compare this to the

US population in 2017; White men over 65 represented only 5.1% of the total US population (based on data in Administration for Community Living, 2018).

White females made up 27.6% of all primary producers, meaning that 95.4% of all primary producers in the US were White (USDA NASS, 2019). Contrast this with the percentage of the US population that was White, 76.6%, or White, not Hispanic, 60.7% (US Census, 2019). African Americans made up 13.4% of the US population but only 1.4% of the primary producers. African American males made up 1.1% of all primary producers and African American females 0.3%. Hispanics of any race made up 18.1% of the US population but only 3.3% of all primary producers: Hispanic males constituted 2.3% and Hispanic females 0.96% of all primary producers. Furthermore, women producers had smaller farms; female primary producers made up 38.8% of farms under 10 acres (4 ha), but only 5% of those over 2,000 acres (809 ha).

Rather than stemming the decline in the number of farms, US agricultural policies have encouraged fewer, larger farms because most subsidies go to the biggest farms. Furthermore, the policies have enriched the already privileged. They have resulted in funneling more income and wealth to households who earn more and have more wealth than the average US household. And those subsidies primarily favor an already very privileged group: old White men. US agricultural policies function to perpetuate gender and racial inequality.

US agriculture and its workers

Those who are doing the work in agriculture are less privileged. Most are foreign-born and many do not speak English. Their work is hard and dangerous. Many work very long hours, yet live in poverty. It is estimated there are 2.5 to 3 million agricultural workers in the US (NCFH, 2018), another 109,000 workers on dairies and feedlots (NCFH, 2014), and about 500,000 are employed by slaughterhouses and meat processors (Food Empowerment Project, 2019).

Of the total number of agricultural workers in the US, 37% work in vegetables, 32% in fruit and nuts, 19% in horticulture, 10% in field crops, and 3% in mixed operations (Hernandez and Gabbard, 2018). Over three-quarters of US agricultural workers are foreign-born, with 69% from Mexico, 6% from Central America, and 1% from other countries. Of the foreign-born, 78% have been in the US for at least ten years. Nearly half of agricultural workers are undocumented, while 29% are US citizens, 21% are legal permanent residents, and 1% had an H2-A or other visa. The primary language of 77% of agricultural workers is Spanish. The average age is 38 years old, the average education is eighth grade, 68% are male, 57% are married, and 55% have children. They work an average of 45 hours a week for US$ 10.60 per hour. One-third have household incomes below the poverty level and 53% have no form of health insurance at all. In other words, agricultural workers are largely Latinos who work long hours for little pay.

Among the workers on dairies and cattle ranches, 41% are foreign-born, of which three-quarters are from Mexico and one-quarter are from Central America (NCFH 2014). They tend to be young, male, and uneducated. They work even longer hours for even less pay: an average of 62 hours per week in dairies for US$ 554, or US$ 8.94 per hour. Workers in feedlots earn somewhat more: US$ 743 per week. Their work is also dangerous, and their injury and illness rates are 68% above the average for private industry. However, 88% do not have health insurance.

Meatpacking is also dominated by the foreign-born. The work is dangerous because each worker on the line has a single, repetitive task, using knives or cutting equipment. At times, workers cannot keep up with line speed or do not have time to sharpen knives. This can result in injuries. Among slaughterhouse workers in the US, an average of two amputations a week occur (Wasley, Cook, and Jones, 2018). Yet the industry is pushing to remove the cap on line speeds. In addition to adversely affecting the safety of workers, increased line speed also poses a risk to consumers because it increases the chances of workers accidentally puncturing animals' intestines, leading to salmonella or E. coli contamination of meat (van der Zee et al., 2020). Salmonella incidence is on the rise, with one in ten poultry processing plants failing government tests. Yet during early 2020, poultry plants were allowed to increase their line speed at the same time that the number of government inspectors fell by 10%, and many plants were hit by a shortage of workers due to COVID-19 (Kendall, 2020). Although short-staffed, the remaining workers have had to contend with increased line speeds, leading to safety issues. As a result, anonymous safety complaints in the first half of 2020 have increased by 30% compared to 2019. The US government's response has been that they do not have the staff to process the complaints, but they will allow companies that meet certain conditions to increase line speeds from 140 birds a minute to 175.

Workers also suffer chronic ailments due to performing repetitive tasks; 42% of poultry workers have been found to have carpal tunnel syndrome (Kendall, 2020). Hazardous cleaning chemicals and slippery floors covered in blood and guts also result in injuries (Food Empowerment Project, 2019). The US government relies on companies to voluntarily report workers' injuries and, therefore, underreporting is chronic. Furthermore, immigrant workers are often afraid they will lose their job if they report injuries, or are actively discouraged from reporting.

Meatpacking workers used to be mostly undocumented immigrants from Mexico and Central America (Miroff, 2018). However, slaughterhouses and processing plants have been targeted by Immigration and Customs Enforcement (ICE) raids. In one of the largest ICE operations, 1,300 workers at Swift slaughterhouses in six states were arrested on December 12, 2006. After the ICE raids, the Brazilian company JBS bought out Swift and had to increase wages by 25%. It replaced undocumented workers with those with refugee status. At a single plant, over 20 languages were spoken and refugees came from Burma, Thailand, Malaysia, Sudan, and Somalia. The Trump administration's cuts in refugee admissions have created a shortage of these workers in slaughterhouses. Wages now average US$ 17 per hour, plus health insurance, and free English classes. Despite this, one employee said he has seen only two or three White Americans cutting meat in ten years. He reported that half the workers were Hispanic, mostly immigrants, and the other half were refugees. Non-Hispanic White Americans in the nearby town claimed they would not work in the meatpacking plant unless it paid US$ 30 an hour.

The approximately 2.5 to 3 million agricultural, livestock, and meatpacking workers in the US work for far less, and the work is hard, dangerous, and often involves exposure to toxic chemicals, dangerous accidents, and chronic ailments. Because of the danger and low pay, the workers are largely foreign-born. Farmers claim they cannot raise wages, while slaughterhouses have only done so because of immigration enforcement. Yet employers complain there is a shortage of workers, while at the same time increasing production targets and line speeds that result in even more injuries and deaths. Obviously, if wages were higher and working conditions were better, there would be no worker shortage. Aside from higher profits, keeping wages low is one way of ensuring that workers are vulnerable, living paycheck to paycheck, making them unwilling to complain or take part in organized labor, lest they lose their job.

COVID-19 has added an additional danger; as essential workers, agricultural and food processing workers have had high rates of infection. At some plants, 20-30% of workers have tested positive (Ho, 2020; Kendall, 2020). One plant that produces about 5% of the pork in the US closed due to hundreds of workers testing positive for COVID-19 (van der Zee et al., 2020). Workers complain that companies have not provided protective gear, have not allowed for social distancing, have not informed them when co-workers test positive, have not given them paid leave as mandated by federal law when they become ill, and have fired workers who have complained or attempted to mobilize themselves. Yet they continue to go to work because they have families to support and may not have access to unemployment benefits.

Consumers rarely spare a thought for the working conditions of those who harvest or process their food: the pesticides workers are exposed to, the injuries, the chronic respiratory problems, the amputations, or the exploitation. The question is why should they? Is it unreasonable to expect farms and companies to keep their workers safe? Is it unreasonable to expect the government to ensure that workers are protected? Why do we have a food system built on the exploitation of vulnerable workers, often immigrants? The US is not alone in this respect; plantations in Malaysia and Indonesia, which produce 85% of the world's palm oil, have been accused of enslaving workers, child labor, and rape (Mason and McDowell, 2020). However, over its history, US policies have been deliberate and persistent in exploiting the labor of slaves and immigrants in our food system. Colonial policies actively rewarded the use of indentured servants and slaves. Until the Civil War, the minimum size of US public land sales was so large it could only be farmed with slave labor. Even after the Homestead Act, only 16% of the public lands went to farmers. With the implementation of direct subsidies via Farm Bills, these have benefited the largest farms, encouraged farms to get larger, and fostered dependence on immigrant labor.

Do US agricultural policies ensure people get access to food?

Putting aside the impacts of our food system on the environment, on most farmers, and on agricultural workers, surely our food system must be providing cheap food to those in need? Despite having the lowest proportion of food to total expenditures of any country in the world, or at any time in its history, 40 million Americans, 1 in 8, received government food assistance in 2018 (USDA FNS, 2018), costing taxpayers US$ 65 billion (Farm Bureau, 2018). There is some overlap with another 46 million Americans, 1 in 7, who received assistance through a non-profit network of food banks and food pantries (Feeding America, 2019). Clearly, the US food system has not addressed the issues of food access because many Americans are struggling to obtain adequate food.

Food insecurity does not just affect the 39.7 million people who are officially poor in the US (US Census Bureau, 2018). It does not even affect all the poor; only half of all those living below the official poverty line are food insecure (Gundersen and Ribar, 2011), while 20% of US households earning two to three times the US poverty level experience food insecurity, and 10% of households earning three or more times the poverty level experience food insecurity (Schanzenbach et al., 2016).

Food insecurity arises due to a number of reasons, including inadequate incomes, job loss, debt, and medical bills. Food has become a way to manage budgets for those who are living paycheck to paycheck (Zepeda, 2018). With wages stagnant or effectively cut due to the increasing contributions to benefits like health insurance, 78% of US workers are living paycheck to paycheck (Milligan, 2019). Americans are notorious for their low savings rates: 61% of workers do not have US$ 1,000 in savings to cover an emergency. This means that in order to cover fixed expenses like rent or mortgage, utilities, transportation, medical bills, or the US$ 1.4 trillion in student loans, even people with relatively high incomes will resort to skipping meals or eating cheap starches to make ends meet (Zepeda, 2018). Along with adverse health impacts, their inability to afford food affects their ability to socialize, creating isolation. Many hide their food insecurity from their co-workers, friends, and even family members, often feeling a sense of shame and societal blame.

The inability of large portions of the US population to afford adequate food is compounded by the poor quality of the American diet. What we eat is dominated by empty calories and is lacking in appropriate nutrients. Americans are faced with over 40,000 different items in the average grocery store (Toops, 2017). Yet this appearance of choice masks a highly dysfunctional food system: over 60% of the foods we eat are highly processed (Poti et al., 2015) and 10% of all calories consumed by Americans come from HFCS (Institute for Agriculture and Trade Policy, 2009). Companies have so filled foods with added sugars that an Irish court was asked to rule whether the baked good Subway uses for its sandwiches is bread; they determined it is not, because it contains five times the maximum amount of added sugars allowed in bread (Sullivan, 2020).

A predictable result of these empty calorie options (and lack of exercise) is that over 70% of Americans are overweight or obese, which has led to numerous health conditions that have reduced life expectancy and quality of life (CDC, 2017a, 2017b). The medical costs of obesity alone in the US are estimated at US$ 147 billion per year and the annual economic loss in the US due to reduced productivity, at between US$ 3 and 6 billion per year (CDC, 2017b). On average, US households now spend more on health care than on food eaten at home, despite the fact that food-related illnesses are the leading medical conditions.

Furthermore, consumers are asked to pay to extract the pollutants emitted by large commercial farms and CAFOs. Water utility users are paying an estimated US$ 1.7 billion annually in the US to remove the excess nitrogen due to agricultural practices (Ribaudo et al., 2011). In addition, the annual environmental and economic costs to consumers of pesticide use are estimated at US$ 10 billion, with health costs expected to rise (Pimentel, 2005). Hence, US agricultural and food policies are failing to reduce food insecurity and exposing consumers to externalized direct and indirect economic and health costs due to agricultural practices.

Then who benefits from the US food system?

This begs the question, if consumers are unable to get adequate and nutritious food and are suffering from food-related illnesses and contaminants from agriculture, agricultural workers and most farmers are struggling financially, and the impacts of US agricultural policies are detrimental to the environment, who then is benefiting?

Large farmers of subsidized crops certainly benefit, particularly corn (maize) and wheat farmers. US$ 13.8 billion was spent in direct government subsidies in FY2018 (USDA ERS, 2019). While only 31.5% of all farms received subsidies, 74.1% of government payments went to farms over 500 acres (202 ha) (USDA NASS, 2019).

Companies selling agricultural chemicals, seeds, and animal genetics also gain because they have oligopolies. Four companies control over half of the seed market, over 60% of the agrochemical market, and two-thirds of the swine genetics; three companies control 95% of the broiler genetics; and only two companies control 94% of the laying hen genetics (Hendrickson, Howard, and Constance, 2017). Farmers not only have little choice in what seeds, chemicals, or genetics they can use, they also have very little choice whom to sell to. For example, Ardent Mills controls one-third of the wheat flour market, while four companies in the US control 85% of beef slaughter (Hendrickson, Howard, and Constance, 2017).

Indeed, in 2016, US farmers received on average less than 19% of the retail price of foods and beverages in grocery stores (Stewart, 2018). For bread, the share wheat farmers receive is even lower, 3%, while the farm share reached 32% of the retail price of cheddar cheese. Grocery sales at US supermarkets and clubs are ten times larger than the aggregate net income of farmers (Dudlicek et al., 2018; USDA ERS, 2019). US farmers receive an even smaller portion of the expenditure on eating out: only 4% on average (Stewart, 2018).

Along with large farms and agrochemical companies, food brands, retailers, restaurants, and food services also profit from our food system. Food brands, retailers, and restaurants offer consumers the appearance of choice, but essentially a few companies control what is offered and reap the profits. The world's five largest food companies own two out of three global food brands (Ramsey, 2003). The top five food retailers in the US sold 48% of the groceries in the US (Costco, 2018 Dudlicek et al., 2018). Four companies sell 40% of the fast food in the US, and two companies sell most of the food to restaurants, hotels, hospitals and other institutions (Hendrickson, Howard and Constance, 2017).

The US food system produces vast amounts of food with incredible amounts of water and chemicals. It relies on the exploitation of natural resources and immigrant labor. Yet most farmers are dependent on a handful of companies for their agro-chemical, seed, and genetic inputs, and have equally few options to sell their products. The result is a system that exploits farmers to produce cheap inputs for processed foods sold by a handful of food companies to a handful of retailers and restaurant/institutional food suppliers. About 20 companies dominate most aspects of our food system. The market power they wield is immense: they can set the prices they buy and sell at; they sell us products that are unhealthy for workers, the environment, and our health; and all these costs of the food system are externalized so that someone else has to pay for the effects.

Exercise: Look in your refrigerator

Look in your refrigerator, cupboards, pantry, or wherever else you store food. What do you see? What foods do you have? What are their ingredients? What food companies are represented?

References

Administration for Community Living. 2018. 2017 profile of older Americans. April.
https://acl.gov/sites/default/files/Aging%20and%20Disability%20in%20America/2017OlderAmericansProfile.pdf, accessed March 28, 2019.

Akil, L. and Ahmed, H. A. 2011. Relationship between obesity and cardiovascular disease in four southern states and Colorado. Journal of Health Care for the Poor and Underserved, 22 (4 Supplemental), 61–72.
https://www.ncbi.nlm.nih.gov/pmc/articles/PMC3250069/,
accessed March 15, 2019.

Angadjivand, S. 2018. U.S. Farm Commodity Support: An Overview of Selected Programs. CRS Report, April 17. Congressional Research Service.
https://fas.org/sgp/crs/misc/R45165.pdf, accessed February 11, 2019.

Barnes, A. S. and Coulter, S. A. 2011. The epidemic of obesity and diabetes: trends and treatments. Texas Heart Institute Journal, 38(2), 142–144.
https://www.ncbi.nlm.nih.gov/pmc/articles/PMC3066828/,
accessed March 18, 2019.

Benbrook, C. M. 2016. Trends in glyphosate herbicide use in the United States and globally. Environmental Sciences Europe, 28(3), 1–15.
https://www.ncbi.nlm.nih.gov/pmc/articles/PMC5044953/,
accessed March 21, 2019.

Boseley, S. 2020. Obesity increases risk of Covid-19 death by 48% study finds. The Guardian, August 26.
https://www.theguardian.com/world/2020/aug/26/obesity-increases-risk-of-covid-19-death-by-48-study-finds?CMP=Share_AndroidApp_Other,
accessed August 27, 2020.

Cardiology Magazine. 2018. Cover story: obesity and cardiovascular disease risk. American College of Cardiology. July 23.

https://www.acc.org/latest-in-cardiology/articles/2018/07/06/12/42/cover-story-obesity-and-cardiovascular-disease-risk, accessed March 15, 2019.

CBS News. 2018. Appeals court orders EPA to ban sales of widely-used farm pesticide chlorpyrifos. August 10. https://www.cbsnews.com/news/epa-dow-chemical-farm-pesticide-chlorpyrifos-scott-pruitt-appeals-court-ban-sales/, accessed March 21, 2019.

CDC. 2002. Public health statement for DDT, DDE, DDD. Agency for Toxic Substances and Disease Registry. https://www.atsdr.cdc.gov/phs/phs.asp?id=79&tid=20, accessed March 18, 2019.

CDC. 2013. Nitrates/nitrites poisoning: Patient education care instruction sheet. https://www.atsdr.cdc.gov/csem/nitrate_2013/docs/nitrate_patient-education.pdf, accessed March 18, 2019.

CDC. 2017a. Data & statistics. https://www.cdc.gov/obesity/data/index.html, accessed March 14, 2019.

CDC. 2017b. Adult obesity causes and consequences. https://www.cdc.gov/obesity/adult/causes.html, accessed March 13, 2019.

CDC. 2017c. Table 53. Selected health conditions and risk factors, by age: United States, selected years 1988–1994 through 2015–2016. Health, United States. https://www.cdc.gov/nchs/data/hus/2017/053.pdf, accessed September 30, 2020.

CDC. 2017d. Heart disease facts. https://www.cdc.gov/heartdisease/facts.htm, accessed March 15, 2019.

Center for Sustainable Systems, University of Michigan. 2018. Carbon Footprint Factsheet. Publication number CSS09-05. http://css.umich.edu/factsheets/carbon-footprint-factsheet, accessed March 22, 2019.

Central California Irrigation District. 2019. 2019 water supply information. Water supply and rates: Water management. February 4. https://ccidwater.org/water-management/water-supply-and-rates/, accessed March 21, 2019.

Circle of Blue. 2018. The price of water. https://www.circleofblue.org/waterpricing/, accessed March 21, 2019.

Costco. 2018. Annual report 2018, fiscal year ended September 2, 2018. http://investor.costco.com/Mobile.view?c=83830&d=10&v=100, accessed February 28, 2019.

CPI Inflation calculator. 2019. US Inflation Rate, $500 in 1870 to 2017. http://www.in2013dollars.com/1870-dollars-in-2017?amount=500, accessed March 25, 2019.

Cummings, R. O. 1941. An American and His Food: A History of Food Habits in the United States, revised edition. Chicago: The University of Chicago Press.

Davies, S. 2019. EPA given 90 days to make decision on chlorpyrifos. Agri-Pulse, April 19. https://www.agri-pulse.com/articles/12122-epa-given-90-days-to-make-decision-on-chlorpyrifos accessed May 17, 2019.

Dudlicek, J. 2018. Top 50 grocers: Amazon in 8th place while rest of industry restrategizes, reshuffles. The Progressive Grocer, May 7. https://progressivegrocer.com/top-50-grocers-2018-ranked, accessed February 28, 2019.

Dudlicek, J., Goldschmidt, B., Hofbauer, R., and Martin, K. 2018. 85th annual report of the grocery industry. Progressive Grocer, 97(4), 26-30. http://www.nxtbook.com/nxtbooks/ensembleiq/pg_201804/index.php#/30, accessed February 28, 2019.

Dufault, R., Lukiw, W. J., Crider, R., Schnoll, R., Wallinga, D. and Deth, R. 2012. A macroepigenetic approach to identify factors responsible for the autism epidemic in the United States. Clinical Epigenetics, 4. https://clinicalepigeneticsjournal.biomedcentral.com/articles/10.1186/1868-7083-4-6, accessed March 20, 2019.

Elert, E. 2010. US food still tainted with old chemicals. Scientific American, April 22. https://www.scientificamerican.com/article/chemical-tainted-food/, accessed March 18, 2019.

FAO. 2011. Global food losses and food waste—Extent, causes and prevention. Rome: Food and Agriculture Organization. http://www.fao.org/3/a-i2697e.pdf, accessed March 22, 2019.

FAO. 2016. Water withdrawals by sector, around 2010. AQUASTAT. November. http://www.fao.org/nr/water/aquastat/tables/WorldData-Withdrawal_eng.pdf, accessed March 18, 2019.

FAO. 2017. Water pollution from agriculture: a global review. http://www.fao.org/3/a-i7754e.pdf, accessed March 18, 2019.

Farm Bureau. 2018. Reviewing the 2018 Farm Bill baseline. December 17. https://www.fb.org/market-intel/reviewing-the-2018-farm-bill-baseline, accessed February 11, 2019.

Feeding America. 2019. https://www.feedingamerica.org/hunger-in-america, accessed April 1, 2019.

Food Empowerment Project. 2019. Slaughterhouse workers. https://foodispower.org/human-labor-slavery/slaughterhouse-workers/, accessed March 28, 2019.

Gilbert, N. 2012. One-third of our greenhouse gas emissions come from agriculture. Nature, October 31. https://www.nature.com/news/one-third-of-our-greenhouse-gas-emissions-come-from-agriculture-1.11708, accessed March 22, 2019.

Gonzales, R. 2019. Jury awards $80 million in damages in Roundup weed killer cancer trial. National Public Radio, March 27. https://www.npr.org/2019/03/27/707439575/jury-awards-80-million-in-damages-in-roundup-weed-killer-cancer-trial, accessed March 31, 2019.

Gundersen, C., and Ribar, D. 2011. Food insecurity and insufficiency at low levels of food expenditures. Review of Income and Wealth, 57(4), 704–726.

Harvard Medical School. 2019. Diet & weight loss. https://www.health.harvard.edu/topics/diet-and-weight-loss, accessed March 18, 2019.

Hendrickson, M. K., Howard, P. H., and Constance, D. H. 2017. Power, food and agriculture. Implications for farmers, consumers and communities. University of Missouri, College of Agriculture, Food & Natural Resources Division of Applied Social Sciences Working Paper. https://philhowardnet.files.wordpress.com/2017/11/hendrickson-howard-constance-2017-final-working-paper-nov-1.pdf, accessed February 28, 2019.

Hernandez, T. and Gabbard, S. 2018. Findings from the National Agricultural Workers Survey (NAWS) 2015-2016. A Demographic and Employment Profile of United States Farmworkers. Research Report No. 13. JBS International. https://www.doleta.gov/naws/pages/research/docs/NAWS_Research_Report_13.pdf, accessed March 28, 2018.

Hertz-Picciotto, I., Sass, J. B., Engel, S., Bennett, D. H., Bradman, A., Eskenazi, B., Lanphear, B., and Whyatt, R. 2018. Organophosphate exposures during pregnancy and child neurodevelopment: Recommendations for essential policy reforms. PLOS Medicine, October 24. https://doi.org/10.1371/journal.pmed.1002671, accessed March 19, 2019.

History.com editors. 2019. Treaty of Guadalupe Hidalgo. A&E Television Networks. February 6. https://www.history.com/topics/mexican-american-war/treaty-of-guadalupe-hidalgo, accessed February 20, 2019.

Ho, V. 2020. "Everyone tested positive": Covid devastates agriculture workers in California's heartland. The Guardian, August 8. https://www.theguardian.com/us-news/2020/aug/08/california-covid-19-central-valley-essential-workers?CMP=Share_AndroidApp_Gmail, accessed August 27, 2020.

Institute for Agriculture and Trade Policy. 2009. Mercury and high fructose corn syrup: Frequently asked questions. https://www.iatp.org/sites/default/files/421_2_105091.pdf, accessed March 22, 2019.

Kendall, L. 2020. "Incredibly dangerous job": concerns safety is slipping at US meat plants. The Guardian, October 1. https://www.theguardian.com/environment/2020/oct/01/incredibly-dangerous-job-concerns-safety-is-slipping-at-us-meat-plants?CMP=Share_AndroidApp_Other, accessed October 1, 2020.

Mason, M. and McDowell, R. 2020. Palm oil labor abuses linked to world's top brands, banks. Associated Press, September 24. https://apnews.com/article/virus-outbreak-only-on-ap-indonesia-financial-markets-malaysia-7b634596270cc6aa7578a062a30423bb, accessed September 24, 2020.

Mekonnen, M. M. and Hoekstra, A. Y. 2012. A global assessment of the water footprint of farm animal production. Ecosystems, 15, 401–415. https://link.springer.com/article/10.1007/s10021-011-9517-8, accessed March 21, 2019.

Mekonnen, M. M. and Hoekstra, A. Y. 2016. Four billion people facing severe water scarcity. Science Advances, 2(2), e1500323. http://advances.sciencemag.org/content/2/2/e1500323/tab-figures-data, accessed March 21, 2019.

Milligan, S. 2019. Stretched thin. US News and Reports, January 11. https://www.usnews.com/news/the-report/articles/2019-01-11/stretched-thin-majority-of-americans-live-paycheck-to-paycheck, accessed April 1, 2019.

Miroff, R. 2018. After an ICE raid, few Americans showed up to work at this Texas meatpacking plant. The Texas Tribune, March 5. https://www.texastribune.org/2018/03/05/even-after-ice-raid-few-american-workers-showed-work-texas-meatpacking/, accessed March 28, 2019.

Mohan, G. 2020. California banned a pesticide from your food. Now it won't be manufactured. The Los Angeles Times, February 6. https://www.latimes.com/business/story/2020-02-06/california-chlorpyrifos-ban-production, accessed August 31, 2020.

Murphy, S. L., Xu, J., Kochanek, K. D., and Arias, E. 2018. Mortality in the United States, 2017. NCHS Data Brief, No. 328. November. https://www.cdc.gov/nchs/data/databriefs/db328-h.pdf, accessed March 15, 2019.

NASA. 2007. Causes of deforestation: Direct causes. March 30. https://earthobservatory.nasa.gov/features/Deforestation/deforestation_update3.php, accessed March 18, 2019.

NCFH (National Center for Farmworker Health). 2014. Dairy workers. http://www.ncfh.org/uploads/3/8/6/8/38685499/fs-dairyworkers.pdf, accessed March 28, 2019.

NCFH (National Center for Farmworker Health). 2018. Agricultural worker fact sheet. http://www.ncfh.org/uploads/3/8/6/8/38685499/fs-facts_about_ag_workers_2018.pdf, accessed March 28, 2019.

NRDC. 2017. Wasted: How America is losing up to 40 percent of its food from farm to fork to landfill. https://www.nrdc.org/sites/default/files/wasted-2017-report.pdf, accessed March 22, 2019.

Obesity Action Coalition. n.d. Obesity and stroke fact sheet. https://www.obesityaction.org/wp-content/uploads/Obesity-and-Stroke-Fact-Sheet.pdf, accessed March 18, 2019.

Osteen, C. D. and Fernandez-Cornejo, J. 2016. Herbicide use trends: a backgrounder. Choices, 31(4). https://ageconsearch.umn.edu/bitstream/250108/2/cmsarticle_544.pdf, accessed March 21, 2019.

Our Documents. n.d. Homestead Act (1862). https://www.ourdocuments.gov/doc.php?flash=false&doc=31, accessed February 15, 2019.

Pimentel, D. 2005. Environmental and economic costs of the application of pesticides primarily in the United States. Environment, Development and Sustainability, 7(2), 229–252.

Poti, J. M., Mendez, M. A., Ng, S. W., and Popkin, B. M. 2015. Is the degree of food processing and convenience linked with the nutritional quality of foods purchased by US households? American Journal of Clinical Nutrition, 101(6), 1251–62.

Ramsey, J. 2003. Whither global branding? The case of food manufacturing. Journal of Brand Management, 11(1), 9–21.

Ribaudo, M., Delgado, J., Hansen, L., Livingston, M., Mosheim, R., and Williamson, J. 2005. Nitrogen in agricultural systems: Implications for

conservation policy. USDA Economic Research Service, Economic Research Report 127.
https://www.ers.usda.gov/webdocs/publications/44918/6767_err127.pdf?v=0, accessed April 1, 2019.

Roser, M. and Ritchie, H. 2018. Yields and land use in agriculture. https://ourworldindata.org/yields-and-land-use-in-agriculture, accessed March 18, 2018.

San Diego County Water Authority. 2018. Water Authority's proposed 2019 rates the smallest in years: Successful litigation and Rate Stabilization Fund benefit ratepayers. May 17. https://www.sdcwa.org/water-authoritys-proposed-2019-rate-increases-smallest-years, accessed March 21, 2019.

Schanzenbach, D. W., Bauer, L., and Nanzt, G. 2016. Twelve facts about food insecurity and SNAP. The Hamilton Project, The Brookings Institute. http://www.hamiltonproject.org/papers/twelve_facts_about_food_insecurity_and_snap, accessed August 30, 2016.

Stewart, H. 2018. Monitoring trends in retail prices and farm shares of food products. USDA ERS August 6. https://www.ers.usda.gov/amber-waves/2018/august/monitoring-trends-in-retail-prices-and-farm-shares-of-food-products/, accessed April 1, 2019.

Stokstad, E. 2018. New global study reveals the 'staggering' loss of forests caused by industrial agriculture. Science, September 13.
https://www.sciencemag.org/news/2018/09/scientists-reveal-how-much-world-s-forests-being-destroyed-industrial-agriculture, accessed March 18, 2019.

Sullivan, H. 2020. Irish court rules Subway bread is not bread. The Guardian, October 1.
https://www.theguardian.com/world/2020/oct/01/irish-court-rules-subway-bread-is-not-bread?CMP=Share_AndroidApp_Other, accessed October 1, 2020.

Tarazona, J. V., Court-Marques, D., Tiramani, M., Reich, H., Pfeil, R., Istace, F. and Crivellente, F. 2017. Glyphosate toxicity and carcinogenicity: A review of the scientific basis of the European Union assessment and its differences with IARC. Archives of Toxicology, 91(8), 2723–2743.

https://link.springer.com/article/10.1007%2Fs00204-017-1962-5, accessed March 22, 2019.

Transparency Market Research. 2018. Glyphosate market for genetically modified and conventional crops to gain revenue worth US$8.79 bn by 2019. June 12. https://www.globenewswire.com/news-release/2018/06/12/1520433/0/en/Glyphosate-Market-for-Genetically-Modified-and-Conventional-Crops-to-Gain-Revenue-Worth-US-8-79-bn-by-2019.html, accessed March 21, 2019.

Toops, D. 2017. Chapter 2: How did the food industry get (from there) to here? Accelerating New Food Product Design and Development, Second Edition. Edited by J. H. Beckley, L. J. Herzog, and M. M. Foley. Hoboken, NJ: John Wiley & Sons Ltd and the Institute of Food Technologists. http://www.ift.org/~/media/Knowledge%20Center/Publications/Books/Samples/IFTPressBook_ANFPDD_Chapter1.pdf, accessed February 4, 2019.

US BLS 2018. Table 1101. Quintiles of income before taxes: Annual expenditure means, shares, standard errors, and coefficients of variation, Consumer Expenditure Survey, 2017. September. https://www.bls.gov/cex/2017/combined/quintile.pdf, accessed February 6, 2019.

US Census Bureau. 2018. Income and poverty in the United States: 2017. Report number P60-263. September 12. https://www.census.gov/library/publications/2018/demo/p60-263.html, accessed April 1, 2018.

US Census Bureau. 2019. Quick Facts United States. https://www.census.gov/quickfacts/fact/table/US/PST045218, accessed May 17, 2019.

USDA n.d. Census of agriculture historical archive. 1850 to 2002. http://agcensus.mannlib.cornell.edu/AgCensus/homepage.do, accessed March 22, 2019.

USDA ERS. 2018a. Table 30-US high fructose corn syrup (HFCS) supply and use, by calendar year. April 17. https://www.ers.usda.gov/data-products/sugar-and-sweeteners-yearbook-tables/sugar-and-sweeteners-yearbook-tables/#Corn%20Sweetener%20Supply,%20Use,%20and%20Trade, accessed March 20, 2019.

USDA ERS. 2018b. Irrigation and water use. December 14. https://www.ers.usda.gov/topics/farm-practices-management/irrigation-water-use/, accessed March 21, 2019.

USDA ERS. 2019. Highlights from the March 2019 Farm Income Forecast. March 7. https://www.ers.usda.gov/topics/farm-economy/farm-sector-income-finances/highlights-from-the-farm-income-forecast/, accessed April 1, 2019.

USDA FNS. 2018. Supplemental Nutrition Assistance Program (SNAP). Participation and costs. December 7. https://fns-prod.azureedge.net/sites/default/files/pd/SNAPsummary.pdf, accessed March 20, 2019.

USDA NASS. 2014a. 2012 Census of agriculture, Introduction, p VIII https://www.nass.usda.gov/Publications/AgCensus/2012/Full_Report/Volume_1,_Chapter_1_US/usintro.pdf, accessed March 25, 2019.

USDA NASS. 2014b. 2012 Agricultural Census, Table 64, summary of size by farm. https://www.nass.usda.gov/Publications/AgCensus/2012/Full_Report/Volume_1,_Chapter_1_US/st99_1_064_064.pdf accessed March 27, 2018.

USDA NASS. 2018. Table 1. Historical highlights: 2012 and earlier census years. https://www.nass.usda.gov/Publications/AgCensus/2012/Full_Report/Volume_1,_Chapter_1_US/st99_1_001_001.pdf, accessed March 22, 2019.

USDA NASS. 2019. 2017 Census of Agriculture. Report AC-17-A-51, April https://www.nass.usda.gov/Publications/AgCensus/2017/#full_report, accessed May 17, 2019.

US Department of Commerce. 1928. United States census of agriculture 1925. p III. http://usda.mannlib.cornell.edu/usda/AgCensusImages/1925/02/00/1925-02-00-intro.pdf, accessed March 25, 2019.

US Department of Commerce. 1954. US Census of Agriculture, Chapter V, Size of Farm. p 341. http://usda.mannlib.cornell.edu/usda/AgCensusImages/1954/02/05/1954-02-05.pdf, accessed March 25, 2019.

US Department of Commerce. 1973. 1969 Census of agriculture, Chapter 2, Farms: number, use of land, size of farm. p1. http://usda.mannlib.cornell.edu/usda/AgCensusImages/1969/02/02/1969-02-02-intro.pdf, accessed March 25, 2019.

US DHHS. 2013. Managing overweight and obesity in adults. Systematic evidence review from the obesity expert panel, 2013 https://www.nhlbi.nih.gov/health-topics/managing-overweight-obesity-in-adults, accessed March 13, 2019.

US EPA. 2017a. Report of pesticide industry sales and usage, 2008–2012 market estimates. https://www.epa.gov/sites/production/files/2017-01/documents/pesticides-industry-sales-usage-2016_0.pdf, accessed March 18, 2019.

US EPA. 2017b. Global greenhouse gas emissions data. https://www.epa.gov/ghgemissions/global-greenhouse-gas-emissions-data, accessed March 22, 2019.

US EPA. 2018. Sources of greenhouse gas emissions. https://www.epa.gov/ghgemissions/sources-greenhouse-gas-emissions, accessed March 22, 2019.

US EPA. 2019. Chlorpyrifos. Updated July 25. https://www.epa.gov/ingredients-used-pesticide-products/chlorpyrifos, accessed August 31, 2020.

US National Archives and Records Administration. 2016. The Homestead Act of 1862. https://www.archives.gov/education/lessons/homestead-act, accessed February 15, 2019.

van der Zee, B., Levitt, T., and Wasley, A. 2020. 'No way food safety not compromised': US regulation rollbacks during Covid-19 criticised. The Guardian, April 20. https://www.theguardian.com/environment/2020/apr/20/no-way-food-safety-not-compromised-us-regulatory-roll-backs-during-covid-19-criticised?CMP=Share_AndroidApp_Gmail, accessed April 20, 2020.

Varney, S. 2020. US obesity epidemic could undermine effectiveness of Covid-19 vaccine. CNN Health, August 5. https://www.cnn.com/2020/08/05/health/obesity-covid-vaccine-effectiveness-wellness/index.html, accessed August 27, 2020.

Verburg, S. 2019. DNA evidence traces drinking water hazards back to farms and manure. Wisconsin State Journal, February 28. https://madison.com/wsj/news/local/govt-and-politics/dna-evidence-traces-drinking-water-hazards-back-to-farms-/and/article_daf21447-0b24-5b0e-a1a6-ab3f5f17094c.html, accessed March 22, 2019.

Wasley, A., Cook, C. D. and Jones, N. 2018. Two amputations a week: the cost of working in a US meat plant. The Guardian, July 5. https://www.theguardian.com/environment/2018/jul/05/amputations-serious-injuries-us-meat-industry-plant, accessed March 28, 2019.

World Population Review. 2017. Life expectancy by country 2017. http://worldpopulationreview.com/countries/life-expectancy-by-country/, accessed March 15, 2019.

Yan, H. and Holcombe, M. 2019. Jurors say Roundup contributed to a 2nd man's cancer. Now thousands more cases against Monsanto await. CNN, March 20. https://www.cnn.com/2019/03/20/health/monsanto-verdict-federal/index.html, accessed March 22, 2019.

Zepeda, L. 2018. Hiding hunger: Food insecurity in middle America. Agriculture and Human Values, 35(1), 243–254.

Zhang, L., Rana, I., Shaffer, R. M., Taioli, E., and Sheppard, L. 2019. Exposure to glyphosate-based herbicides and risk for Non-Hodgkin Lymphoma: A meta-analysis and supporting evidence. Mutation Research-Reviews. https://doi.org/10.1016/j.mrrev.2019.02.001, accessed March 21, 2019.

Zimmer, K. 2018. How toxic is the world's most popular herbicide Roundup? The Scientist. February 7. https://www.the-scientist.com/news-opinion/how-toxic-is-the-worlds-most-popular-herbicide-roundup-30308, accessed March 22, 2019.

CHAPTER FIVE

WHERE ARE WE GOING?

Our current food system is incredibly productive in terms of calories; we produce more than enough food to feed ourselves. The FAO (2017) estimates the caloric need across all age groups at an average of 1,950 calories per person per day.[4] However, average daily availability in high-income countries is 3,350 calories per person per day, and 2,750 calories in low and middle-income countries. Yet, there were 815 million hungry people in 2016, and 2.5 billion suffered from anemia (InterAcademy Partnership, 2018). Furthermore, in 2014, 40% of people globally were overweight or obese (FAO, 2017). The problem with our food system is not lack of food, but unequal distribution; many people do not have the means to access sufficient food because they are too poor or are displaced because of conflicts or natural disasters.

While our food system produces enough calories for everyone, it is failing us all in terms of nutrition. Globally, life expectancies have plateaued and half of all deaths are attributable to four risk factors: high blood pressure, smoking, high blood glucose, and high body mass index (Horton, 2017). Recent analysis of 15 dietary recommendations across 195 countries found that average unhealthy food consumption exceeded recommendations for all 21 regions (GBD 2017 Diet Collaborators, 2019). Intake of healthy foods was below recommendations for almost all foods in all regions, except vegetables in Central Asia, seafood Omega 3 fatty acids in high-income Asia Pacific, and legumes in five of the 21 regions.

Worldwide, we ate only 23% of the recommended amount of whole grains, 12% of the recommended nuts and seeds, less than half the recommended fruit, a little more than half the recommended vegetables, and nearly twice the recommended sodium (GBD 2017 Diet Collaborators, 2019). Meat

[4] While the calorie requirements of adults are higher, around 2,200 for adult women and 2,800 for adult men, the FAO estimate takes into account infants and children, the age distribution of the world population, and their calorie requirements.

consumption globally exceeded recommendations, although it varied by region, with Australasia, Southern Latin America, and the US and Canada eating more than twice as much meat as is recommended. Indeed, North Americans eat nearly 10 times more processed meat than is recommended. The researchers found that globally, 22% of all deaths (11 million) can be attributed to diet. Half of these deaths were attributable to excess sodium, too few whole grains, and too few FAV. They found that cardiovascular disease (CVD) due to poor diet resulted in 10 million deaths annually, while there were over 900,000 deaths annually from diet-related cancers, and over 300,000 type-2 diabetes deaths annually.

The diets we eat around the world not only have adverse effects nutritionally, but they also contribute to environmental problems, because animal products and processed foods are land, water, chemical, and energy intensive. Food waste increases these impacts because one-third of the food produced is wasted. Our food system is also failing us by contributing to climate change, habitat loss, and resource degradation. Agriculture is the biggest user of land and water resources, and a large contributor to GHG that exacerbates climate change. Agriculture not only contributes to climate change, but climate change is also increasing droughts, floods, and fires that adversely affect food production and displace people. Agriculture is exacerbating water scarcity and contributes nitrates from fertilizer and livestock, emerging pathogens and chemicals from livestock, and pesticides, which are all deteriorating water quality.

Our food system is also failing us economically and socially. The health and environmental impacts due to our food system pose huge, externalized costs for consumers and health systems. These affect daily well-being and quality of life. Furthermore, as our food system becomes more and more concentrated and vertically integrated, market power converges in the hands of a few large food processors, and increasingly, a few food retailers, while only the largest farmers can make a living. This places small farmers, small food and retail businesses, and workers across the agro-food industries at an economic disadvantage and results in increasing income inequality.

Where then are we headed in the future? Will we have enough food for everyone? What about the environmental impacts? How will we get our food? How will our diets change?

Will there be enough food?

The world population is expected to be 9 billion by the mid-century and 11 billion by the end of the 21st century (FAO, 2017). Population growth is slowing in most parts of the world. As such, the global population is aging; currently 8.3% of the world's population is 65 years or older; by the end of the 21st century, it will be 22.7%. Populations in Africa and South Asia will continue to rise; this is expected to increase out-migration from rural areas of the young who are seeking jobs. Out-migration contributes to rapid urbanization; currently, 54% of the world's population live in urban areas; by 2050 it will be two-thirds.

Population growth, while slowing, will continue because 85 million pregnancies annually, or 40% of all pregnancies worldwide, are unplanned (Sedgh, Singh, and Hussain, 2014). In the US, the percentage is even higher: 51% of pregnancies are unintended (7.1 million annually). These are conservative estimates of the number of unintended pregnancies; the method of collecting data retrospectively has been shown to underestimate unintended pregnancies because people rationalize births after the fact.

The primary reasons there are so many unintended pregnancies are the lack of access to contraception and failure to use contraception appropriately. In developing countries, there were 222 million women who had an unmet need for contraception in 2012 (Sedgh, Singh, and Hussain, 2014). Had they had contraception, this would have avoided 54 million unintended pregnancies, or 64% of global unintended pregnancies. Lack of access to contraception is due to disempowerment and discrimination against women; across 105 countries, the correlation between fertility rates and a measure of discrimination against women was 0.66 (Doepke and Tertilt, 2018). Across 51 countries with data, these researchers found men on average wanted women to have more children than women wanted to have. Saad (2018) found the same in the US. Analyzing within-couple data, Doepke and Tertilt (2018) found that the more educated the woman, the closer were her desired and actual fertility. The fact that men on average want women to have more children does not mean men provide for their children, and this, in part, explains why women, on average, want fewer children than men; they are the ones left to care for the children physically and economically. Globally, 14% of the world's 2.3 billion children live with a single parent, mostly women, and the numbers are rising (Chamie, 2016). In the US, one in four mothers raise children alone (Livingston and Bialik, 2018) and only 44% of custodial parents receive the full amount of child support they are owed (US Census Bureau, 2018). The upshot is that while population growth is slowing, there is much room to slow population growth further by increasing access to birth control and empowering women.

Given that the population is projected to rise by 22% by mid-century, and we already produce 44% more calories than are needed, in theory, we could feed everyone by 2050, even if production remained at current levels. Reducing the enormous amount of food wasted would further increase the availability of food. A further cushion to feed the increased population is that technology and the output of food are expected to increase, albeit at slower rates than in the past (FAO, 2017). However, demand for agricultural products is expected to increase by 50% between 2012 and 2050, due in part to population growth, but also growth in urbanization, incomes, demand for meat and milk, and demand for energy. Between 2000 and 2011, one-third of the increase in cereal consumption was due to biofuel production in the US alone. Biofuel production will continue to rise, from 130 billion liters in 2015 to 140 billion liters in 2020. By 2024, one-quarter of the world's sugarcane production will be used to manufacture ethanol. Hence, increasingly, our food supply is being diverted from people who are hungry to people with cars.

While agricultural production is sufficient in quantity to feed the world, in regions of conflict, food availability and access can be disrupted. All recent famines can be traced to conflicts, the main drivers of which are ethnic and religious differences (FAO, 2017). Competition for land and water, and climate change exacerbate these conflicts. Half the world's poor live in conflict zones and conflicts are on the rise; there were 424 in 2014, of which 46 were very violent. In 2015, 65 million people were forcibly displaced. Most were residing in low-income countries: 89% of international refugees and 99% of those internally displaced were located in low-income countries. Given these countries were the least able to afford assistance to refugees and the displaced, 80% of humanitarian funding was allocated to conflict zones. Reducing conflict is clearly imperative to minimize hunger.

Global trade is also crucial to food security. Many countries depend on food exports for earnings, and many more depend on food imports to feed their populations and keep food prices low. At the extremes, Argentina, Australia, and the US export more than 50% of their domestic food supply, while the Near East and North Africa import more than 50% of their food supply (FAO, 2017). However, global trade is expected to slow, due to the rise in protectionism and failure to negotiate multilateral agreements. In addition to fostering agricultural trade, trade agreements include rules on food safety, animal and plant health, food product standards and names, plant patent protections, agricultural export subsidies, and the dates when agricultural export restrictions can be imposed. These rules facilitate the safety, quality, and transparency of the food supply. Hence, when trade agreements fail, they not only affect the availability and prices of food, but also the safety, quality, and information about food. However, not all trade agreements are equal; how they are negotiated can also affect food quality and availability.

Income and wealth inequality also pose threats to food production and access, and foster rural out-migration, as people seek better opportunities. Income and wealth inequality do not appear to be slowing down and are growing fastest in rapidly growing countries like China, India, Indonesia, and South Africa (FAO, 2017). Disparate income distribution means food access is low for some groups. Women, in particular, are vulnerable; 60% of the world's hungry are women and most of the 2 billion people suffering from micronutrient deficiencies are women. Rural women, in particular, are most vulnerable, despite the fact that women supply 43% of agricultural labor in developing countries. The rising number of men in developing countries leaving rural areas has resulted in a "feminization" of agriculture, yet despite this, women are the most vulnerable to hunger. Male out-migration is only expected to increase as they seek earnings in cities and other countries. Internal migrants in 2013 were estimated at 740 million. In 2015, the estimated 150 million global migrant workers remitted US$ 500 billion annually; that is US$ 3,333 per migrant worker per year. In many countries, this exceeded per capita GDP, providing a clear incentive for workers to migrate.

So, in theory, globally, there is plenty of food now and sufficient food in the future to feed everyone. In practice, however, the problems of distribution, waste, conflict, and lack of resources and money impede access to adequate food for some. So, if the present is any indication of the future, food will continue to be wasted and much of it will be squandered by the overfed. Indeed, predictions by the FAO (2017) are that the number of hungry globally will not decline.

Within the US, there is obviously enough food to feed Americans. The US has one of the highest levels of agricultural output and efficiency in the world and is also a major food exporter. Agricultural productivity has grown at a rate of about 1.5% per year since 1948 (Wang et al., 2015). Yet, it has not been agricultural production and policies that have reduced hunger in the US, but social programs that transferred income to the poor, especially those programs that targeted food such as SNAP and WIC. However, beginning under President Reagan, and continuing under Bush Sr. and Clinton, social programs were cut.

In 1995, an indicator of food insecurity was developed; it revealed 12% of the US population was food insecure (Nord and Andrews, 2002). Food insecurity remains at 12% (Feeding America, 2018). The characteristics of the food insecure in the US may be surprising; not only are they mostly employed, often they have more than one job. Often, they must choose between housing, utilities, healthcare, or food. That food insecurity should remain stubbornly high in the US is not due to a lack of growth in agricultural productivity or lack of effort on the part of those who are food insecure, but the lack of political will to provide wages that Americans can live on.

What about the environmental impacts?

One of the consequences of the increased demand for agricultural products expected over the 21st century will be to put further stress on our planet's natural resources. One-third of the world's farmland is already moderately to highly degraded (FAO, 2017). Given there is no suitable land to expand agriculture, there is a need to intensify agriculture, which may lead to further degradation of resources. However, productivity growth is slowing due to lack of investments in agriculture and in technological innovation, degradation of resources, transboundary pests and diseases, resistance to pesticides and antimicrobials, and private ownership of new technologies that increase costs to farmers, thereby limiting their diffusion. Furthermore, half of all agricultural subsidies provided in OECD countries in 2010-12 were harmful to the environment because they incentivized an increased demand for fertilizer and fossil fuels, thereby increasing GHG.

Globally, climate change is expected to reduce yields through increased and more extreme floods, drought, and heat. Most adverse effects of climate change on agriculture will occur in low and middle-income countries, while, on average, positive effects are predicted for high-income countries (FAO, 2017). Extreme weather and natural disasters also contribute to conflict and migration, with 200 million climate refugees expected by 2050. As stated above, conflict and migration hinder access to food and, therefore, are a root cause of hunger. Hence, climate change is expected to exacerbate access to food directly through adverse effects on agriculture and indirectly by creating conflict.

It is estimated that globally, we will need to invest more than US$ 89 trillion to deal with climate change over the next 15 years, or nearly US$ 6 trillion per year (FAO, 2017). The needs for investment in developing countries are well beyond the current global aid of US$ 1.5 trillion per year. However, there is neither the political will nor willingness to pay for these needed investments to combat climate change. Hence, the effects of climate change will likely be borne by those with the least resources. It should also be noted that the rising number and intensity of natural disasters due to climate change already disproportionately kill more women than men. This is just one more example of the inequities of the impacts of climate change.

Climate change is also expected to make crops and livestock more vulnerable to transboundary diseases and pests. These include diseases in livestock like foot and mouth disease, lumpy skin disease, African swine fever, and Newcastle disease; plant pests like locusts, army worms, and fruit flies; and crop-specific viruses (FAO, 2017). There are also disease risks to humans from climate change; more than 70% of new diseases in humans since 1940 can be traced back to animals, including: Ebola from wildlife, H5N1 avian flu from chickens, H1N1 swine flu, MERS from camels, and COVID-19, from either pangolins or bats. As habitat is being destroyed and intensive livestock operations increase, so do pathogens and foodborne illnesses that affect humans. Furthermore, growing antimicrobial resistance means we do not have the medications for humans or animals to combat some diseases.

The environmental, economic, and social impacts of our current food system are illustrated by the WHO's 17 sustainable development goals for 2030 (SDG17) on poverty, hunger, health, equity, and sustainability. Not one single country is on the path to achieving these goals (Horton, 2018). This is due to a lack of political will and insufficient allocation of public expenditure to achieve the goals that countries have set for themselves.

The FAO's (2017) suggestion that cooperation with private commercial interests could fill the huge gap in funding to achieve SDG17 is best answered by examining the stewardship of commercial interests with respect to agriculture. Agricultural input companies have promoted the use of practices that have contributed to the degradation of natural resources, erosion, habitat loss, reduced quantity and quality of water, eutrophication, and have had adverse impacts on the health of humans and other species. Food processors have used their vast market power to pay farmers little for their crops and to produce foods for consumers that are not merely devoid of nutrients, but are reducing consumers' quality of life and life expectancy. The overall effect of the private sector's influence on the food system is that 22% of people globally die of a diet-related illness. Therefore, to believe that private commercial interests will change what they have been doing to help achieve SDG17 is, at best, optimistic.

Will our food be safe?

Another concern about the future of food is food safety. Globally, in 2010, there were 420,000 deaths due to foodborne illness, 600 million illnesses, and 40% of the illnesses were among children under five (FAO, 2017). One in six Americans get a foodborne illness each year, resulting in 320,000 hospitalizations and 3,000 deaths per year (Braden and Tauxe, 2013). The most common source identified is norovirus, which accounts for 58% of foodborne illness. However, salmonella causes 35% of hospitalizations and 28% of deaths. We experience norovirus as food poisoning: vomiting, diarrhea, and stomach cramps. It is the most frequent cause of foodborne illness because it is highly contagious, and is often passed to us by infected food handlers. Salmonella bacteria have thousands of varieties, some of which are resistant to antibiotics. Contamination occurs via contact with feces. Poultry was the leading source of illness, followed by leafy greens, beef, and dairy products. Since the 1970s, fresh produce has risen as a vehicle for salmonella bacteria. In the 1970s, fresh produce was responsible for just 1% of outbreaks and illnesses. More recent data indicates that half of all foodborne illness in the US is caused by bacteria on fresh FAV (Karthikeyan and Garber, 2019).

In the US, the Food and Drug Administration and Department of Agriculture are tasked with protecting the safety of the food supply (US FDA, 2018). Recalls of processed foods and produce remained about the same between 2013 and 2018 in the US, but recalls of meat and poultry increased by 67% during the same period (Karthikeyan and Garber, 2019). Identifying the cause of foodborne illnesses is difficult. Processing and globalization mean that the products we eat may contain hundreds of ingredients, produced in intensive agricultural systems that increase the chances of contamination, and are sourced from all over the world; 75% of processed foods in the US contain ingredients from another country (IOM, 2012).

To illustrate the complexity of the food system, within the US, two million farms produce foods that are processed and distributed through 167,000 facilities and sold at 114,000 retail stores or 935,000 food service outlets. So, tracing the exact cause of food poisoning is difficult (IOM, 2012). However, meat and poultry are often contaminated during slaughter when feces from animal intestines come in contact with meat or contaminate equipment (Schlosser, 2002). Increased line speeds in slaughterhouses are associated with increased contamination because workers are unable to keep up with the line speed or have time to sharpen knives, leading to accidental puncturing of intestines. Since slaughterhouses do not stop lines to remediate the problem when this happens, carcasses are cross-contaminated. Ground meat is at the greatest risk, since an individual package of meat can contain meat from dozens of animals. The scope of cross-contamination is illustrated by the October 2018 JBS recall of 12 million pounds of beef contaminated with antibiotic-resistant salmonella (Karthikeyan and Garber, 2019). While inspections are the first line of defense for food safety, their effectiveness is limited because many companies ignore citations and fines; Foster Farms (a US privately held company) was cited 480 times by federal inspectors in 2013 before their 2013-14 poultry recall for salmonella.

Given that the source of salmonella is feces, it should not be a surprise that recalls of processed foods and produce in the US have been linked to livestock production: romaine recalled in March 2018 is thought to have been contaminated by water tainted by E. coli from a nearby Concentrated Animal Feed Operation (CAFO), while the July 2018 Ritz Crackers (owned by Swiss Modelez) and Goldfish (owned by US Campbell Soups) recalls were thought to be due to salmonella-contaminated whey powder produced by AMPI, a milk producer cooperative in the Upper Midwest (Karthikeyan and Garber, 2019). It is not clear how Honey Smacks cereal (owned by US Kellogg) or Caito melon (owned by US food retailer SpartanNash) were contaminated with salmonella in May and June of 2018, respectively. However, the products or equipment must have come into contact with animal or human feces.

Contamination by human feces is linked to the lack of enforcement of sanitary regulations. By law in the US, agricultural workers are supposed to have access to toilets, handwashing facilities with potable water, soap, and single-use towels (Hancock, 1998). However, one study in North Carolina showed that one-third of agricultural workers did not have access to water to wash their hands, 36% reported more than eight people per bathroom, and over half did not have access to soap or towels (Whalley et al., 2009). One-third of the workers said they were able to wash their hands once or fewer times during work. Given that there were only seven inspectors in the state to inspect the 6,000 to 10,000 registered camps for agricultural workers, it is little wonder that so many farmers flout the laws regarding agricultural workers. Furthermore, farmers voluntarily register camps for inspection, hence, a farmer not wishing to be inspected simply does not register their work camp. It is also illegal for farmers to hire undocumented workers, yet 43% of the workers in this study were undocumented. The researchers found that one impact of employer compliance with immigration laws was that it significantly increased the probability of workers having access to soap and towels.

Having legal status also protects agricultural workers from retaliation by their employers; undocumented workers may be afraid to complain about sanitation, or anything else, for fear of being detained and deported. Even if workers have access to toilet facilities, they may not be able to use them. There may be pressure by employers not to take breaks or the facilities may be unclean. So even when there are facilities "available," workers may be required to, or prefer to, eliminate in the fields. This creates a risk of fecal contamination of the food by the workers. Similar issues with inability to use facilities exist in slaughterhouses, where workers resort to wearing diapers (Chuck, 2016). The upshot is that agricultural workers handling the food we eat may be the source of foodborne illness because employers fail to comply with sanitation standards, the government is unable to enforce sanitation standards for lack of personnel, or workers may be unable or unwilling to use facilities that might exist.

Some researchers see the increase in food recalls as an indication that regulation is working (IOM, 2012). However, understaffing of government inspectors makes it unlikely that offenders are caught (Whalley et al., 2009), and even when caught and fined, some companies choose to make no changes (Karthikeyan and Garber, 2019). Despite this, the government is viewed by the public as primarily responsible for food safety (Arnot, 2018). Food companies, then farmers, are also seen as having a responsibility, but to a lesser degree than the government. However, there is a gap between who the public views as being responsible and their trust in those organizations; the public ranks the government as eighth out of 11 organizations in terms of trust to protect the safety of food, and has the least trust in food companies to protect food safety.

Regardless of perceptions about food safety, with the growing production of meat and animal products, there will be more animals slaughtered and processed, which means more CAFOs and more feces. So, unless production, slaughtering, processing, and distribution practices change, one can expect more outbreaks of food poisoning. With greater globalization and eating of processed foods, one can expect more cross-contamination of plant-based processed foods. CAFOs also pose a risk to contaminating water used to irrigate FAV, and until farms, processing plants, and food services comply with sanitation requirements for their workers, the workers are also potential sources of contamination. Regulators in the US are hamstrung because they simply do not have the inspectors to examine every facility regularly. Furthermore, the concentration and size of operations mean that even when caught, companies, e. g. Foster Farms, can choose to pay citations as a cost of doing business. Apparently, doing so is much cheaper than shutting down operations for cleaning, or changing practices to avoid contamination.

Consumers can protect themselves by cooking their meat thoroughly and cleaning anything touching raw meat. However, the alternatives for consumers to protect themselves' from contaminated processed foods and FAV are not particularly realistic. There is little one can do to protect against potential food poisoning from processed foods except avoid them. As to fresh FAV, one can avoid cut or prepared FAV that are raw or cook FAV to reduce risk. Growing one's own FAV or buying directly from a producer would allow one to identify the source if one were to become ill. Consumers are unlikely to take these measures unless there is a large recall, and then only for a short time. Therefore, the risk of food poisoning is likely to increase until such time as there is the political will to fund sufficient food inspectors, increase transparency by making violations public, and increase fines such that farms and processing companies find it cheaper to comply with government safety standards.

How will we get our food?

Our food system was transformed in the 20th century by food processing. It has required the standardization of food production, and has encouraged the concentration of production and the consolidation of land. As a result, agriculture is increasingly characterized by vertical integration of primary production, processing, and distribution, and automated large scale processing that is capital intensive. Large scale, vertically integrated, concentrated food processing companies have increased the availability of cheap foods with empty calories; the increase in overweight, obesity, and food-related disease is evidence of their effectiveness (FAO, 2017).

Global food brands along with global retailers have also: reduced access of small-scale producers and family farmers to viable markets; generated high levels of food waste; created food safety problems; exacerbated plant disease and animal health issues; and increased energy use and the ecological footprint by lengthening food chains. The concentration of food retailers during the late 20th and early 21st centuries has given retailers the market power to negotiate the quality, quantity, and price of food. Small farmers, in particular, are unable to access these markets for lack of sufficient production, inability to meet standards, or because the prices offered are too low. Furthermore, these global food processing chains and retailers may have a larger ecological footprint because of transport, processing, and food waste.

The market power of large retailers is linked to their concentration and control over consumers' access to food. In North America, 93% of food is purchased through hypermarkets, large grocery chains, and convenience stores; almost all the rest is purchased through drug stores and hard discount stores (FAO, 2017). In the rest of the world, hypermarkets, large grocery chains, and convenience stores sell 55% of the food in Europe, 46% in Latin America, 38% in the Middle East and Africa, and 36% in Asia. Small grocery stores sell a further 20% of the food in Europe and Latin America, while hard discount stores sell another 12% of the food in Europe.

The consolidation of food retailers may have begun as a way to deal with thin profit margins, but slotting fees and private labels have become the keys to retail profits. Slotting fees, or listing charges as they are called in Europe, are fees charged to brands for shelf space in grocery stores. Grocery store profits increased in the US after slotting fees came into effect in 1982 (Achrol, 2012). Slotting fees originated as small, one-time fees to compensate stores for introducing new products. They grew as retailers consolidated and realized they could charge ongoing fees for shelf space. The fees can take many forms: outright cash payments to discounts on goods, or free goods. By 2000, slotting fees were equal to 2% of all US grocery sales or US$ 9 billion. In 2018, the annual profit margin of grocery stores was only 2.52% (CSI Market, 2019), meaning that slotting fees represent a substantial component of grocery store profits.

Slotting fees allow retailers to collect rents from brands to place their products in locations that enhance their sales. Brands are willing to pay because the amount of space and location of items on shelves affects their sales. Hence, shelf space and location have become a source of bargaining power for retailers to generate additional income (Adam et al., 2017). Achrol (2012) analyzed three decades of food retailing data to assess whether slotting fees were consistent with the efficient allocation of shelf space or rent-seeking behavior that increased the market power of food retailers. His analysis found evidence for increased market power by retailers and that the introduction of slotting fees was consistent with higher retail food prices, lower cost of goods to retailers, and higher retail profits.

Slotting fees are even paid to small retailers, the kind of stores that often serve food deserts. Laska et al. (2018) found that among 72 small stores, the managers had an average of six slotting fee agreements per store. Some agreements were one time and others were recurring. They included fees for sugary beverages, salty snacks, frozen desserts, sweet snacks, and candy. Sugary beverages were the most profitable for the small stores, with annual fees ranging from US$ 80 to US$ 25,000. Nearly half of all managers had agreements with competitors, Coca-Cola and PepsiCo. Note that all the slotting agreements in this study were for unhealthy foods; these are the foods being promoted in food deserts by food companies.

While slotting fees originated as a way to introduce new products within the limited space of a grocery store, they have become a way of ensuring that the location of a product favors its sales. Researchers have found that shelf location affects purchases. For this reason, slotting fees and related incentives were banned in 1995 in the US by the Bureau of Alcohol, Tobacco and Firearms for alcohol, but interestingly, not for tobacco (Achrol, 2012). The implementation of this policy provides evidence of the effect of slotting fees on the average price of food. After the slotting fee ban on alcohol was implemented, alcoholic beverages fell in price relative to food prices and the price indices have continued to diverge. The implication is that slotting fees have raised food prices over what they would have been and the effect is increasing over time.

Looking at shelf space allocations across ten countries, researchers found that not only did supermarket shelf space affect what types of foods people ate, but the amount of shelf space allocated to different foods was correlated with the average BMI of the countries (Norman, Hoffman, and Cheskin, 2014). They found the greater the average proportion of shelf space devoted to FAV, the lower the national BMI, while greater shelf space devoted to starchy foods, junk food, and dairy was correlated with higher national BMI.

The implications of these studies are as follows: that slotting fee agreements affect what we buy; that most of what is promoted through slotting fees is unhealthy, particularly in food deserts; that food prices have increased as a result of slotting fees; and that the promotion of unhealthy foods in stores is related to increased BMI. From a public health perspective, policies to ban or regulate slotting fees could be used to promote healthier food choices.

Another way that retailers influence consumer food choice is through their private food labels. Private labels make up over US$ 50 billion in sales in the US, or about 20% of the items sold by food retailers in the US; in Europe, they represent 23% of sales (Hyman, Kopf, and Lee, 2010). Private labels are brands owned by a retailer, or in some cases, a wholesaler. This does not imply that food retailers are in the food processing business; they contract with food processors to produce private label products for them. The advantages for branded food processors are that they can contract sales with retailers at known prices and quantities and it allows processors to reduce risks and utilize processing capacity, thereby reducing the average cost of production for their own products. These advantages mean that half of branded food processors produce products for private labels. Indeed, some national brands produce private label products for multiple, competing retailers. Private labels can further increase the profits of national or global brands because they serve as a pretext for brands to increase the prices of their own products; it is assumed national or global brand prices should be above private-label prices. Thus, private-label prices serve as a baseline price signal to brands. Private labels increase the profits of both brands and retailers by increasing consumers' expenditure on product categories, by permitting market segmentation of consumers, and by fostering tacit collusion between brands and retailers over consumer prices.

While private-label foods have been used for decades, their use has increased and they have shifted in terms of actual and perceived quality (Hyman, Kopf, and Lee, 2010). They are popular with consumers because their retail prices are less than brands. Thus, 97% of food shoppers in 2018 purchased at least one private label product (Food Marketing Institute, 2018). However, while the quality of private labels decades ago may have been inferior to food brands, premium private labels have grown in popularity today. The actual quality of private-label products has increased, thereby reducing the perceived differences between national/global and private label brands. Therefore, private labels can offer consumers a higher quality for a lower price than national/global brands. Having consistent high quality across all products using a private label is crucial to generating profitability of private labels to retailers. Setting a large price differential with respect to national/global brands can also enhance retailers' profits, as it increases the demand for private labels by price-sensitive consumers.

The advantages of private labels for food retailers are that they generate higher profits than selling brands, they reduce retailers' risks, they attract price-sensitive consumers, and they enhance store loyalty (Hyman, Kopf, and Lee, 2010). Private labels increase profits directly because the wholesale price of private-label products is less than brands, R&D costs are less because retailers copy rather than develop products, marketing costs are lower than brands because retailers do not need to launch and develop brand loyalty for individual products, and the volume of sales is high. Indirectly, private labels give retailers more bargaining power with national brands, allowing them to negotiate more lucrative margins and slotting fees from brands. Given the low cost of developing new private label products, because they contract out production and do not need much more than a recipe, retailers can use even the threat of introducing a private label product to get concessions from brands. Retailers can piggy-back on the market research done by brands by imitating new products. Private labels are also less risky because retailers copy successful products rather than introducing a brand that could potentially fail. Furthermore, the prevalence of high-quality private label products creates a positive image for the retail chain, attracting price-sensitive customers, enhancing customer loyalty, and differentiating the retailer from other chains. At the same time, private labels reduce price competition between retailers because private labels are only available within each retail chain.

Private labels are particularly useful to retailers when serving niche markets (Hyman, Kopf, and Lee, 2010). National or global brands may be discouraged from launching products that serve, for example, organic, sustainable, or ethnic markets due to the high cost of product launch and advertising, and the high risk of failure. For retailers, the costs are low to introduce a line of organic, gluten-free, or other niche products, that can be sold at premium prices. Retailers' cost advantages in contracting production, the familiarity of their customers with their private label, and their ability to introduce an entire range of products mean that they can offer such products at lower prices than national brands. This enhances their sales success.

Organic sales, in particular, have attracted private labels in the US. The success of Whole Foods' "365" private label has encouraged other retailers to introduce lines of private-label organic foods. Both Albertsons' "O Organics" and Kroger's "Simple Truth Organic" private labels have each exceeded US$ 1 billion in sales (Albertsons, 2018; Patel, 2017). So far, the introduction of private labels for organic foods appears to be quite successful. Private label organic products are generally cheaper than other organic brands, more visible as private labels, and are promoted by the retailers. This increased access and mainstreaming of organic products has contributed to increasing overall organic sales.

The marketing of private-label organic and gluten-free foods also implies that retailers are attempting to expand their brand appeal. There are many examples of private labels being used to promote products that were considered incongruent with a retail image; Sears, K-Mart, and Wal-Mart all failed to shift their image by introducing private label high fashion clothes (Hyman, Kopf, and Lee, 2010). Indeed, this strategy of emphasizing private label products incongruent with the retail image contributed to the demise of both K-Mart and Sears. However, grocery retailers appear to have tapped into unmet demand by making private-label organic and gluten-free products available. Unlike high fashion, organic and gluten-free foods in the US have been difficult to find, being available largely in food cooperatives and health food stores that tend to have limited locations. The availability of private-label organic and gluten-free foods means that shoppers can buy them at grocery stores located in their neighborhoods.

Just as online sales have transformed the purchase of other goods, online grocery sales are beginning to transform the grocery industry. A total of 34% of US food shoppers have purchased food online in the past 12 months, with 28% ordering from online-only retailers (Food Marketing Institute, 2018). Many grocery stores offer online orders and home delivery. However, Peapod is the largest online grocer in the US, serving 24 cities in the Northeast, mid-Atlantic, and Midwest (Ahold Delhaize, 2019). Peapod is part of Ahold Delhaize USA, one of the top five food retailers in the US and a subsidiary of the Dutch food retailer with US$ 44 billion in food sales in the US in 2018. Along with Ahold Delhaize USA, Wal-Mart, Kroger, Albertsons, and Costco sold US$ 403 billion or nearly half of all groceries in the US in the same year (Costco, 2018; Dudlicek, 2018; Dudlicek et al., 2018). The immense market power of food retailers due to the concentration of the industry allows them to negotiate with brands and commodities over price and perhaps more importantly, shelf or web space, and location (Achrol, 2012).

Amazon is ranked ninth in retail food sales (Dudliceck, 2018). Amazon's 2017 purchase of retail grocery chain, Whole Foods, makes economic sense since six of the world's top ten retailers are primarily food retailers: Wal-Mart, Costco, Kroeger, Schwarz Group (Lidl), Aldi, and Carrefour (Deloitte, 2018). Purchase of an existing high-end brick and mortar chain is a way to expand online grocery sales through congruent branding.

Online groceries offer retailers a way to promote their private labels. As mentioned above, private labels are highly profitable. Canadian online grocer, "GoBio!" features only private label products, while most online grocers simply offer private labels prominently. Another lucrative revenue stream for online groceries is charging brands fees for online promotion. These are equivalent to slotting fees. For example, Kroger offers a self-service marketing platform that lets brands promote their products when consumers search for relevant products online (Kelso, 2018).

Some online grocers also charge monthly membership fees and/or delivery fees to shoppers. For some retailers, online shopping is an extra service for existing customers or to attract customers. They may offer home delivery or easy pickup. They may source all the products from their brick and mortar stores or have a centralized warehouse to fulfill orders. In contrast to supermarkets that add online groceries to their services, online-only grocery stores, like Peapod in the US or Ocado in the UK, operate only in select markets. This facilitates profitability by ensuring the density of customers keeps the number of orders high and transport costs low.

Online sales can provide consumers with greater convenience by saving them time. Online grocery delivery may even be able to reduce the transportation footprint over individual shopping trips if the density of deliveries is high enough. Deliveries have drawbacks, however. If they are attended, the delivery window can be hours, which means the consumer must be at home to take delivery. Unattended deliveries risk theft or spoilage. Either form may involve additional packaging which increases waste. Dedicated coolers can reduce packaging, but are an additional expense for consumers.

The COVID-19 pandemic has increased the attractiveness and use of online shopping. It allows shoppers to avoid going to grocery stores and risking exposure to COVID-19. If they are working from home or in quarantine, there is no inconvenience taking delivery at home, even if the delivery window is large. Some stores offer delivery for free if the amount purchased exceeds a certain minimum, but whether there is a fee or not, adding a tip is expected. Often the people assembling and delivering groceries are not retail employees, but gig workers, who rely on tips for all or much of their income.

While the pandemic has increased the popularity of online grocery shopping, having an easy-to-use and attractive website helps businesses to appeal to and retain customers, especially those who seek convenience or niche products. Large, national retailers may use online sales to feature organic, local, gluten-free, and kosher foods prominently, or to make them easy to find. Some online services are set up specifically to serve niche food markets, such as local or organic food. These may have started as a CSA, e.g., Skarsgard Farms in New Mexico, which has expanded to essentially be a food hub that supplies a range of products, or as an online delivery service like Doorstep Farmers in California, which specializes in organic and local foods (Zepeda and Reznickova, 2018). Terre2sens provides a similar service in France that features local foods. However, they are neither associated with a farm nor deliver to homes, but rather to multiple drop points. All these services can be set up to order weekly bundled items and one can easily substitute or add additional products. Another model of online shopping is Local Harvest, a non-profit umbrella organization, which has a website that allows consumers to connect directly with individual farmers.

Online shopping provides consumers with convenience and options to select products that might otherwise be difficult to find. It can also be a convenient way for small producers to sell to consumers directly or through an intermediary. Online-only grocers have used convenience and niche products to attract customers in select markets. Large retailers are piggy-backing on these efforts by using niche products, as well as their existing customer base, to expand online grocery shopping. They can offer online shopping as an additional service to their customers. They can also provide a full range of products, including organic, local, and other niche products, as well as feature their private labels, and charge brands fees for marketing their products online. For example, Amazon offers brands the option of selling their products directly to consumers on the Amazon platform through Seller Central and/or selling their products wholesale to Amazon via Vendor Central, with Amazon then setting prices and handling delivery (Smucker-Brian, 2018). All these options provide consumers with a sense of choice, but they obscure the fact that a handful of food retailers control the distribution of food in the US, and increasingly globally. Retailers also make us believe that we are freely making choices.

What will we eat? Retailers nudge consumers

The immense marketing power of retailers means that the marginal cost of promoting their private label products within their usual advertising and promotional channels is very low. The potential impact on demand for these niche products is huge, as is the market power that it gives retailers in negotiating with the producers and processors of organic and other niche foods. On the one hand, by promoting their private-label organic products, retailers increase the demand for organic products. On the other, the sheer size of their markets means that retailers will be able to dictate prices and will prefer dealing with fewer and larger operations. For organic producers to maintain their ability to negotiate fair terms, they will perceive the need to become larger. However, given the sheer size of retailers, producers may need to become immense to be able to negotiate good terms for themselves. An effective strategy to address the market power of retailers is for producers to organize cooperatives and negotiate as a group. In the US, there are 1,953 farmer cooperatives with nearly two million members (National Council of Farmer Cooperatives, 2020). Yet their market power is dwarfed by that of retailers, particularly in influencing consumers' food choices.

The success of organic private labels demonstrates the market power of retailers and their ability to nudge consumers. They also illustrate how private labels could be used to promote demand for other sustainability and/or health targets. For example, private labels could be used to inform consumers about the water footprint of food to encourage food choices that conserve water. Plant foods generally use less water per calorie, per gram of protein, or per gram of fat, than animal foods (Mekonnen and Hoekstra, 2012). As an example, beef uses 20 times the water per calorie as cereals or starchy roots, and six times the water per gram of protein as pulses. Per gram of protein, milk, eggs, and poultry are somewhat more water-thrifty;

they require 1.5 times the water needed by pulses for a gram of protein. Butter is the only animal fat that has a smaller water footprint than oil crops.

In France and Finland, the supermarket chains, Groupe Casino and Raisio Group, respectively, have introduced private label products that feature carbon footprint labels (Feucht and Zander, 2017). Both labels use carbon dioxide equivalents (CO2e) per hundred grams as well as color-coding to indicate the carbon footprint of their private label products. Only their private label products are labeled with CO2e, so shoppers cannot compare between brands, but the labels do provide consumers with information about the carbon footprint of their purchases. E. Leclerc, a French cooperative food retail chain, provides information on the carbon footprint of all products and indicates the CO2e of consumers' purchases on their receipts. Making such information accessible gives consumers the option to make choices that are more sustainable.

Some confusion about carbon labels stems from the way they have been implemented. In Japan and South Korea, the national governments have set standards for carbon labels (Feucht and Zander, 2017). In Canada, the US, and the UK, non-profit organizations have developed carbon labels, and in some cases, multiple labels, while in Thailand, a non-profit has developed a carbon label with collaboration from the national government. Labels are voluntary, even in countries where the government has set standards. Therefore, retailers and food processors have a primary role in implementing their use. There are also a variety of ways of presenting the information: either as the absolute grams of CO2e; the grams per 100 grams of product; color-coding; certification that a product is low carbon or that it is the "front-runner" with the lowest carbon footprint within a category; or that a product is carbon neutral through carbon offsets. Some of the presentation methods are combined, such as color-coding and CO2e grams per 100 grams. The certification schemes are usually through non-profits.

A problem with the CO2e certification schemes is that although consumers indicate concern about climate change, they do not understand the labels and do not believe their own actions impact climate change. Both of these seem to justify consumers' lack of willingness to change their behaviors. A survey of over 6,000 consumers in Germany, the UK, France, Italy, Spain, and Norway indicated that while over 70% of consumers supported carbon labels, and nearly 80% felt climate change threatened the future, most consumers admitted they had a low level of knowledge about climate change and believed their personal actions had little impact (Feucht and

Zander, 2017). Furthermore, most were not willing to pay more for climate-friendly products and few were willing to consume less meat or dairy products. Interviews confirmed the lack of knowledge about climate change and the role of personal food choices in climate change, as well as a failure to look at or notice food labels; none of the people involved in extended interviews had noticed the carbon labels, despite them being available in their countries. The interviews also revealed a lack of concern about the effects of climate change on daily life, the belief that individuals' food choices had no effect on climate change, and interviewees viewed climate change as the responsibility of the government to enact laws and education programs to address it. The latter is consistent with the approaches Japan and South Korea have taken with respect to food labels. Other countries have largely left non-profits to establish standards and labels, and retailers and manufacturers to voluntarily utilize them. The UK supermarket chain, Tesco, offers an example of voluntary CO2e food labels; they have phased them out because they claim the labels are too costly and British consumers did not understand them.

The upshot appears to be that consumers do not understand how their food consumption affects the climate and believe that it is the responsibility of the government to address climate change. Yet governments have done little to inform people, set standards, or take action against climate change. Meanwhile, only a few food retailers have made an effort to provide consumers with information to make informed choices. Much of the work to inform consumers and set standards has been left to non-profits, which lack the ability to make and enforce policy decisions. Clearly, a voluntary, underfunded effort will fail to inform, much less change consumers' behaviors.

Telling us what to eat: culture, diets, and media

What we eat is an expression of our culture. What, when, where, and with whom we eat reflect where we grew up, where we live, our families, our values, and possibly our religion. In historical agrarian societies, we grew what we ate. Thus, local foods evolved into local cuisine. Trade introduced new ingredients and new dishes, which became synonymous with local cuisines; imagine Italian food without pasta introduced from China or tomatoes introduced from the Americas. Globalization has made foods from all over the world available; one can eat croissants in Tokyo, injera in Seattle, pho in Paris, or a hamburger in Bangkok. Local interpretations of foreign foods can be surprising; in China, they put ice cubes in red wine, while the French wrap french fries and meat in flatbread and call it a taco. Traditionalists may be appalled or amused at such violations of traditional foods, but just like culture and language, cuisine is always evolving.

Yet, nations retain their food habits. Spaniards have five meals a day, whereas Italians generally eat two. In France, outside of Paris, do not attempt to eat a midday meal at a restaurant after 1:30 pm. Whereas, in Spain, other than in tourist restaurants, do not attempt to eat a midday meal before 1 pm. Americans' eating habits may appear to have changed dramatically, but they retain the legacies of early America's "hog and hominy" diet and ever westward movement. Today, as was the case historically, food in America must be cheap, convenient, have large portions, and contain processed meat. Americans still hate vegetables and disproportionately prefer their processed, salted meats and their corn products; however, the latter is now mostly in the form of HFCS. The appearance of variety masks the fact that so much of America's food is processed and still stems largely from pork, beef, chicken, corn, and wheat.

While culture still has a hold on our eating habits, increasingly in English-speaking countries, personal food choice is an expression of identity. Everyone in these countries, it seems, is on a special diet or has personal dietary requirements. There are vegetarians and vegans, and a rising number of "food allergies." While about 4% of Americans have food allergies (CDC, 2018), 19% of Americans self-diagnose as having food allergies (Gupta, Warren, Smith et al., 2019). A meta-analysis concluded that, while different studies identified a wide variation in the prevalence of any food allergy, self-diagnosis yielded values about three times higher (3% to 35%) than verified symptomatic and sensitized allergies (1% to 10.8%) for any food (Rona et al., 2007). There is no doubt that many people may find their food does not agree with them. However, allergies, along with celiac disease, are immunological, while food intolerances are not (Moneret-Vautrin, 2013). Food intolerances may cause digestive discomfort, though they tend to be related to the amount and frequency of the food eaten, hence their treatment is similar to allergies: avoid the offending food. This is potentially why people self-identify as having allergies; the treatment is the same as for food intolerances or food preferences.

At the extreme, personal dietary requirements can lead to eating disorders like anorexia, bulimia, or orthorexia, an obsession with eating only "healthy" foods, or at least foods that are perceived to be healthy. Much like anorexics and bulimics, orthorexics experience anxiety, guilt, control, and self-esteem issues around eating (Adamiec, 2013). Eating acts to isolate and separate orthorexics from the people around them, yet they take their cues from the many people promoting fad diets. Adamiec points out that "eaters have lost the ability to determine on their own what is harmful to them" (p 159). There is no doubt this is also true at the societal level, given the role diet plays in global disease and deaths.

In hunter-gatherer societies, our ability to identify what was food allowed us to survive. It is no less true today, but rather than choosing foods from our surrounding natural world, which has remained the same over centuries, we may be faced with 40,000 competing products in a supermarket, most of which were created in our own lifetimes. Since the products are new, we do not have elders or a culture that has experience with these new products to guide us. In the past, accumulated experience guided communities to survive and thrive. Now we rely on food labels. However, for many people, reading labels might be as informative as reading entrails, for all that labels mean to them. Many people cannot decipher what the labels mean because they have no nutrition knowledge, they may not understand the labels, or they view the information as too complicated.

So, we humans do what we have always done, we look for someone to give us advice. And there are plenty of people willing to do that. There is any number of diets and groups that support various food fads: Paleo, Atkins, Mediterranean, Keto, Pritikin, Weight Watchers, Jenny Craig, etc. Every celebrity has a special diet and diet book. There are cooking shows, podcasts, celebrity chefs—a whole industry of people making money by telling us what to eat. Social media is particularly insidious, with influencers paid to promote global brands. A study of the most popular child and youth influencers on YouTube found that 90% of their videos that featured food promoted unhealthy foods (Airuwaily et al., 2020).

The rise in the number and popularity of cooking shows is particularly ironic. Households with children in the US prepare and eat dinner with their family only 3.8 times a week, and households without children do so 4.1 times a week (Food Marketing Institute, 2018). Cooking shows promise to help us eat healthier, but most seem designed to introduce new food fads or provide remedial assistance on how to order trendy food in a restaurant. Cultural appropriation abounds; Anglo men show viewers how to cook "authentic" Mexican, Asian, Middle Eastern, or Southern dishes. Sometimes Asians are allowed to demonstrate how to cook Asian food, but no other person of color is apparently allowed to host a cooking show in the US. We are told to stock our pantries with hundreds of ingredients, and add dozens of ingredients to each dish. It is unheard of to simply prepare a dish so that the flavor of the food comes through; chicken must never taste like chicken; it must have the savor of rosemary-harissa-pesto-barbeque-garlic-hoisin-fish sauce. The combinations of flavors are presented as sophisticated, but often they are sophomoric. The original TV chef, Julia Child, must be spinning in her grave; her objective was to teach people how to cook traditional French foods, to demystify and make classic recipes accessible by demonstrating techniques. Today's video chefs either own restaurants or sell cookbooks; they appear to have no intention of teaching people anything, rather, their goal appears to be to promote their brand.

Cooking contests are another interesting trend in the media. Making food has ceased to be something one does to share with others; it has become something one does to compete with or humiliate others. Apparently, producers realized viewers were never going to actually make any of the dishes shown in cooking shows, so the only way to retain viewers' interest was to make cooking a competition where someone wins and many lose. It speaks volumes that in the midst of epidemic levels of obesity and diabetes, baking shows are so popular; we obsess and glorify the very foods we should not eat. It makes about as much sense as a show in which contestants compete to access opioids.

While food shows seem to be designed to tell us what to order in restaurants, food manufacturers have been developing prepared foods to eat in homes for over 100 years and retailers have promoted them. Convenience products are aimed at deskilling the cooking process—heat-and-eat, whether it is soup in a can, frozen foods, foods precut and ready to eat, or already prepared foods. Cooking skills have so eroded that a new product has taken hold: the meal kit. Meal kits contain all the ingredients to make a meal, including little packets of mayonnaise or herbs. The kits are sold as a "convenience" because consumers are deemed to be too busy (and/or lacking in skill) to plan or shop for a meal. Five percent of US shoppers say they have purchased a meal kit in the past year (Food Marketing Institute, 2018). Not even half those who have used them claim they are convenient, although convenience is the most cited reason for buying them. The second most popular reason is to explore new food, and one-third buy meal kits because "I don't have to think about what to cook." Only a quarter of purchasers buy kits because they are healthy and a fifth say they buy them because they do not know how to cook. Purchasers appear to use them as a way to force themselves to cook a meal and eat with others rather than go out; they become a commitment to cook and eat together. The kits generally include every ingredient, except possibly staples like oil, and detailed instructions about how to prepare the meals. Some, like Blue Apron, are offered as a subscription service: choose X number of meals a week and pick which meals you want each week. Most food retailers in the US with online shopping offer meal kits to be purchased ad hoc. All meal kits use enormous amounts of packaging.

Some researchers have argued that meal kits are more environmentally sustainable than grocery store purchases (Heard et al., 2019). However, the conclusions of this particular study indicate that the choice of food (meat versus plant-based) has a much bigger environmental impact than the mode of delivery. The environmental benefits they find for meal kits are largely due to the smaller portions the kits use as compared to grocery store items and the assumption, therefore, that less food is wasted. The researchers compared meal kits to grocery store shopping assuming identical ingredients for one to five meals, and assuming that meal kits replaced all grocery shopping. First, meal kits do not replace all meals and do not replace grocery shopping. Indeed, online food shoppers make 1.6 grocery shopping trips a week, while those who do not buy food online make only 1.5 shopping trips a week (Food Marketing Institute, 2018). Nor do food shoppers go to the grocery store to only buy the ingredients for a single meal. If they did so, they would need to go to the grocery store three times a day or more. In fact, people shop for groceries on average 1.6 times a week (Food Marketing Institute, 2018), or once for every 13 meals, on average. Nor do people buy all the ingredients for a meal or even five meals when they shop; most people have items stored in their kitchens that they use. Thus, the study's conclusion that meal kits are sustainable is based on a series of unrealistic assumptions.

Meal kits are marketed as "healthy" or as fulfilling a specific diet, e.g., "Mediterranean." As such, one might assume portion sizes are appropriate, but one would be wrong. Each serving of protein generally exceeds the MyPlate daily recommendation of five ounces, whole grains are notably absent, and FAV are mere garnish; they rarely occupy half the plate. Indeed, only a quarter of meal kit buyers buy the kits because they consider the food healthy. Although one-third claim meal kits save them time, it is unclear how the kits do that; one could prepare a meal in the time it takes simply to unpack and unwrap the ingredients, let alone read through the instructions. The packaging includes individually wrapped items, cold packs, and boxes, most of which will wind up in a landfill. Meal kits are essentially the TV dinners of the 21st century, except they are much more work and produce far more waste.

In an era where 70% of Americans are overweight or obese, many of the diets, podcasts, books, cooking shows, and meal kits are aimed at weight loss. The fact is that any diet will help one lose weight if the calories eaten are less than those expended and if one exercises. However, some diets are easier for some people to stay on than others, many diets may lack essential nutrients, and nearly all diets will result in gaining back weight lost once you stop. If the goal is weight loss, a "diet" will not solve this, it requires changing one's eating habits and activity levels, permanently, and ensuring that one is getting essential nutrients, routinely. That does little to pay the bills of the people and companies promoting different diets, so no one says as much. We are told there is a miracle cure and we desperately want to believe it.

Our food system

There is hope for the future of our food system…if we can make some adjustments. There is plenty of food and there will continue to be plenty of food for the world's increasing population. The problem globally, and even within a rich country like the US, is the lack of income to access food that is healthy and nutritious. Furthermore, conflicts can prevent access to food. Even when there is sufficient income, the choices we make, or more precisely the choices that we are offered, may not be very healthy or nutritious. On average, we are not eating enough whole grains, FAV, or seeds and nuts, and we are eating too much processed food, particularly refined starches, sugars, sugary beverages, meat, and alcohol. And we do not get enough exercise. The results are overweight, obesity, heart disease, strokes, diabetes, and diet-related cancers. We could live longer and better if we ate fewer empty calories, more nutritious foods, and got more exercise.

The environmental consequences of our diets high in meats and processed foods are monocultures, erosion, habitat loss, species extinction, CAFOs, water shortages, water contamination, and increased GHG. A diet high in whole grains and FAV, with fewer processed foods and less meat is not just good for our health and well-being, it is good for the planet. It is also safer since reducing meat consumption means fewer animal feces that could contaminate our food supply.

The human side of the US food system is that extreme concentration of production and processing means exploitation of mostly immigrant and largely undocumented workers. Anti-immigrant rhetoric masks the crucial labor immigrants provide, and keeps immigrants, with and without legal status, vulnerable and unable to access basic rights. For example: toilets, the ability to use them when needed, water and soap to wash hands, and towels. Public health and safety are put at risk when agricultural and food workers are denied these basic rights.

Globally, the increased concentration of brands, trade, and retail stores means a handful of companies control most of the food we eat. Despite this concentration, we are told that these few companies with logistical capabilities to negotiate prices, sources, and distribution of products all over the world are unable to trace the source of food safety issues. Clearly, if they are able to trace profits, they have the capability to trace safety issues. Along with this lack of transparency, the lack of funding for government enforcement agencies means it is difficult to identify public health problems to prevent them. Even when problems are identified, the size of fines is so minuscule compared to the scope of operations of companies that they can choose to ignore citations if it is cheaper to pay the fines than rectify the safety issues.

The power of retail stores to promote specific brands, for a fee, or their own private labels, means we are faced with little real choice of what to buy. Retail stores are able to guide us to buy things in-store and online that are neither healthy nor sustainable, but highly profitable for themselves. Traditional knowledge and culture regarding food have been supplanted not just by retail stores, but by diet gurus, cooking shows, and restaurants. After thousands of years of taking cues from our cultures and environments about what to eat, we find ourselves following personalized diets to regain some control over our bodies and health, and perhaps as a way to exert our identity. We want to believe in a magic bullet, we are willing to make sacrifices for a short time, but the fact is, we are surrounded by foods that are simply unhealthy. So, is it any wonder that we have trouble making healthy changes in our eating habits?

Exercise: Keep a 24-hour time diary

Keep track of how much time you spend eating during one 24-hour period. Count all the time that you ate, even if you are doing something else. Also keep track of how much time you spent preparing food, cleaning up from cooking and eating, and food shopping. Were these typical? If not, what is typical? Did you cook or prepare food for someone other than yourself? Did you eat with someone else?

How much time did you spend on social media, videos, TV, podcasts? How much time did you spend driving or in transportation? How much time did you spend actually working? How much time did you spend exercising? Sleeping?

Look at how you spent the 24 hours: is this how you want to spend your day? If not, what could you change so your allocation of time aligns with your values?

References

Achrol, R. S. 2012. Slotting allowances: a time series analysis of aggregate effects over three decades. Journal of the Academy of Marketing Science, 40(5), 673-694. doi:10.1007/s11747-011-0260-7.

Adam, A., Jensen, J. D., Sommer, I., and Hansen, G. L. 2017. Does shelf space management intervention have an effect on calorie turnover at supermarkets? Journal of Retailing and Consumer Services, 34, 311–318.

Adamiec, C. 2013. When healthful eating becomes an obsession, in Selective Eating: The Rise, Meaning and Sense of "Personal Dietary Requirements" C. Fischler, editor. Translated by C. Schoch and W. Snow. Paris: Odile Jacob.

Ahold Delhaize. 2019. All the facts about our stores in the US. https://www.aholddelhaize.com/en/brands/united-states/our-brands-in-the-united-states/, accessed April 8, 2019.

Albertsons Companies. 2018. Albertsons Companies' O Organics hits $1 billion brand milestone. January 11. https://www.globenewswire.com/news-release/2018/01/11/1287576/0/en/Albertsons-Companies-O-Organics-hits-1-billion-brand-milestone.html, accessed April 11, 2019.

Airuwaily, A., Mangold, C., Greene, T., Arshonsky, J., Cassidy, O., Pomeranz, J., and Bragg, M. 2020. Child social media influencers and unhealthy food product placement. Pediatrics, October, e20194057. doi:

https://doi-org.ezproxy.library.wisc.edu/10.1542/peds.2019-4057, accessed October 26, 2020.

Arnot, C. 2018. The dangerous disconnect: Food and agriculture trust gaps. Food Processing, January 17. https://www.foodprocessing.com/articles/2018/power-lunch-food-ag-trust/, accessed February 18, 2019.

Braden, C. R. and Tauxe, R. V. 2013. Emerging trends in foodborne diseases. Infectious Diseases Clinic of North America, 27(3), 517–533. http://dx.doi.org/10.1016/j.idc.2013.06.001, accessed February 18, 2019.

CDC. 2018. Food allergies: Knowledge and attitudes of restaurant managers and staff. Environmental Health Services. https://www.cdc.gov/nceh/ehs/ehsnet/plain_language/food-allergies.htm, accessed April 15, 2019.

Chamie, J. 2016. 320 million children in single-parent families. Global Issues, October 15. http://www.globalissues.org/news/2016/10/15/22568, accessed April 5, 2019.

Chuck, E. 2016. Poultry workers denied bathroom breaks, wear diapers: Oxfam report. NBC News, May 12. https://www.nbcnews.com/business/business-news/poultry-workers-denied-bathroom-breaks-wear-diapers-oxfam-report-n572806, accessed April 19. 2019.

Costco. 2018. Annual report 2018, fiscal year ended September 2, 2018. http://investor.costco.com/Mobile.view?c=83830&d=10&v=100, accessed February 28, 2019.

CSI Market. 2019. Grocery stores industry profitably: Profitability & trends. https://csimarket.com/Industry/industry_Profitability_Ratios.php?ind=1305, accessed April 11, 2019.

Deloitte. 2018. Global powers of retailing 2018. https://www2.deloitte.com/content/dam/Deloitte/at/Documents/about-deloitte/global-powers-of-retailing-2018.pdf, accessed February 28, 2019.

Doepke, M. and Tertilt, M. 2018. Women's empowerment, the gender gap in desired fertility, and fertility outcomes in developing countries. IZA Institute of Labor Economics. Discussion Paper IZA DP No. 11262, January. http://ftp.iza.org/dp11262.pdf, accessed April 3, 2019.

Dudlicek, J. 2018. Top 50 grocers: Amazon in 8th place while rest of industry restrategizes, reshuffles. The Progressive Grocer, May 7. https://progressivegrocer.com/top-50-grocers-2018-ranked, accessed February 28, 2019.

Dudlicek, J., Goldschmidt, B., Hofbauer, R., and Martin, K. 2018. 85th annual report of the grocery industry. Progressive Grocer, 97(4), 26-30. http://www.nxtbook.com/nxtbooks/ensembleiq/pg_201804/index.php#/30, accessed February 28, 2019.

FAO. 2017. The future of food and agriculture: Trends and challenges. http://www.fao.org/3/a-i6583e.pdf accessed April 3, 2019.

Feeding America. 2018. Facts about poverty and hunger in America. https://www.feedingamerica.org/hunger-in-america/facts, accessed February 12, 2019.

Feucht, Y. and Zander, K. 2017. Consumers' attitudes on carbon footprint labelling: Results of the SUSDIET project. Thünen working paper number 78, Johann Heinrich von Thünen-Institut, Braunschweig, Germany. https://www.econstor.eu/bitstream/10419/173086/1/1009605887.pdf, accessed April 15, 2019.

Food Marketing Institute. 2018. US grocery shopper trends 2018. http://www.mmibusinessadvisors.com/wp-content/uploads/2018/06/shopper-trends-report-2018.pdf, accessed April 24, 2019.

Frazier, M. 2006. Home Depot, Wal-Mart sell vendors web ads. Advertising Age, 77(29) July17, 26.

GBD 2017 Diet Collaborators. 2019. Health effects of dietary risk in 195 countries, 1990-2017, a systematic analysis for the Global Burden of Disease Study 2017. Lancet, published online April 3. http://dx.doi.org/10.1016/S0140-6736(19)30041-8, accessed April 4, 2019.

Gupta, R .S. Warren, C. M., and Smith, B. M. 2019. Prevalence and severity of food allergies among US Adults. JAMA Network 2(1), e185630. doi:10.1001/jamanetworkopen.2018.5630. https://jamanetwork.com/journals/jamanetworkopen/fullarticle/2720064, accessed April 15, 2019.

Hancock, M. 1998. Handwashing and toilet facility requirements for agricultural operations. Standard Number: 1928.110(b) 1928.110(c)(2). US Department of Labor, June 5. https://www.osha.gov/laws-regs/standard interpretations/1998-06-05, accessed April 19, 2019.

Hendrickson, M. K., Howard, P. H., and Constance, D. H. 2017. Power, food and agriculture. Implications for farmers, consumers and communities. University of Missouri, College of Agriculture, Food & Natural Resources Division of Applied Social Sciences Working Paper. https://philhowardnet.files.wordpress.com/2017/11/hendrickson-howard-constance-2017-final-working-paper-nov-1.pdf, accessed February 28, 2019.

Heard, B. R., Bandekar, M., Vassar, B., and Miller, S. A. 2019. Comparison of life cycle environmental impacts from meal kits and grocery store meals. Resources, Conservation and Recycling, 147(August), 189–200. https://doi.org/10.1016/j.resconrec.2019.04.008, accessed April 24, 2019.

Horton, R. 2018. GBD 2017: a fragile world. The Lancet, 392(10150), 1683. https://doi.org/10.1016/S0140-6736(18)32858-7, accessed October 22, 2020.

Hübner, A., Kuhn, H., and Wollenburg, J. 2016. Last mile fulfilment and distribution in omni-channel grocery retailing. International Journal of Retail & Distribution Management, 44(3), 228–247. doi: 10.1108/IJRDM-11-2014-0154.

Hyman, M. R., Kopf, D. A., and Lee, D. 2010. Review of literature - Future research suggestions: Private label brands: Benefits, success factors and future research. Journal of Brand Management, 17(5), 368–389. doi: 10.1057/bm.2009.33.

IOM (Institute of Medicine). 2012. Improving food safety through a One Health approach. Washington, DC: The National Academies Press.

InterAcademy Partnership. 2018. Opportunities for future research and innovation on food and nutrition security and agriculture. November. https://www.interacademies.org/node/50845, accessed October 22, 2020.

Karthikeyan, V. and Garber, A. 2019. How safe is our food? Recent trends and case studies, and what they mean for our health. US PIRG Education Fund, January. https://uspirg.org/sites/pirg/files/reports/WEB_USP_Safe-Food-Report_Jan19.pdf?_ga=2.236751811.396103287.1555626538-1657785805.1555626538, accessed April 18, 2019.

Kelso, A. 2018. Kroger will launch tool for suppliers to reach online shoppers. Grocery Dive, June 1. https://www.grocerydive.com/news/grocery--kroger-will-launch-tool-for-suppliers-to-reach-online-shoppers/533969/, accessed April 15, 2019.

Laska, M. N., Sindberga, L. S., Ayala, G. X., D'Angelo, H., Horton, L. A., Ribisl, K. M., Kharmats, A., Olson, C., and Gittelsohn, J. 2018. Agreements between small food store retailers and their suppliers: Incentivizing unhealthy foods and beverages in four urban settings. Food Policy, 79, 324–330.

Livingston, G. and Bialik, K. 2018. 7 facts about US moms. Pew Research Center, May 10. https://www.pewresearch.org/fact-tank/2018/05/10/facts-about-u-s-mothers/, accessed April 5, 2019.

Mekonnen, M. M. and Hoekstra, A. Y. 2012. A global assessment of the water footprint of farm animal production. Ecosystems, 15, 401–415. https://link.springer.com/article/10.1007/s10021-011-9517-8, accessed March 21, 2019.

Moneret-Vautrin, D. A. 2013. Diet and food allergy: Truth, error, ignorance and myth, in Selective Eating: The Rise, Meaning and Sense of "Personal Dietary Requirements" C. Fischler, editor. Translated by C. Schoch and W. Snow. Paris: Odile Jacob.

National Council of Farmer Cooperatives. 2020. About National Council of Farmer Cooperatives. http://ncfc.org/about-ncfc/, accessed September 9, 2020.

Nord, M. and Andrews, M. 2002. Reducing food insecurity in the United States: Assessing progress toward a national objective. USDA ERS Food Assistance and Nutrition Research, Research Report 26-2, May. https://naldc.nal.usda.gov/download/36551/PDF, accessed April 19, 2019.

Norman, M., Hoffman, J., and Cheskin, L. J. 2014. Shelf space devoted to nutritious foods correlates with BMI. American Journal of Food and Nutrition, 2(2), 18–22. doi:10.12691/ajfn-2-2-1.

Patel, H. 2017. Simple Truth: Kroger's gem. Seeking Alpha, March 8. https://seekingalpha.com/article/4053209-simple-truth-krogers-gem, accessed April 11, 2019.

Robles, P. 2017. Is Amazon's ad business the new slotting fee? Ecoconsultancy, October 20. https://econsultancy.com/is-amazon-s-ad-business-the-new-slotting-fee/, accessed April 9, 2019.

Rona, R. J., Keil, T., Summers, C., Gislason, D., Zuidmeer, L., Sodergren, E., Sigurdardottir, S. T., Lindner, T., Goldhahn, K., Dahlstrom, J., McBride, D., and Madsen, C. 2017. The prevalence of food allergy: A meta-analysis. Journal of Allergy and Clinical Immunology, 120(3), 638–646. https://doi.org/10.1016/j.jaci.2007.05.026, accessed April 17, 2019.

Saad, L. 2018. Americans, in theory, think larger families are ideal. Gallup, July 6. https://news.gallup.com/poll/236696/americans-theory-think-larger-families-ideal.aspx, accessed April 3, 2019.

Schlosser, E. 2002. Fast Food Nation. New York: Perennial.

Sedgh, G., Singh, S., and Hussain, R. 2014. Intended and unintended pregnancies worldwide in 2012 and recent trends. Studies in Family Planning, 45(3), 301–314. https://www.ncbi.nlm.nih.gov/pmc/articles/PMC4727534/, accessed April 3, 2019.

Smucker-Brian, Z. 2018. Grow your food brand on Amazon, if you constantly optimize. Marketplace Strategy, September 6. https://test-foodfinance.pantheonsite.io/blog/2018/grow-your-food-brand-amazon-optimize/, accessed April 15, 2019.

US Census Bureau. 2018. 44 percent of custodial parents receive the full amount of child support. January 30. https://www.census.gov/newsroom/press-releases/2018/cb18-tps03.html, accessed April 5, 2019.

US FDA. 2018. What we do. https://www.fda.gov/aboutfda/whatwedo/ accessed April 18, 2019.

Wang, S. L., Heisey, P., Schimmelpfennig, D., and Ball, E. 2015. Agricultural productivity growth in the United States: Measurement, trends, and drivers. USDA ERS Economic Research Report 189, July. https://ethanolrfa.org/wp-content/uploads/2017/07/Agricultural-Productivity-Growth-in-the-US_Wang-et-al_2015.pdf, accessed April 19, 2019.

Whalley, L. E., Grzywacz, J. G, Quandt, S. A., Vallejos, Q. M., Walkup, M., Chen, H., Galvan, L., and Arcury, T. A. 2009. Migrant farmworker field and camp safety and sanitation in Eastern North Carolina. Journal of Agromedicine, 14(4), 421–436. https://www.ncbi.nlm.nih.gov/pmc/articles/PMC2774916/pdf/nihms140383.pdf, accessed April 19, 2019.

Zepeda, L. and Reznickova, A. 2018. Potential demand for local fresh produce by mobile markets. US Department of Agriculture, Agricultural Marketing Service Research Publication. http://localandorganicfood.org/wp-content/uploads/2018/05/Potential-Demand-for-Local-Fresh-Produce-by-Mobile-Markets-05-18-1.pdf, accessed October 22, 2020.

CHAPTER SIX

WHY DO WE CHOOSE THE FOODS WE DO?

Processed foods contain high levels of sugar, salt, and fat because we are hardwired to like them. In addition, sugar and salt cover up the bland and canned flavor of processed foods (Bentley, 2014) and are preservatives, while fat is used to enhance the feel of food in the mouth (O'Sullivan, 2020). The food industry has manipulated the levels of salt, sugar, and fat to get us to like processed foods, not just in adult food, but in baby foods (Bentley, 2014). For nearly a century, most Americans have been reared since infancy on diets of processed foods high in sugar, salt, and fat. This has shaped our food preferences and health problems later in life.

However, social scientists mostly look at our food choices as autonomous. They often fail to see the context within which decisions are made. This chapter examines the way social science disciplines generally view our food choices and behavior change, their contributions to understanding behavior change, and their blind spots.

The economics of food demand

Economists mostly do not try to understand people's motivations or objectives, rather, they assume these are revealed through peoples' choices. They use observable information, primarily prices and income, to predict choices. They assume preferences are fixed and our choices are rational; we maximize our happiness (utility) given our budget, or minimize our costs given our target level of happiness (Just and Payne 2009). Neoclassical theory dispenses with measuring happiness directly by assuming that what people buy maximizes their utility and therefore "reveals" their preferences. Economics frames questions in terms of constrained optimization. All decisions are assumed to be constrained by something: money, time, or a goal. In contrast, other disciplines often operate as though people have no constraints and that decisions do not involve trade-offs. The premise that all decisions are constrained and involve trade-offs is perhaps the most important contribution of economics, while the assumptions of rationality and fixed preferences are its greatest failings.

Key questions economists examine regarding consumers include: how much do they buy given prices and incomes; and what is their price and income responsiveness? For example, food has an inelastic (unresponsive) demand. That is, the amount of food purchased does not vary much if prices change because we have a limited capacity to eat. Thus, if a staple food price goes up, we may buy somewhat less of it, or substitute it with something else, but generally, we continue to buy it. If the price goes down, we can afford more, but may not choose to because we already have enough. When demand for a food varies a lot with respect to income, these foods are deemed luxuries, while foods that are unresponsive to income changes are deemed necessities.

The practical application of estimating price and income responsiveness is for those selling the products. Sales of foods with inelastic demands will not change much, hence increasing the price of such foods will increase the seller's total revenues, while decreasing the price will decrease their total revenues. This creates an incentive for sellers of products with inelastic demand to restrict supply in order to keep prices high. In contrast, foods that have an elastic demand are those for which a decrease in price increases the demand proportionally more. Hence a decrease in price will increase total revenues, while an increase in price will decrease revenues. Thus, producers of foods with an elastic demand have an incentive to expand production and lower prices. Therefore, identifying whether a product has an inelastic or elastic demand affects a company's production and pricing strategies. To increase revenues, we must restrict the production and raise the prices of inelastic products, while expanding the production and lowering the prices of elastic products.

Measuring the relationship between products and income helps identify to whom one markets products. Income elasticities measure whether a good is a luxury or a necessity. If the product is a luxury, demand increases (or falls) with the rise (or fall) in income. If the product is a necessity, demand will not change much with rising (or falling) incomes. Knowing this, marketers advertise products as luxuries to groups with rising incomes, or as necessities to groups with falling or unchanging incomes.

These are market-level applications of elasticities, but those selling food are also interested in the preferences of individuals within a market. Economists do not try to measure preferences directly; they use proxy variables, often demographics. Furthermore, they assume individual preferences are fixed and consumers are rational. Thus, economists assume consumer choices can be captured by income, prices of a good or service, prices of competing or complementary goods or services, and characteristics like one's gender, age, race, ethnicity, and education. Since they assume preferences are fixed and consumers are rational, economists focus on prices and income as the key to changing consumption.

Is it reasonable to believe that one's choices are rational? Is it reasonable to assume that gender, age, race or ethnicity determine one's preferences? Do all White men aged 40 choose the same thing given prices and income? Economists seem to think so, but a 60-year-old Latina economist would beg to differ. Using demographics is clearly a matter of convenience; it is easier to measure demographic characteristics than to measure preferences. However, the reliance on gender, age, race, and ethnicity to explain consumer decisions also reveals the misogyny, ageism, and racism that economists use as a lens through which to view and dissect the economy; everyone within a demographic group is seen as the same.

Furthermore, analysis of revealed preferences is often problematic. Economists claim they can predict consumer behavior. Often, they do not account for out-of-sample variation, meaning that the farther one predicts outside their data, the wider the margin of error, and hence the less accurate their predictions are. Their statistical estimates are subject to a margin of error because there is variation in the relationships among the data, and most importantly, because the data does not capture all the variation in demand. There are missing variables, such as direct measures of preferences, which obviously are neither fixed according to one's demographic characteristics, nor fixed in time. However, it is not uncommon to publish results where the statistical models explain less than 10% of the variation in the dependent variable. Clearly, such an analysis has missed major explanatory factors.

Often, published papers conspicuously omit measures of fit, presumably because such measures are so low. Instead, researchers focus on the statistical significance of explanatory variables. However, statistical significance is easily manipulated; one can simply add or delete explanatory variables until one gets the desired results, or one can add more observations. For example, if 20 years of data do not show that there is a significant relationship between price and demand, use monthly data over the same period; 240 months will surely indicate a significant relationship.

Even if there is a relationship between the variables, significance does not show causality; two measurements can move together without causing each other. Indeed, two measurements could move mostly together because of random chance or a third excluded factor.

Perhaps the most neglected area of economics is data: data quality, missing data, and the relationship between theory and data. Economists and other social scientists rarely question the secondary data they use. It is always assumed to reflect what it is supposed to measure and often assumed to be representative. However, it is worth understanding and examining one's data. How was it collected? Was it, as I was told by statisticians in one Ministry of Agriculture, simply taking census data from decades ago and adding 2% each year? Furthermore, does the definition of the variable in question change over time? For example, if one used the same definition of "farm" as was used in the US in the 1860 Agricultural Census, there would be less than half as many farms as were reported in the latest US Agricultural Census. Hence, it is important that variables are defined in the same way over the sample examined.

The interest in behavioral economics is one way of addressing data quality to find cleaner relationships. However, behavioral economics rarely addresses the fact that the samples are too small to be representative, that there is likely selection bias among those who participate, that there may be missing variables, and whether the data collected really represents what it is purported to measure.

The economics of behavior change

With regard to food-related health problems, such as obesity, economists often regard these as mistakes in personal choices that are due to a lack of information that places costs on society, for example, by increasing health care expenses (Just and Payne, 2009). The lack of information and costs imposed on others are called market failures that reduce societal well-being, thereby justifying policy interventions, such as nutrition information, taxes on unhealthy foods, or subsidies of healthy foods. However, many of the economic studies use simulations rather than actual policy interventions. Unsurprisingly, simulations find that interventions are effective (Hope et al., 2017), or they would not have been published.

In contrast, Just and Payne (2009) note that interventions like health information are often misused by consumers. They suggest that prices have a limited effect in determining choice since shoppers rarely recall prices correctly. Taking their cue from marketing, they suggest that psychological techniques to manipulate behavior are more effective than information or prices. They identify the shopping and eating environment as causing people to eat too much because there is an information asymmetry: marketers know what makes people buy and eat more food, but people themselves are unaware of these effects. So, to improve eating habits, they suggest using or reversing the techniques used by marketers. These include removing distracting stimuli and setting healthy consumption norms to encourage what and how much is eaten. Their suggestions include: allowing food vendors to charge extra for private rooms with fewer distractions; requiring all-you-can-eat restaurants to use smaller plates; using cash rather than a debit card because the former is associated with healthier food choices; third-party certification for portion size; and requiring people to make decisions about food choice before being exposed to "sensual temptation." While these interventions are not very practical, the take-away of this research is that one should look to the field of psychology and to the food environment to understand how to change behavior.

Other economists have focused on the role cognitive load has on poor choices (e. g. Fudenberg and Levine, 2006; Carroll et al., 2018). The idea is that people are too busy and distracted to make good choices. These approaches focus on demonstrating and measuring the impact cognitive load has on making poor choices. The solutions focus on how to nudge consumers to make "better" choices, often through manipulation of the shopping environment.

Behavioral economics provides a rationale for incorporating theories from other disciplines into economic models. It provides a framework to conduct experiments to measure the impacts of psychological factors. However, while experimental economics can control many factors, given the small and nonrandom nature of these experiments, they are by definition, anecdotal.

Natural experiments provide a more robust measurement. These occur when policies are implemented in some areas and not others. Having a control group allows researchers to compare the results and attribute the change to the policy. As an example, Guagnano et al. (1995) analyzed a natural experiment in recycling. They found that ease of recycling was more important than one's attitude in determining whether one recycled. Even those who did not espouse pro-environmental attitudes tended to recycle if it was easy. The researchers developed the Attitude, Behavior, Context (ABC) theory which posits that attitudes align with behaviors when the context is facilitating or at least neutral. The implication for behavior changes with respect to diet is that even if there is a strong desire to change ones' behaviors, it is unlikely to happen if one's environment (context) does not make it easy. This is a basic premise of Weight Watchers; provide portion-controlled foods that make dieting easy and a peer group for accountability and support.

Often policies are implemented across the board, allowing only for comparison of behavior before and after, which may be subject to confounding influences. In other words, there is no control group. Sugar and sodium taxes are examples of policies that local and national governments have implemented to foster behavior change. In 2014, Mexico implemented a one peso per liter tax on sugary beverages to reduce the consumption of added sugar; they targeted sugary beverages because a 2012 study found that 9.8% of the calories Mexicans consumed were from sugar-sweetened beverages (Colchero et al., 2017). In the first two years after the implementation of the sugar tax, per capita consumption of sugar-sweetened beverages in Mexico fell by an annual rate of 5.5% in 2014, with a larger reduction in 2015 (9.7%). A similar but smaller tax on sugary beverages (5% versus 10% of the price) implemented in Chile resulted in a 4.0% reduction in calories from sugary beverages, amounting to a decrease of less than 34 calories per month (Caro et al., 2018). Mexico's soda tax was accompanied by an extensive public education campaign, while Chile's tax was not. Is the difference in the effects of the policies due to the difference in the size of the taxes or the difference in public education? Since there were no control groups and no randomization in either case, it is difficult to say.

Municipalities have also implemented soda taxes. Berkeley, California implemented a relatively large tax of one cent per ounce and found that while most of the tax was passed on to consumers, and sales of sugary drinks in Berkeley fell by 9.6%, they rose in surrounding communities by 6.9%, and that the overall impact on consumption of sugary beverages was insignificant because Berkeley residents were low consumers of sugary beverages to begin with (Silver et al., 2017). In Philadelphia, the short-term effects of a 1.5 cent per ounce tax, equivalent to a 20% price increase, on sugary and diet drinks yielded a 38% reduction in consumption in the first two months (Zhong et al., 2018). The results provide support for taxes as a policy tool to improve dietary choices. However, since none of the implementations involved a control group or randomization, we cannot be sure of the degree to which their effectiveness depends on the size of the tax, the initial levels of consumption, whether taxes are accompanied by public education campaigns, or some combination of these factors.

The upshot is that the contributions of economists to understanding food-related behaviors are that prices can influence behaviors; that some products generate more price responsiveness than others; and that consumers face economic, time, and information trade-offs and constraints in making decisions. We have to look at other fields to understand how to influence preferences and price responsiveness, as well as how to address constraints.

Why do people eat what they do? The psychology of changing food choices

While economists tend to adhere to a single theory and try to get their data to fit it, psychologists are somewhat more curious; they often collect data to test different theories. There are many psychological theories, and only a few are covered here.

Kurt Lewin is considered the founder of social psychology and action research. One of the important questions he examined was how to change eating behaviors. He used experiments to test theories to come up with practical recommendations. Just before WWII began, he was asked to participate in a National Research Council committee to address how to improve nutrition in the US. The advent of WWII made the issue crucial because of the high rate of defects among American men of draft age, many related to diet. As Cummings (1941) noted, more than half of the men drafted in WWI had defects. Apparently, this was still an issue during WWII. The issue is no less crucial today; in 2017 only 17% of 17 to 24-year-olds in the US would qualify for military service and of those who actually try to enlist, 31% are disqualified immediately because they are obese (Maxey et al., 2018). Hence, researchers like Lewin are motivated by national security to understand how to improve dietary choices.

Lewin (1943) developed Channel Theory to explain why people eat what they do. While noting that there were practical, cultural, and psychological factors that influence what people eat, his premise was that people ate what was on the table, hence the real issue for him was, how did food arrive at the table? The notion that people eat at a table with others needs a bit of adjustment in contemporary America or Britain. It is no longer the norm to eat a meal at a table with others at a specified time. One-third of Britons eat most of their meals alone and 37% replace at least one meal a week with snacks (Fleming, 2019). While many people eat distracted, looking at screens, whether eating alone or even with others, eating alone has spawned the phenomenon of *mukbang*—watching recorded or live videos of others eating. Clearly, eating customs have changed.

Today, there are no temporal or spatial limits as to when or where Americans eat. Americans eat in cars, in classrooms, in bed, at their workspace, and in public. They eat any time of day or night. If one happens to eat with others in the US, it is considered normal to refuse to eat what is served; parents and hosts are expected to cater to the dictates of children and guests. However, Channel Theory still has relevance if we modify the premise from people eating what is put on the table, to people eating what they put in their mouth. The issue still is: how does that food get there?

To understand what was eaten, Lewin (1943) stated that one needed to identify the channels by which food arrived. These included, and still do, stores, deliveries, food already in the house, and restaurants. He introduced the concept of a gatekeeper who decided what food was purchased and how it made it to the table, and stated that it was important to understand the psychology of the gatekeeper. While he was talking about the housewife, the gatekeepers of today might be considered food retailers because they are the ones who determine what choices one can make, or social and other media, because they influence what people eat. Lewin also posited that different forces may act on the different channels, and that the person who controls a channel influences the food that is eaten.

Lewin (1943) identified five factors that could be used to alter food behavior: the psychology of the gatekeeper; food availability; food channels; frames of reference; and eating groups. The gatekeeper defines what is food, when meals are eaten, and the eating situation. We take for granted what we think to be food, but it varies; some people consider sugared beverages to be food, while others eat insects. Some foods are associated with specific groups; Lewin found that meat was considered a "husband's food," and in 1941, vegetables were considered as food for children. In America today, vegetables are assumed to be a child's natural enemy and children's food is defined as highly processed junk foods: hot dogs, french fries, chicken nuggets, and anything with large amounts of sugar. Parents reinforce this behavior by stating in front of their children that, "children do not eat vegetables," by buying them "kids' meals," and by buying them breakfast cereals, desserts, candies, and beverages full of sugar. Observing adults feeding children in the US, one is reminded of force-fed geese, except rather than producing foie gras, the adults seem determined to create a diabetic. Most American children, as a consequence, have learned that sugar and processed foods are children's foods, and vegetables are not.

Not only are some foods perceived as pertaining to particular people, but certain foods are also seen as appropriate for specific meals or times of the day. For example, meat during Lewin's time was considered essential for dinner, and it remains so today for many Americans. Eggs are usually eaten in the morning in the US, not in the evening. Pizza is eaten in the evening in Italy, not for the main meal in the middle of the day. Cultural norms tell us what foods to eat when.

Today, food availability is limited mainly by price; even seasonal food can be obtained out of season if one is willing to pay for food shipped from another region or hemisphere. Food channels appear to be diverse, but in fact, food retailing and processing are highly concentrated globally. In the US, we purchase 93% of the food eaten at home from hypermarkets, large grocery chains, and convenience stores, almost all the rest is purchased through drug stores and hard discount stores (FAO, 2017). Of the food we buy, the five largest food companies own two out of three global food brands (Ramsey, 2003). Retailers use their shelf space to promote products, charging slotting fees to brands. The placement of products on shelf space influences what we choose and that, in turn, affects our weight (Norman, Hoffman and Cheskin, 2014), and ultimately health. Hence, the fact that food channels are highly concentrated and controlled means we need to be mindful of how our choices are being manipulated.

Lewin (1943) identified four main values as frames of reference that motivate food choice: taste, expense, health, and status. These are still relevant today. The environment, and social justice or equity, are additional frames we could add to Lewin's Channel Theory. Obstacles may be prices or time, conceived as constraints by economists; and skill, which economists rarely consider because people are assumed to have perfect knowledge. Furthermore, Lewin stated that there were often conflicts in values around foods that were considered essential, such as meat or dessert.

Eating groups are who one eats with; they influence how and what one eats, as well as how one thinks about food. One can eat with different groups, each of which has a specific culture. For example, eating habits may be quite different at a family dinner, on a first date, or at an all-you-can-eat buffet. For us today, social media may be our most common eating influencer.

Given the context of WWII, Lewin (1943) tried to understand the role of group and democratic processes to get people to change their behavior, specifically, to ration food. He implicitly recognized that individuals are at a disadvantage, and that groups help reinforce behavior change. He conducted experiments in which groups were asked to set goals for behavior change democratically and compared them to groups with the same targets given as an order. Not surprisingly, groups with democratically chosen goals were more likely to reach them, and the greater the majority and the more modest the goal, the more likely the goal was achieved. Overly ambitious goals led to attrition, whereas modest goals not only facilitated reaching the goal, but they also encouraged continued adherence, as well as supporting increased targets. Decisions made by a simple majority led to dissension by the minority, whereas compliance by the minority was higher when the decision had a strong majority. Another set of experiments involved comparing behavior change between groups given a lecture by an expert versus a democratic decision process with an expert consultant. Unsurprisingly, the latter was more effective in achieving behavior change.

Lewin's experiments illustrate how eating groups can encourage and support behavior change, and why simply providing information or directing people to make changes in their diet does not work. People have to want to make a change, they need an achievable goal, and support and accountability to reinforce the goal.

A related psychological framework for behavior change was developed from work with addicts: the Transtheoretical or the Stages of Change model (Prochaska and DiClemente, 1983). When it was originally conceived, there were five stages to behavior change: pre-contemplation, characterized by lack of awareness or not being ready for change; contemplation, the recognition of a problem; action; maintenance or the ability to sustain changed behavior; and relapse. A sixth stage, preparation, defined as the intention to act, was added to the original model. After analyzing data on addiction, Prochaska and DiClemente concluded that successful treatment required categorizing the stage people were in currently to identify which of the ten processes of change would best assist them. The ten processes are: consciousness-raising, i.e. getting the facts; environmental reevaluation or realizing the effect one's behaviors have on others; social liberation or noticing public support for healthy behavior; self-reevaluation or creating a new self-image; dramatic relief or paying attention to one's feelings; self-liberation or making a commitment to change; stimulus control or managing one's environment to encourage healthy behavior and restrict unhealthy behaviors; helping relationships that support change; counter-conditioning or substituting healthy ways of acting and thinking for unhealthy ways; and reinforcement management or rewarding positive behavior.

There are many adaptations of the Stages of Change model for situations other than addiction. Figure 6.1 conceptualizes the model for any crisis or external shock. The framework acknowledges that a natural reaction to a sudden shock is denial and resistance (MacDonald Boyd and Associates, 2009). Information is helpful to come to terms with a crisis, but if change is difficult, it is predictable that one will despair. However, reaching the bottom can motivate one to explore options for action. Support helps one get through this despair, rather than facts or inspiration. Moving forward requires acceptance and commitment, which require inspiration. What is interesting about this adaptation of the Stages of Change model is that facts are not presented as a way to facilitate action, but as a way to cope with strong emotions. Support is only useful when one has "hit bottom" as a way to encourage intentions and exploration, while inspiration is most useful in the decision-making and action phases.

This model can be applied to diet to explain responses to shocks: a doctor tells someone they are obese; they learn their favorite foods are unhealthy; or they find out a food involves the unethical treatment of people or animals. A natural reaction is denial and anger. Without factual information, it is likely that the person will rationalize their behavior. For example: I am not obese, the obesity measure, BMI, is incorrect; if I stop drinking soda it won't matter because I will still get HFCS from other foods; or even if I stop buying shrimp, other people will still buy it, so shrimp workers will still be enslaved. However, factual information may lead to despair: no matter what measure is used, I need to lose weight and that is hard; I need to get my blood sugar under control, but how will I ever get rid of added sugars from my diet; or I don't want to support slavery, but I really like shrimp. In the first two cases, a dietician would be extremely helpful, but in all three cases, there are support groups. There are dieting services, like Weight Watchers, support groups for diabetics, and consumer groups interested in ethical consumption, like Buy Nothing. Within these groups are success stories that can inspire participants to take action and move forward.

Figure 6.1 Stages of Change model

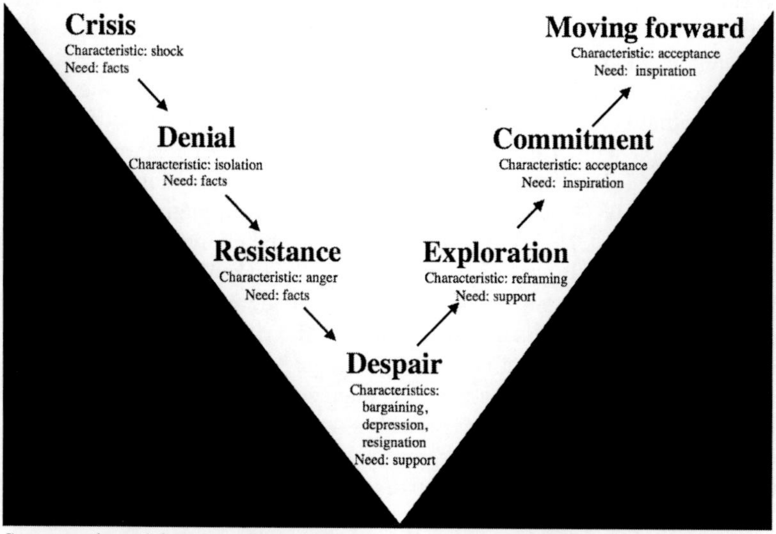

Source: adapted from MacDonald Boyd and Associates, 2009.

The Stages of Change model illustrates how consumer behavior is often not guided by rationality, as economists believe, but by emotions. Despite this, the model posits that information is useful, not to make rational decisions, but to counteract rationalization and denial. Indeed, facts serve to move one from one emotional state to another. This explains why denial and rationalization are such common reactions to unpleasant information; accepting bad news will lead to despair, and who does not wish to avoid despair? However, the inability to accept reality means one is stuck, unable to address the problem, and indeed, may exacerbate the problem. This may result in relapse and, ultimately, in despair. One can also get stuck in despair. However, despair can serve to motivate one to seek or be receptive to the support needed to address the problem. Inspiration provides the motivation to tackle the problem and keep moving forward. The Stages of Change model provides a way to understand why changing our food-related behaviors is so difficult. First, we can get stuck somewhere in the process of denial, resistance, or despair. Second, rather than serving to encourage rational behavior, the Stages of Change model posits that information leads to anger, resistance, and despair. Third, these emotions are necessary; the acceptance and ability to address our behaviors happens after we have been through these negative emotions and also found support and inspiration.

Weinstein (1988) developed a psychological model for preventative or self-protective behavior that is similar to the Stages of Change model, called the Precaution Adoption Model. The structure of his model is linear. He posited that people are in different stages of behavior change, that they need different things in each stage, and that there is no guarantee that they will reach the next stage. He also incorporated the concept of costs and benefits into his model. Weinstein's first stage is similar to that of Prochaska and DiClemente (1983): awareness that a risk exists. Information is the key to moving beyond stage 1 and being in stage 2: the belief that precautionary behavior is generally effective at mitigating the risk. Weinstein notes that personal experience can be as relevant as outside information. The third stage is the belief in personal susceptibility: the risk is personally relevant and the precaution is effective. Getting to stage 3 depends on the clarity and credibility of the information, personalized risk information, one's experience, and one's peers' experiences with the hazard. The fourth stage is the decision or intention to take action. This is based on beliefs about the likelihood and severity of failure to take action, and beliefs about the costs, difficulties, and benefits of taking action. The final stage is action.

Applying Weinstein's model to food, suppose one reads or hears a credible source that low consumption of whole grains is linked to lower life expectancy. Weinstein posits that one has to believe that it is true in general before one can accept it as personally relevant. Perhaps there is a family medical history that is relevant, or a specific condition that encourages the person to think that it might be a good idea to substitute some whole grains for refined products. The more severe the condition and the closer to one personally, the more likely action will be taken. Obstacles include the difficulty and cost of changing one's diet.

Weinstein's (1988) model does not have an explicit stage for relapse like the Stages of Change model, nor is it explicit about how emotions are tied to the stages. However, a major contribution of his model is recognition of the intention–behavior gap and why it exists; many people do not change their behavior even when they say they intend to. The intention–behavior gap has been widely recognized in many behaviors. For example, meta-analysis of pro-environmental behavior studies shows that, on average, intentions only explain about 27% of the variation in behavior (Bamberg and Moser, 2007). That intention plays such a small role in behavior change needs to be understood by practitioners. Weinstein explains the intention–behavior gap as a function of the strength of intention, reminders, the actual costs and time to take action, the complexity of the action, and the ease or difficulties of the effort to take action. This points to the need for a facilitating environment, support, and accountability to encourage intentions to translate into actions.

Rather than being concerned with the process of behavior change, Badura (2004) focused on a single reason, self-efficacy, as a means to segment people into groups for different strategies to facilitate health behavior change. He does not explore why people have different capacities for self-efficacy. He simply divides people into three groups: those with a high level of efficacy and belief in positive outcomes for behavior change; those who have self-doubt about efficacy and outcomes; and those who believe their health habits are beyond their personal control. The purpose is to identify what support is needed by different people to encourage behavior changes. Badura posited that health campaigns worked for people with high efficacy because they needed little guidance. However, he predicted that health campaigns were insufficient for the other two groups. His suggestions were that those with self-doubt may give up easily; they need support and guidance, while those who believe their habits are beyond their control require a very structured program with strong guidance. Badura found that social support and guidance in the early phase of behavior change increased long-run adherence. He recommended interactive computerized feedback as a convenient way to provide an oversight and called for the social diffusion of information. Today, we see the proliferation of apps and wearable devices to monitor and reinforce behavior. Indeed, Singapore is paying its citizens to use a health app designed for Apple watches to encourage exercise (Toh, 2020). The use of social networks through or outside these apps can provide support for adherence. Badura also saw the potential of entertainment, such as soap operas or reality shows (e.g., The Biggest Loser), to inspire self-efficacy.

Self Determination Theory (SDT) is a theoretical approach that focuses on the reasons for behaviors, rather than the process of behavior change. SDT provides mechanisms to use these reasons to induce behavior change. It offers an explanation for self-efficacy. SDT is used to explain human motivations, the pursuit of goals, and behaviors within the context of innate psychological needs for autonomy, competence, and relatedness (Deci and Ryan, 2000). These differ from physical needs because we are seldom conscious of them, and if they are not met, we tend to address them indirectly, e.g., through avoidance or defensive behaviors. When our psychological needs are met, we thrive, when they are not, it affects our mental health and well-being.

Deci and Ryan (2000) argue that motivations for behaviors are derived unconsciously to fulfill our basic psychological needs. If we are self-motivated to perform a behavior, it is often because it fulfills a psychological need. However, if the behavior is motivated externally, it may not necessarily fulfill our psychological needs. This explains why simply providing people with dietary and exercise recommendations does not necessarily result in changed behavior, even if the external factor is a medical condition. External forces can result in lasting behavior change if we are able to identify and internalize the behavior such that we willingly perform it, thereby fulfilling our psychological needs. For example, if one finds their new diet and exercise program does help them lose weight, lower their cholesterol, feel better, or if it tastes delicious, they may continue the diet and exercise willingly because of the positive feedback.

In addition to providing an explanation for efficacy, SDT provides an explanation for the results of Lewin's (1943) experiments. Lewin found that groups who chose their target for a behavior change performed better than groups that were mandated to achieve the same target. SDT attributes the success of groups who selected their own target to exercising and fulfilling their psychological needs for autonomy. Furthermore, groups who chose more moderate targets not only continued achieving their goals, but they were also motivated to set higher goals. The SDT interpretation of this is that the choice of moderate goals fostered a sense of competence, thereby encouraging continued adherence and more ambitious goals. Finally, Lewin found groups that had greater consensus also did a better job of reaching their targets; an SDT explanation is that consensus fostered greater relatedness by creating a group goal as opposed to the winner's goal. SDT provides a theoretical explanation for Lewin's findings: there is greater behavior change if people arrive at the decision themselves, have achievable goals, and a group that supports those goals because these foster the psychological needs for autonomy, competence, and relatedness.

The upside of these psychological theories is that there seems to be a good understanding of how to change behavior. It is generally a stepwise process that requires different types of information, support, and inspiration at different stages of the behavioral change process. We know that different people have different efficacy in making these changes, but that all of us want to feel as though we are autonomous, competent, and related, hence giving people choice, small goals, and a support group are effective in changing behavior. The downside is that the process can be complex and lengthy. Furthermore, we have a food system that provides us with an unhealthy food environment, and we are up against an industry spending billions manipulating the contents, placement, and advertising of their products to get us to eat unhealthy foods.

Shaping consumer preferences

Social science theories assume autonomous individuals making decisions about what to eat. However, our eating habits may be formed long before we have cognition or can exercise choice. As infants and children, what we eat is determined by our caregivers, and guidelines for infant feeding have changed radically over the past 100 years.

During the 1920s, infant formula had already made large inroads in replacing breastfeeding, and mass-produced baby foods were introduced in the US. The age that babies were fed solids declined. By 1950, mothers were advised to introduce solids when babies were just weeks old (Bentley, 2014). Advertising played on mothers' insecurities about their baby's health and their own social status; baby food was a way to demonstrate competency as a mother, as well as status because one could afford to give their child the best. Except they were not, because manufactured baby foods were highly processed and full of sugar and salt. It took decades before infant feeding practices were criticized as harmful and lacking in nutrients (Citizens' Committee on Infant Nutrition, 1974). It was two more decades before Gerber, the largest brand with a market share of 74%, eliminated sugar, salt, and modified starch from most, but not all, of its products in 1996 (Bentley, 2014).

Currently, the American Academy of Pediatrics (2014) recommends that infants be breastfed for 12 months and be fed breastmilk only during the first six months, with solids added gradually thereafter. Critics liken spoon-feeding younger babies to force-feeding; young infants have no way to indicate satiation other than trying to turn away (Bentley, 2014). Many experts advocate baby-led weaning; give babies a variety of cut-up healthy foods with different textures and tastes and allow them to feed themselves. This necessitates sufficient motor skills to be able to manipulate food and put it in their mouth, that is, being at least six months old. Furthermore, self-feeding is unlikely to result in overfeeding. It also trains infants to try different foods and to explore foods. In other words, it can help infants develop lifelong good eating habits.

However, self-feeding has gained little traction; 73% of American infants four to six months old are fed commercial baby food at least once a day, while 95% of seven- to eight-month-olds are fed it at least once a day (Bentley, 2014). This is the result of a consistent marketing strategy that appeals to mothers' material and maternal insecurities. To appeal to trendy moms, companies have introduced new flavors and recipes: avocados, mango, kale, Greek yoghurt, and pasta primavera (Gerber, 2016).

Brands have also come up with their own twist on baby-led weaning: pouches. Babies self-feed by sucking food out of composite plastic pouches. Pouches make up about one-third of baby food sales (Bentley, 2014). Using pouches, infants no longer need to be confined by highchairs or mealtimes; they can eat lying down and without adult supervision. Pouches cleverly circumvent the point of baby-led weaning; rather than developing motor skills, exploring food, or participating in family mealtimes, pouches allow babies to force-feed themselves because infants suckle innately. The food in the pouches also develops the babies' taste for highly processed, textureless foods.

While sugar, salt, modified starch, and preservatives have been largely eliminated from commercial baby foods in the US, infant eating habits today are far from healthy. American infants eat too many calories, consume candy and soda as young as seven months, and older infants and toddlers do not eat sufficient FAV (Bentley, 2014). One can conclude that generations of parents raised on processed foods high in salt, sugar, and fat, feed their children processed foods high in salt, sugar, and fat.

Breaking the cycle is difficult. Changing consumer preferences is a slow process, as the theories on behavior change discussed in the previous sections have shown. Furthermore, people tend to stick to old habits (Samuelson and Zeckhauser, 1988). This is known as status quo bias. In contrast, food contamination outbreaks have rapid and sometimes lasting impacts on behavior. Policies to tackle obesity such as education, subsidies, or taxes are somewhere in between (OECD/FAO, 2018). Samuelson and Zeckhauser (1988) conducted experiments that examined the dominance of status quo bias in decision-making. They found little support for transaction costs, uncertainty, or cognitive misconceptions as explanations of status quo bias in decision-making. Rather, they determined that psychological anchoring was the dominant reason: using past decisions to rationalize current behavior. Their research provides support that it is indeed hard to change habits, even when it is rational to do so. We are, in effect, creatures of habit.

Most marketers are much more optimistic about behavior change; their goal is to get people to buy things they may not have heard of, did not know they wanted, or might not be able to afford. The goal of marketing firms is to influence consumer choice through manipulating the behavior setting, and through patterns of functional and symbolic reinforcement (Foxall, 2010). In his Behavioral Perspective Model, Foxall posits that three emotions are used to manipulate consumers to purchase products or services: pleasure, arousal, and dominance. Each emotion is linked to the product's function, symbolism, and behavioral setting, respectively.

Much of the work on persuasion and advertising uses or modifies the Elaboration Likelihood Model (ELM), which argues that motivation and ability are influenced directly through logic and need, and indirectly through emotional cues like fear and desire (Jacoby et al., 1998). Research of this type has focused on emotional cues and how the composition and content of advertising can increase persuasion. Repeated exposure and association with stimuli, e.g., music or images, have also been studied for their influence on conditioning consumers to make purchases. Marketing research has also examined the role of consumers' characteristics on purchases. These characteristics include demographics, identity, mood, and perceptions.

In contrast, sociological researchers have focused largely on the effects of persuasion rather than how to persuade. Brand communities are an example of such research; they represent an extension of consumption communities. Brand communities are shared communities around branded products (Muniz and O'Guinn, 2001). Harley Davidson is an example of how a brand can become a lifestyle and create a community; owning one of these motorcycles makes one part of a community, with its own style, and commitment to others. Brand communities have the characteristics of communities: connection with each other and differences from others; rituals or traditions; and obligations to those within the community. Muniz and O'Guinn argue that rather than being tied to place, contemporary communities are virtual, imagined, or limited in scope; they exist because of mass and social media.

The amount spent on advertising reflects its perceived value in persuading consumers to buy products. Spending on advertising in the US in 2017 was US$ 254.3 billion, of which television advertising was US$ 70.1 billion (PwC, 2018). Food and restaurant advertisements represented about 5.3% of US advertising spending, but 15.5% of US spending on television advertising (Harris et al., 2019; PwC, 2018). While food and restaurant advertising expenditures are dropping, this is linked to a decrease in television advertising expenditures, driven by falling television viewing, as Americans spend more time online.

Like so many things in the US, advertising is highly concentrated. While it may appear that there are many different food brands advertising, most brands are part of large parent companies. Just 31 companies paid for 69% of all food ads and 72.4% of all food ads on television (Harris et al., 2019). Together, these 14 restaurants and 17 food and beverage brands spent US$ 9.3 billion on food advertising and US$ 7.9 billion on television ads in the US in 2017. The highest-spending restaurants were Yum! Brands (Taco Bell, KFC, and Pizza Hut), which spent US$ 765.9 million on ads, and MacDonald's, which spent US$ 744.4 million. The highest-spending food and beverage brands were PepsiCo, which spent US$ 718.4 million on advertising in the US, Mondelez-Kraft-Heinz, which spent US$ 658.7 million, and Coca-Cola, which spent US$ 561.7 million.

Of the food companies that spent more than US$ 500,000 on television advertising in 2017, restaurants made up 52% of the advertising spending, soda and sugary drinks represented 10%, candy/gum/mints 10%, and just 3% of all food advertising was spent on "healthier" foods: water, juice, nuts, and fruit (Harris et al., 2019). No vegetable brand exceeded the US$ 500,000 cut-off. Given that 97% of food advertising in the US is for food that is patently unhealthy, is it any wonder that Americans are overweight and have so many diet-related health problems?

Food advertising and promotion have been particularly effective at manipulating the littlest consumers. Children are directly targeted via ads and indirectly through product placement within media programming. US children aged 2-11 viewed an average of ten television ads for food per day in 2017, while youths aged 12-17 viewed an average of 9.4 television ads for food per day (Harris et al., 2019). Food is the most prevalent category of promotion to children and almost all of the foods promoted to children are high in added sugars, salt, fat, and are energy-dense and processed, while promotion of healthy foods to children, such as FAV, is near zero

(Cairns et al., 2009). One result is that globally, 44% of children consume soft drinks every day (Ratcliffe, 2018). The influence of food marketing is as important as family and peers in determining the foods children eat (Cairns et al., 2009). Food marketers have figured out how to capture peers by paying social media influencers; among the most popular YouTube influencers under 17 years old, 90% who promoted food promoted unhealthy foods (Airuwaily et al., 2020). As a result, parents' roles in fostering their children's health is being usurped by food companies. These companies make huge profits, yet do not have to deal with the resulting health consequences and costs; parents and their children bear these costs and pay companies for the privilege of consuming products that harm them.

The majority of food brands belong to the Children's Food and Beverage Advertising Initiative (CFBAI); these brands commit to advertising only foods that meet CFBAI's Uniform Nutrition Standards or to not advertising to children under 12 (Harris et al., 2019). To meet the CFBAI standards, their foods must be lower than conventional products in calories, sugar, sodium, and saturated fat, and provide more beneficial nutrients. However, the actions are voluntary, and reducing some of the adverse components of foods still does not make the foods healthy. Harris et al. note that many of the CFBAI members continue to target unhealthy foods to children of color and have, in fact, increased advertising expenditure to target these children. As a result, in the US, Black children see an average of 16.4 television ads for food a day compared to White children who only see 8.8 per day, while Black youths view 17.1 television ads for food a day and White teens view only 7.8 per day. Paying child influencers to promote junk food (Airuwaily et al., 2020) circumvents the CFBAI's Uniform Nutrition Standards since the influencers' videos are not strictly advertisements, but "entertainment."

Whether from a physiological perspective of creating dopamine rewards (Scalfani et al., 2011) or simply by creating habits that are prone to status quo bias (Samuelson and Zeckhauser, 1988), children are attractive targets for brands because they represent lifelong customers. They are also access points to their parents. They are "surrogate salesmen." Indeed, marketing campaigns encourage them to use their "pester power" to whine for specific products (Schlosser, 2002). Children do not have the knowledge or experience to understand how they are being manipulated or the impact that eating processed foods will have on their health. The result is they are manipulated to line the coffers of food companies, while undermining their own health and their parents' best intentions.

The adverse effects of the advertising of unhealthy products, especially on children, are widely recognized. Policy responses have included nutrition education campaigns, limiting or banning ads, especially to children, warning labels, and sugar taxes. The industry has responded by sponsoring research that frequently serves its economic interests, by lobbying for voluntary self-regulation, by donating to campaigns of elected officials, and by promoting sports and wellness events to induce a halo effect that masks the effects of their products (Borges et al., 2017).

Access to Nutrition (2018) recommends five ways companies could voluntarily improve public health: reformulate products so they are healthier; improve their product mix; stop marketing unhealthy foods to children; shift their company's marketing budget to promote healthier foods; and adopt comprehensive labeling. Brands have taken some steps to offer reformulated products, but in the case of substituting artificial sweeteners for sugar, there is no solid evidence that artificial sweeteners lead to healthier outcomes (Borges et al., 2017). Part of the problem is that much of the research is sponsored by the industry and tends to produce results that favor the economic interests of the industry, be it the sugar or the artificial sweetener industry. However, reformulation may have a limited impact, given that of 23,000 packaged products assessed in nine countries, 69% were determined to be of low nutritional quality (Access to Nutrition, 2018). Reformulation would only work if more or less all products were reformulated, which is unlikely to happen voluntarily. The InterAcademy Partnership (2018) calls for incentives to companies to offer healthier foods. However, they offer no specifics of what these incentives might be. Presumably, they mean governments would pay companies to offer healthier foods.

What most policy analysts avoid stating is the obvious: governments have the power to regulate what companies do. Governments license businesses to operate; they facilitate commerce through physical and regulatory infrastructure; and they protect companies' property and commercial rights. It is illogical that governments should not have a say in the public health effects of companies that only exist because of the protections and services provided by that same government. It is simply audacious that rather than recommending the regulation of ads and marketing, policymakers recommend that governments bribe companies not to harm their citizens.

Why should companies be entitled to advertise and promote the consumption of products that make people unwell and shorten their lives? If only foods that were healthy were allowed to be advertised, voluntary reformulation might actually occur.

Public health is vital to the functioning of a nation and, therefore, central to the responsibilities of government. Clearly, preventable health costs create a burden on society, indirectly through productivity and services, and directly through public health care costs. Even in the US, which does not have a universal health care system, the government shoulders the burden of the health care costs of the poor and those over 65 years old. Older and poor Americans have the highest incidences of preventable health problems linked to diet: overweight and obesity, diabetes, hypertension, etc. It makes sense that the government should try to mitigate the effects of unhealthy food "choices" by restricting the ability of companies to influence those "choices."

We eat what we are given to eat

Why do we eat what we do? Different disciplines contribute something to understanding why we eat the foods we do. Dietitians and health care professionals may assume that people are motivated to change their behaviors and just need information about foods and recipes; that is because they are often working with patients who have been referred to them to address a specific health concern. Economists assume individuals act independently and rationally, their preferences are fixed, and that relative prices and incomes influence behaviors. Hence, they suggest taxing "bad" behaviors and subsidizing "good" ones. Marketers assume that people's preferences can be influenced and manipulated by others, yet many claim that consumers dictate to retailers and producers what is sold. Marketers treat consumers as dupes, but say they are kings. Psychologists examine how psychological needs are met and offer many theories and insights about what needs, emotions, and processes drive behaviors. Sociologists examine sociological forces and groupings around consumption. The upshot is that while each discipline sees behavior through their own lens, they all view eating as an issue of individual choice, whether conscious or not. Each discipline recognizes external factors: health, prices, advertising, symbolic value, or brand communities, but ultimately what we eat is viewed as our "choice."

Given that 71% of American adults are overweight or obese (CDC, 2017), experts recommend we change our choices and exercise more to reduce the economic and health costs. Health care professionals see people who are having health problems, so they often assume that people are motivated to change and that providing information will lead to better outcomes. An economic approach is to nudge consumers into making "good" choices through subsidies or credits, and away from "bad" choices through taxes; veggie prescription programs and soda taxes are examples. Psychologists look at ways to address needs or emotions, while sociologists examine how social pressure or the community can encourage or support behavior changes. Marketers rely on promotion and advertising that appeal to emotions, and strive to identify and craft ads to different demographic groups.

What most disciplines fail to acknowledge is that the entire food system presents people with bad choices and has been doing so for generations from infancy. Processed foods account for over three-quarters of calorie intake in the US (Poti et al., 2015). We consume processed foods because that is what is available. It is what we were raised on. It is what we know. Of the more than 40,000 items in US grocery stores, most are highly processed (Toops, 2017). In a study of ten countries, 41% of all shelf space was allocated to soda and junk food alone, and the greater the shelf space devoted to unhealthy foods, the higher was the national BMI (Norman, Hoffman, and Cheskin, 2014).

Not only is our food environment dominated by processed foods, but practically the only message we get through advertising is to eat processed foods: 97% of the US$ 13.5 billion spent on food advertising in the US was for unhealthy products (Harris et al., 2019; PwC, 2018). We can try eating out less; the average American only prepares about four meals a week at home (Food Marketing Institute, 2018). However, 93% of the food eaten at home is purchased from hypermarkets, large grocery chains, and convenience stores, and the rest is purchased mostly from drug stores and hard discount stores (FAO, 2017). The choices offered in grocery stores are largely highly processed, calorie-dense foods. Borrowing from Lewin (1943), we eat what is put in front of us.

What this means is that there is no way to create a healthy food environment around us. We would need to remove ourselves from society, cut ourselves off from all media, and grow or forage our own food. This is not a realistic option for the vast majority of us. A heroin addict can at least stop using heroin and remove themselves from the places and people who use drugs. We do not have the option of not eating, nor do we have the option of removing ourselves from either unhealthy foods or unhealthy eaters. We can try to create a healthy food environment immediately around us, in our own home, but that requires navigating the constant exposure to and promotion of unhealthy foods. Even if we manage to create a healthy home food environment, every time we leave our home, in virtually every social situation, and any time we try to buy food or eat out, we are faced with unhealthy food options. Our only "choice" is to be surrounded by harmful substances and by people who ingest them.

It isn't much of a choice.

The only way we can move forward is to realize that our food-related problems are not a matter of personal choice. They are systemic and the result of public policy.

Exercise: Set a food goal with someone

Ask a friend or family member to identify and set a food goal with you. Discuss your food goals; it might be weight loss, reducing sugar intake, or increasing FAV consumption. Find common ground, for example, if you disagree about a specific food or class of foods, move to a different food goal. Identify one goal you would both like to achieve. Make sure your target is reasonable, yet meaningful; for example, rather than 100% adherence or elimination, set a lower target, but not so low that it is meaningless. Try it for a week. Support each other in achieving that goal.

Debrief after a week: Did you meet your goal? Why or why not? Was it too ambitious? Did you need more support or communication? Talk about how you can get or offer that. Did you need more information? If so, use reputable sources: government, academic, or non-profit research. Avoid social media, blogs, and other sources that have a financial interest.

References

Access to Nutrition Foundation. 2018. Access to Nutrition Index, 2018. Global Index 2018. www.accesstonutrition.org/index/global.2018, accessed February 14, 2018.

Airuwaily, A., Mangold, C., Greene, T., Arshonsky, J., Cassidy, O., Pomeranz, J., and Bragg, M. 2020. Child social media influencers and unhealthy food product placement. Pediatrics, October, e20194057.

https://doi-org.ezproxy.library.wisc.edu/10.1542/peds.2019-4057, accessed October 26, 2020.

American Academy of Pediatrics. 2014. Where we stand: Breastfeeding. https://www.healthychildren.org/English/ages-stages/baby/breastfeeding/Pages/Where-We-Stand-Breastfeeding.aspx, accessed October 7, 2020.

Badura, A. 2004. Health promotion by social cognitive means. Health Education & Behavior, 31, 143–64. https://journals.sagepub.com/doi/abs/10.1177/1090198104263660, accessed May 2, 2019.

Bamberg, S. and Moser, G. 2007. Twenty years after Hines, Hungerford, and Tomera: A new meta-analysis of psycho-social determinants of pro-environmental behavior. Journal of Environmental Psychology, 27, 14–25.

Bentley, A. 2014. Inventing Baby Food: Taste, Health, and the Industrialization of the American Diet. Oakland, CA: University of California Press.

Borges, M. C., Louzada, M. L., de Sá, T. H., Laverty, A. A., Parra, D. C., Fellegger Garzillo, J. M., Monteiro, C. A., and Millett, C. 2017. Artificially sweetened beverages and the response to the global obesity crisis. PLOS Medicine, 14(1), e1002195. https://doi.org/10.1371/journal.pmed.1002195, accessed October 22, 2020.

Cairns, G., Angus, K., and Hastings, G. 2009. The extent, nature and effects of food promotion to children: a review of the evidence to December. World Health Organization. https://www.who.int/dietphysicalactivity/Evidence_Update_2009.pdf, accessed May 2, 2019.

Caro J. C., Corvalán C., Reyes M., Silva, A., Popkin, B., and Taillie, L. S. 2018. Chile's 2014 sugar-sweetened beverage tax and changes in prices and purchases of sugar-sweetened beverages: An observational study in an urban environment. PLOS Medicine, https://doi.org/10.1371/journal.pmed.1002597, accessed October 22, 2020.

Carroll, K. A., Samek, A., and Zepeda, L. 2018. Food bundling as a health nudge: Investigating consumer fruit and vegetable selection using behavioral economics. Appetite, 121, 237–248 https://doi.org/10.1016/j.appet.2017.11.082, accessed October 22, 2020.

CDC. 2017. Data & statistics. https://www.cdc.gov/obesity/data/index.html, accessed March 14, 2019.

Citizens' Committee on Infant Nutrition. 1974. White paper on infant feeding practices. Washington DC: Center for Science in the Public Interest.

Colchero, M. A., Rivera-Dommarco, J., Popkin, B. M., and Ng, S. W. 2017. In Mexico, evidence of sustained consumer response two years after implementing a sugar-sweetened beverage tax. Health Affairs, 36 (3), 564–571. doi: 10.1377/hlthaff.2016.1231.

Cummings, R. O. 1941. An American and His Food: A History of Food Habits in the United States, revised edition. Chicago: The University of Chicago Press.

Fleming, A. 2019. Table for one: how eating alone is radically changing our diets. The Guardian, May 6. https://www.theguardian.com/lifeandstyle/2019/may/06/table-for-one-how-eating-alone-changing-our-diets?CMP=Share_iOSApp_Other, accessed May 8, 2019.

FAO. 2017. The future of food and agriculture: Trends and challenges. http://www.fao.org/3/a-i6583e.pdf, accessed April 3, 2019.

Food Marketing Institute. 2018. US grocery shopper trends 2018. http://www.mmibusinessadvisors.com/wp-content/uploads/2018/06/shopper-trends-report-2018.pdf, accessed April 24, 2019.

Foxall, G. R. 2010. Theoretical and conceptual advances in consumer behavior analysis. Journal of Organizational and Behavioral Management, 30, 92–109.

Fudenberg, D. and Levine, D. K. 2006. A dual-self model of impulse control. American Economic Review, 96(5), 1449–1476.

Gerber. 2016. Baby food. https://www.gerber.com/product-category/baby-food, accessed October 7, 2020.

Guagnano, G. A., Stern, P. C., and Dietz, T. 1995. Influences on attitude–behavior relationships: a natural experiment with curbside recycling. Environment and Behavior, 27, 699–718.

Harris, J. L., Frazier, W., Kumanyika, S., and Ramirez, A.G. 2019. Increasing disparities in unhealthy food advertising targeted to Hispanic and Black youth. Rudd Report, University of Connecticut, January. http://uconnruddcenter.org/files/Pdfs/TargetedMarketingReport2019.pdf, accessed May 20, 2019.

Hope, S. F., Webster, J., Trieu, K., Pillay, A., Ieremia, M., Bell, C., Snowdon, W., Neal, B., and Moodie, M. 2017. A systematic review of economic evaluations of population-based sodium reduction interventions. PLOS One, 12(3) e0173600. https://doi.org/10.1371/journal.pone.0173600, accessed October 22, 2020.

InterAcademy Partnership. 2018. Opportunities for future research and innovation on food and nutrition security and agriculture. November. https://www.interacademies.org/node/50845, accessed October 22, 2020.

Jacoby, J., Johar, G. V., and Morrin, M. 1998. Consumer behavior: a quadrennium. Annual Review of Psychology, 49, 319–344.

Just, D. R. and Payne, C. R. 2009. Obesity: Can behavioral economics help? The Annals of Behavioral Medicine, 38 (Suppl 1), S47–S55. doi: 10.1007/s12160-009-9119-2.

Lewin, K. 1943. Forces behind food habits and methods of change, in The Problem of Changing Food Habits, Report of the Committee on Food Habits 1941-1943. Bulletin of the National Research Council, Number 108, October. Washington DC: National Research Council. https://www.nap.edu/read/9566/chapter/8, accessed April 25, 2019.

MacDonald Boyd and Associates. 2009. Stages of Change. https://peoplehavethepower.typepad.com/files/stages-of-change-management.pdf, accessed May 1, 2009.

Maxey, H. Bishop-Josef, S., and Goodman, B. 2018. Unhealthy and unprepared: National security depends on promoting healthy lifestyles from an early age. Council for a Strong America. October. https://strongnation.s3.amazonaws.com/documents/484/389765e0-2500-49a2-9a67-5c4a090a215b.pdf, accessed April 29, 2019.

Muniz, Jr., A. M., and O'Guinn, T. C. 2001. Brand community. Journal of Consumer Research, 27(4), 412–432.

Norman, M., Hoffman, J., and Cheskin, L. J. 2014. Shelf space devoted to nutritious foods correlates with BMI. American Journal of Food and Nutrition, 2(2), 18-22. doi: 10.12691/ajfn-2-2-1.

OECD/FAO. 2018. OECD-FAO Agricultural Outlook 2018-2027. Paris: OECD Publishing and Rome: Food and Agriculture Organization. doi: 10.1787/agr_outlook-2018-en.

O'Sullivan, M. G. 2020. Salt, Sugar, and Fat Reduction: Sensory Approaches for Nutritional Reformulation of Foods and Beverages. Duxford, UK: Woodhead Publishing.

Poti, J. M., Mendez, M. A., Ng, S. W., and Popkin, B. M. 2015. Is the degree of food processing and convenience linked with the nutritional quality of foods purchased by US households? American Journal of Clinical Nutrition, 101(6), 1251–62.

Prochaska, J. O. and DiClemente, C. C. 1983. Stages and processes of self-change of smoking: Toward an integrative model of change. Journal of Consulting and Clinical Psychology, 51(3), 390-395. doi: 10.1037/0022-006X.51.3.390.

PwC. 2018. IAB Internet advertising revenue report: 2017 full year results. May. https://www.iab.com/wp-content/uploads/2018/05/IAB-2017-Full-Year-Internet-Advertising-Revenue-Report.REV_.pdf, accessed May 20, 2019.

Ramsey, J. 2003. Whither global branding? The case of food manufacturing. Journal of Brand Management, 11(1), 9-21.

Ratcliffe. R. 2018. 'Diabolical' diets: four in 10 children consume sugary drinks daily. The Guardian, November 29.

https://www.theguardian.com/global-development/2018/nov/29/diabolical-diets-four-in-10-children-consume-sugary-drinks-every-day, accessed May 8, 2019.

Samuelson, W. and Zeckhauser, R. 1988. Status quo bias in decision-making. Journal of Risk and Uncertainty, 1, 7–59.

Scalfani, A., Touzani, K., and Bodnar, R.J. 2011. Dopamine and learned food preferences. Physiology & Behavior, 104, 64–68.

Schlosser, E. 2002. Fast Food Nation. New York: Perennial.

Silver, L. D., Ng, S. W., Ryan-Ibarra, S., Taillie, L. S., Induni, M., Miles, D. R., Poti, J. M., and Popkin, B. M. 2017. Changes in prices, sales, consumer spending, and beverage consumption one year after a tax on sugar-sweetened beverages in Berkeley, California, US: A before-and-after study. PLOS Med, 14(4), e1002283. https://doi.org/10.1371/journal.pmed.1002283, accessed October 22, 2020.

Toh, M. 2020. Singapore says it'll start paying people to work out with Apple's smartwatch. CNN Business, September 17. https://www.cnn.com/2020/09/17/tech/apple-watch-singapore-intl-hnk/index.html, accessed September 21, 2020.

Toops, D. 2017. Chapter 2: How did the food industry get (from there) to here? Accelerating New Food Product Design and Development, Second Edition. Edited by J. H. Beckley, L. J. Herzog, and M. M. Foley. Hoboken, NJ: John Wiley & Sons Ltd and the Institute of Food Technologists. http://www.ift.org/~/media/Knowledge%20Center/Publications/Books/Samples/IFTPressBook_ANFPDD_Chapter1.pdf, accessed February 4, 2019.

Weinstein, N. D. 1988. The precaution adoption process. Health Psychology, 7(4), 355–386.

Zhong, Y., Auchincloss, A. H., Lee, B. K., and Kanter, G. P. 2018. The short-term impacts of the Philadelphia beverage tax on beverage consumption. American Journal of Preventive Medicine, 55(1)26–34. https://doi.org/10.1016/j.amepre.2018.02.017 accessed on October 22, 2020.

CHAPTER SEVEN

HOW DO WE FIX THIS?

We have a dysfunctional food system. It produces more than enough food for humanity in terms of calories (World Food Programme, 2013). The problems with our food system are that of distribution and quality, not quantity. Despite the vast amount of food produced, people go hungry and many more suffer from food-related illnesses, while one-third of all food that is harvested is simply wasted (FAO, 2011). This waste does not count all the food that was not even harvested.

Our food system uses enormous amounts of natural resources; agriculture is the largest user of land and water (Roser and Richie, 2018). Agriculture is driving tropical and subtropical deforestation; 86% of the seven million hectares of forest lost per year between 2000 and 2010 were attributable to agriculture (FAO 2017). Agriculture is responsible for 70% of global water withdrawals and contributes 21% of global GHG. This enormous use of resources has reduced habitat for other species, while contaminating and squandering scarce resources for all species, including ourselves. Species loss is estimated at 1000 times what it would be without human activity, reducing terrestrial species abundance by 85% (UNEP, 2019). Quite simply, our food system is degrading our natural environment.

Notwithstanding the large amount of food produced at the expense of the environment, our food system has done little to reduce the total number of hungry people in the past 25 years. Furthermore, there are increasing levels of food-related illnesses among those getting enough food. Half of all deaths worldwide are attributable to four risk factors, three of which are related to diet: high blood pressure, high blood glucose, and high body mass index (Horton, 2018). Of the nine global nutrition indicators,[5] 100 of 194

---

[5] The nine global nutrition indicators are: child overweight, child wasting, child stunting, exclusive breastfeeding, diabetes among women, diabetes among men, anemia in women of reproductive age, obesity among women, and obesity among men.

countries are on track to meet **zero** of the nine goals. Among these low-achievers are the US, the UK, Russia, and India. The highest number of nutrition goals that are expected to be met are only four out of the nine goals, by only five countries: Armenia, Belize, Kenya, Sao Tome and Principe, and Swaziland. Not one single country in the world is on track to meet their obesity target, which is simply that obesity does not increase. Overweight and obesity affect two billion adults or 38.9% of all adults on Earth, contributing to 7% of deaths globally, 120 million healthy years lost, and US$ 3.5 trillion in direct and indirect costs (Development Initiatives, 2018). Globally, 44% of diabetes and 23% of heart disease cases are attributable to overweight and obesity (FAO, 2017). Our food system is literally killing us.

Despite the adverse health and environmental impacts of our food system, agricultural policies have focused on providing incentives to farmers to increase the production of a few staple crops, rather than improving environmental impacts (UNEP, 2019), health, food quality, or food access. No country has included agriculture completely in carbon pricing or polluter-pays policies. UNEP asserts that farmers need to be given incentives to produce more sustainably, yet the agency does not fully acknowledge that current agricultural policies incentivize farmers to pollute. Governments routinely provide subsidies to farmers through price supports, buying products, fertilizer and pesticide subsidies, irrigation, electrification, and by providing infrastructure and services that reduce the costs of production and marketing. Governments essentially subsidize the overuse of water and land, and chemical use that pollutes land, water, and air. UNEP does not mention removing these subsidies which encourage unsustainable practices in agriculture. Rather, the proposed fix is essentially for governments to pay farmers to pollute and then pay them again not to. The report appears to ignore its own advice that the efficient use of resources "requires well-designed policies."

UNEP (2019) does note that most of the focus in policy is on agricultural production, with little emphasis on reducing food waste, or encouraging healthy and sustainable food consumption. Japan is presented as a model of reducing food waste. Their policies include legislative mandates to control and recycle food waste upstream, and consumer education downstream to reduce consumer food waste. To promote sustainable food consumption, UNEP proposes consumer education and sustainability labeling. Such labels have been implemented in Brazil, Germany, Qatar, and Sweden. The report acknowledges that the likely impact of consumer education and food labeling is low. The ineffectiveness of food labeling to improve health outcomes serves as a predictor of the probable effects of sustainability labels on food: minimal. While labels are necessary to convey information, very few consumers read food labels, and information is not sufficient to motivate behavior, so why would labels alone be an effective means of changing behavior? Oddly, while health taxes on food are acknowledged as effective in changing consumer behavior, taxing the most environmentally harmful foods is not even considered by UNEP.

The UNEP report (2019) ignores the impact of relative prices on improving the sustainability of consumption behavior. Rather, the report focuses on personal choice. In essence, it relies on morality as the mechanism to change behavior. The assumption is that people will change their behavior if given information. However, behavioral researchers know that most people do not read food labels and that changing food habits is very difficult. The latter requires much more than information: it requires motivation, opportunity, support, and minimal or no barriers to behavior change. Since the existing food system subsidizes unsustainable agricultural practices that yield foods that are unsustainable, unhealthy, and far cheaper than they would be if there were no government subsidies, these policies make it cheap, easy, and normal to eat unhealthy, unsustainable food. It is, at best, a mixed message to make unhealthy, unsustainable foods cheap and ubiquitous, and then hope that one can dissuade people from eating them by telling them that these foods are unhealthy and unsustainable.

Continuing our food system as we have will result in continued mass species extinctions, increasing competition and conflict over land and water, and increasing health problems for humans. There simply is not enough land and water to continue on our current path. Many people, especially scientists, are well aware of the trajectory we are on. Many organizations are combating the effects: global warming, water and land scarcity, conflict, human population growth, human health, economic inequality, and refugees and immigrants. Each has advocates and organizations trying to sound the alarm to address these issues…individually.

Leading the charge, non-profit organizations have largely addressed the symptoms. The missions are often very general (hunger, health, protecting the environment, lower GHG, etc.), yet they often focus on micro-level activities (donate and distribute leftover food, eat healthier, ride your bike, micro-enterprises, etc.). What is striking is how the problems are recognized as global, but the focus of the solutions is almost always local. It is a point of view that ties global problems to personal responsibility rather than systematic policy change. It is also a viewpoint that fails to acknowledge how intertwined the problems are and how they are the direct results of our current policies.

Reliance on non-profits to privatize public policy problems

It is understandable in the US that problem resolution is localized; the US has a political system that is highly decentralized. Health care, social policy, education, and many other issues are dealt with at a local level. Furthermore, like all nations, the effects of policies are felt at a local level. For example, it is the local community that deals with the effects of wage and health care policies. The focus on local action in the US developed historically as a cultural practice due to the historical reality of the isolation of communities and distances to services. In the 18th and 19th centuries, communities were simply too isolated to rely on state, let alone federal, assistance. The reliance on local action has been reinforced politically since the country's inception, in part because the founders wanted a weak central government, and in part because of the historical realities that made distance a barrier to services in the US.

The history of reliance on non-profits in the US is reflected in de Toqueville's (2004) travels in the US from 1831–2. He was surprised at how voluntary associations (today's non-profits) did much of the work done by governments everywhere else in the world. He noted that voluntary organizations created hospitals and schools, distributed books, and organized events. He commented that Americans of all ages were involved in associations and nothing was too trivial or wide-ranging to merit an association. This continues today in the US, where the first reaction to any social problem is to privatize it, label it as a personal failing, and create a charity or non-profit to address it, rather than demand government action. If there are hungry people, form an organization to collect unwanted food and distribute it to the hungry. If there are homeless people, collect personal care items to distribute to them, build them a tiny home, or move them to some other place. Mentor a school child struggling with poverty and hence doing poorly in school; but whatever you do, do not work on alleviating poverty or providing public social services.

Privatizing problems makes it simple and doable to address them, albeit at the margins, while not solving the problem in general, or even in individual cases. Privatizing problems has the added benefit of making those involved in organizations helping others feel noble because they are doing something about a terrible problem. It also means that they will have an endless opportunity to feel noble because addressing the symptoms of a few people does nothing to address the systematic policy issues that create the problems in the first place. Hungry people remain chronically hungry, homeless people remain chronically homeless, and poor children remain poor.

As an example, after decades of developing a non-profit network of emergency food banks and pantries in the US, it is clear that the issue of hunger is a chronic problem in the US. Far from being an emergency situation, many families rely consistently on food banks to make ends meet because wages and benefits in the US are insufficient, relative to the cost of living. In response to the immense costs and time involved in gathering and distributing physical food, some food banks have taken the "radical" approach of simply providing the hungry with money for food (Zepeda and Reznickova, 2018). Obviously, providing people with cash is always going to be cheaper than the real cost of mobilizing tens of thousands of volunteers to collect, sort, and distribute donated foods. Indeed, food banks simply purchase most of the food they distribute because it is cheaper to source food this way. However, the costs of sourcing food are rising for food banks. This is due largely to the fact that wholesalers and retailers have been able to reduce their amount of surplus food through improved logistics and selling through high discount stores. Hence, they no longer have as much surplus food to donate or sell at discounted prices to food banks.

Many people erroneously believe that food drives provide most of the food for food banks. They are not aware of the vast amounts of money and resources that go into sourcing food for food banks, and that most food is actually supplied directly by food companies and retailers. Food drives at schools, churches, and other organizations provide a tiny fraction of the actual food distributed. The main purpose of these food drives is not to source food, but to raise awareness about hunger and to involve the community by getting them to volunteer or donate money.

Given the ongoing, persistent demand for food through food banks by so many Americans, personnel at food banks openly talk about the need for a living wage, affordable housing, and universal health care to eradicate hunger. Yet food banks and food pantries are reluctant to communicate the need for political action with their armies of volunteers. They worry about alienating their volunteers and donors by being "political."

This is worth examining; why would volunteers and donors be alienated by addressing the root problems of hunger? In part it is because hunger is viewed as a personal failing, even by those who experience it (Zepeda, 2018). Among many, there is a sense of shame, a need to hide the fact that one is hungry. This narrative makes volunteers and donors de facto heroes for "fighting hunger." They are good people, doing good things. It is non-threatening because they are not giving up anything they do not want to. Any costs to them are voluntary, so their lifestyle is not threatened. More importantly, neither is their world view that the misery of hunger is the result of bad choices or bad luck by others. Companies who donate or sell products to food banks or organize their employees to volunteer at food pantries can say they are helping society, all while avoiding paying their fair share of taxes or providing decent wages or benefits to their workers. It is a charade that allows the status quo to continue to create food insecurity because we are doing "something" about it.

However, if one is working full-time and one must consistently make the choice between paying rent, bills, or medical co-pays versus food, this indicates a systematic problem, one that will never go away by organizing food pantries. While it is possible to point to poor money management skills, those struggling with food insecurity in the US generally exhibit extremely sophisticated knowledge of prices and money management (Zepeda, 2018). They know what foods are offered at different food pantries, they know when there are sales and coupons for particular foods at different retail stores. They make strategic choices to make ends meet: eating the cheapest possible foods to have the money to pay the rent, so that they will not become homeless; turning off the heating so they can afford to buy milk and bread; rescheduling or cancelling medical appointments because they choose to spend their meager wages on groceries that week rather than a medical co-pay. These choices are not the choices of poor money managers, but of people who acutely understand the ramifications of their purchasing decisions. These are choices that no one should have to make. They do not reflect the systematic failures of people, but of public policies that force people to make these choices.

Stagnant wages, rising costs of housing, transportation, and utilities, increasing medical costs, debt from school loans and medical bills—these are the causes of food insecurity in the US (Zepeda, 2018), and these are the direct results of government policies. Local, state, and federal policies set minimum wages. For decades, the minimum wages went unchanged, eroding living standards, while the cost of housing, transportation, medical care, and education have skyrocketed. Business interests have fought raising minimum wages, thereby increasing their profits and resulting in rising income inequality. The minimum wage had to be rebranded as a "living wage" because it was commonly accepted that no one could live on the minimum wage. Much like the minimum wage, the "living" wage has already been eroded since the "fight for $15" began. In 2010, $15 an hour might have been a living wage in some parts of the US, one that would allow a person to pay for their necessities and not have to choose between food and heat. However, most communities that have already adopted living wages are implementing $15 an hour at some point in the future, even though $15 an hour today will not cover basic living costs in these communities.

The fight for a living wage ignores zoning, housing, and tax policies in the US that have made housing unaffordable for many Americans. US tax policies subsidize real estate purchases, benefiting the wealthy and White homeowners in particular (Brown, 2018). In 2018, the government subsidy for mortgage interest in the US was estimated at US$ 92 billion, and the exclusion for the appreciation of home value was estimated at US$ 45 billion. While only 4% of US households have a second home, these wealthy households can deduct mortgage interest for loans up to US$ 750,000. More than three-quarters (77%) of the benefits for all mortgage interest deductions go to households with incomes above US$ 100,000 a year, which equates to less than 29% of US households (US Census Bureau, 2018). The US tax code regarding real estate is extremely regressive; it is a payout to the wealthy.

Meanwhile, public housing has been demolished (Robinson, 2017) and low-income housing has been acquired and gentrified through predatory contracts, evictions, and speculative bulk property buyers (Akers and Seymour, 2018). Local government practices, mortgage and tax foreclosures, and evictions are used to provide profits to local and global capital networks gobbling up property. In Detroit, 88% of property tax foreclosures between 2005 and 2015 were bought by large investors with 50+ properties. In addition to displacing residents, these practices drive up the costs of moderate housing for individuals. City and county councils often call their zoning and development priorities "pro-business." A more accurate name would be "pro-rich" because the policies do little to generate jobs, but involve enormous wealth transfers to the wealthy.

Other factors eroding wages for Americans are rising medical and education costs. They are among the fastest rising expenses. Medical costs are characterized by mystery pricing; the cost of any medical procedure or service is unknown until after the fact, and may differ radically depending upon who receives it and where it occurs. Meanwhile, higher education offers an array of programs or majors that it fails to inform students have no potential for future jobs. Government policies have allowed, indeed promoted, rising medical and education debt, resulting in the world's most expensive health care and higher education systems.

Despite the role of government policies in creating lagging wages and income inequality, and in fostering the rising costs of shelter, education, transportation, healthy food, and medical care, the inability for someone employed full-time to be able to afford basic needs is viewed as a personal failing.

Rather than address the policies that created these problems, the tendency in the US is to form non-profits to address the symptoms. Yet doing so without addressing the government policies that generate these social problems merely ensures that the problems will never end. To solve social problems created by government policies, we need to change the government policies that created or exacerbated the problems in the first place.

The scope and limitations of non-profits

Non-profits do many worthwhile things, from raising money to fight disease, to supporting the arts, to organizing events, to rescue efforts. There were over 1.5 million non-profits registered with the US Internal Revenue Service (IRS) in 2015, generating nearly US$ 1 trillion or over 5% of US GDP (McKeever, 2018). Religious organizations and non-profits with receipts of less than US$ 5,000 annually are not required to register, so the actual number of non-profits in the US is much higher. To illustrate, there were about 345,000 religious congregations in the US in 2010 (Association of Statisticians of American Religious Bodies, 2012), many of which may not be included in the 1.5 million non-profits registered with the US IRS.

In 2017, one-quarter of adults in the US volunteered for a non-profit, including religious organizations, contributing nearly 9 billion hours of their time (McKeever, 2018). About a quarter of that time was spent on social services, 22% on administrative support, and 21% on "other." The value of volunteer time was worth about US$ 195 billion. However, direct private donations to charitable organizations were worth more than twice as much as the value of volunteer time. Private giving by individuals, businesses, and foundations was US$ 410 billion in 2017. Of these donations, 31% went to religious organizations, 14% went to educational institutions, 12% to human services, 11% to foundations, and 9% to health organizations. Clearly, non-profits are a large force in the US economy.

Non-profit organizations in the US shy away from directly trying to influence policy out of fear of losing their tax-exempt status. Tax-exempt status affects expenses by exempting the non-profit from paying taxes on its income. It also affects revenues because donations to non-profits are tax-deductible—an incentive for donors to give to non-profits because it reduces their tax bill. The latter benefit has become less attractive for most individual donors with the recent tax reform in the US; the standard deduction was raised so that for most Americans, itemizing is no longer beneficial, erasing the tax benefits of donating to non-profits. This may impact non-profit funding once people realize this.

Since maintaining a tax-exempt status affects both expenditures and revenues, non-profits guard it carefully. In order to maintain their tax-exempt status, registered non-profits may not expend "a substantial part of its activities … attempting to influence legislation (commonly known as lobbying)" (US IRS, 2018). The IRS indicates that substantial is determined by the amount of time staff and volunteers spend on lobbying efforts and the amount of money spent on such efforts. Churches must follow the same rules if they wish to remain tax-exempt, and in addition, "they must not participate in, or intervene in, any political campaign on behalf of (or in opposition to) any candidate for public office" (US IRS, 2019). In other words, non-profits are allowed to be political, as long as it does not take up a lot of time or money, and religious organizations are, furthermore, not allowed to be partisan.

However, the US IRS specifically states that non-profits "may engage in an unlimited amount of lobbying, provided that the lobbying is related to the organization's exempt purpose" (Reilly and Braig Adam, 2003). Hence, Chambers of Commerce may lobby for legislation that promotes business interests, labor unions may lobby for legislation on labor practices, and environmental groups may lobby for environmental regulations without jeopardizing their tax-exempt status. Things become tricky when a piece of legislation has indirect effects on business, labor, and the environment; the legislation may not be considered directly related to the organization's purpose. Take food banks, for instance—they can lobby for legislation that encourages donations to food banks. However, lobbying to raise the minimum wage or to increase SNAP benefits would likely be considered outside their core mission, even though such legislation would help their clients become more food secure than food donations would. Revising mission statements to focus on poverty rather than food donations can provide cover for such lobbying. Losing non-profit status would not only mean having to pay taxes, but it would also risk losing donations since private donations to registered non-profits are tax-deductible. Given that non-profits do not want to both increase costs and decrease revenues, they are loath to risk losing tax-exempt status by lobbying, even when they understand that changing legislation is the key to solving a problem.

Fear of lobbying is a common problem with small non-profits because it is relatively easy to form a non-profit and highly unlikely that those involved understand the scope and origin of the problems they wish to deal with. As an example, if people are hungry, then the solution must be to give them food. However, after decades of fighting hunger in the US, the number of hungry Americans has increased. To have the power to lobby for legislation that would eradicate hunger, a food bank would have needed to understand why hunger existed and lay out the scope of policies required to eradicate hunger in its mission. Like many non-profits, food banks and food pantries have learned about the problem they are trying to tackle over time. Thus, in 2008, Second Harvest rebranded itself as Feeding America, specifically to expand beyond food distribution, to raise public awareness about hunger, and to advocate "for legislation that protects people from going hungry" (Feeding America, 2008). This gave the organization the grounds to lobby for anti-poverty legislation without losing its tax-exempt status. Yet many food banks maintain narrow mission statements that restrict them from such efforts. For example, the mission of Second Harvest Canada is, "To rescue and deliver fresh, surplus food to feed people experiencing hunger" (Second Harvest, n.d.). This narrow mission statement, common among food banks and food pantries, focuses on distributing surplus food, rather than eradicating hunger.

Focusing on redistributing surplus food will never solve the hunger problem because it addresses a symptom and not the cause of food insecurity. It is clear that food insecurity in the US is not the result of an emergency situation, but is in fact a chronic situation for many households. They simply do not earn enough to cover their basic necessities, even when they work full-time or have multiple jobs. This reflects a systemic problem of low wages and benefits, which is the result of government policy. Non-profits can only address this if they can successfully lobby for higher minimum wages and benefits.

Were the Feeding America network to mobilize its army of volunteers to advocate for higher wages and benefits, such massive political pressure could end poverty and hunger in America. However, it would also end the need for a food pantry/bank system. Given the close ties food banks have with corporate America, this is unlikely to happen; 25% of the board members on food banks work at a Fortune 1000 company, while only two out of 2,817 board members work for a labor union (Fisher, 2017). What then is the likelihood that food bank boards would support advocating legislation for businesses to pay higher wages? Both corporate funding and the corporate culture of food banks have fostered a conflict of interest between the good of the organization and eliminating hunger. Corporations donate billions of dollars, mostly in-kind, so why would food banks jeopardize their relationships with corporate donors by advocating for corporations to pay their workers higher wages? And given that CEOs of food banks earn in excess of $300,000 a year, they would appear to have little incentive to solve the problem of hunger and thereby eliminate their own jobs and lose their exorbitant salaries.

Non-profits cannot solve health issues created by government policies

Globally, Li et al. (2018) estimated that life expectancy could be extended up to 14 years for women and 12.2 years for men if all five healthy habits were adopted as compared to not: not smoking; maintaining a BMI of between 18.5-24.9; moderate to vigorous exercise at least 30 minutes per day; alcohol intake of no more than one serving per day for women or two per day for men; and a diet high in whole grains and FAV.

The impulse is to view these habits as private choices, and not only blame people for their health outcomes, but leave the solution to the individual. Non-profits and for-profits have sprung up to assist individuals: smoking cessation, Alcoholics Anonymous, fitness clubs and businesses, and many people selling or promoting a specific diet. US Health Maintenance Organizations (HMOs) have promoted wellness initiatives to subsidize gyms, CSAs, or other memberships as cost-saving efforts to encourage healthy behaviors and reduce the demand for their medical services.

The US is one of the wealthiest countries in the world, and spends far more than any other country on health care, yet ranks 31st in life expectancy. We can point to smoking, alcohol, diet, and lack of exercise, but why is it that so many Americans smoke and drink too much, are so fat, get so little exercise, and eat so poorly? Are we all just so hopelessly self-indulgent and lazy? Or do we live in a country that has subsidized tobacco, alcohol, unhealthy food, and private transportation, and lacks not only national health care, but also national nutrition and physical education programs? You get what you pay for; we have paid for subsidies for unhealthy lifestyles.

We have explored how US agricultural policy has subsidized, protected, and promoted the very foods that have contributed to the obesity crisis. Agricultural programs in the US are at cross purposes with the country's own nutrition recommendations. The result is that unhealthy processed foods and animal products are relatively cheap and abundant, while healthy FAV and whole grains are relatively expensive. Consequently, it is no surprise that the majority of Americans are overweight. It does little good for doctors and nutritionists to recommend foods that people cannot afford to buy, or even if they could afford to buy, appear far more expensive than the foods they buy normally. US agricultural policies have made unhealthy foods cheap and have made healthy foods relatively expensive.

The same has happened in other sectors of our society. Direct government subsidies of car manufacturers, highways, and roads have contributed to lifestyles with inadequate exercise. The very way we design cities in the US limits how much exercise we get. A car in the US is not a luxury, but a necessity. Cities are designed with no or inadequate public transportation systems, no or few bike lanes, and in some cases no sidewalks. Distances are so far and populations so sparse that public transportation is expensive and infrequent, if it indeed exists. In all rural and suburban areas and most cities, one must have a car for transportation. Driving to get exercise is considered normal in the US, whether it is to go to a gym, a bike trail, a dog park, or a walking area. City and county planning, and state and federal policies and funding, have created a country where people cannot get sufficient exercise in the normal course of their day; they must go out of their way to get exercise. Essentially, the government has invested public monies to ensure that we cannot exercise unless we make a special effort. With multiple jobs and long commutes standard in America, this becomes difficult and costly for the individual. To make exercise part of one's day means reversing decades of zoning and planning and re-designing America's built environment.

Tobacco is another example of how government policies have promoted unhealthy private behaviors. Smoking results in nearly half a million deaths each year in the US, or about one out of five deaths (CDC, 2018). The direct medical costs and lost productivity due to tobacco are estimated at over US$ 300 billion annually in the US (CDC, 2019a). About 14% of the adult population, or 34 million American adults, smoke (CDC, 2019b). This is down from 44% of adults smoking in the US in 1950 (Ravenholt, 1990), but how did cigarette smoking become such a problem?

Tobacco is native to the Americas. It was widely cultivated and used by Native Americans prior to colonization (Ravenholt, 1990). It became the principal crop and export of the colony of Virginia. Indeed, Virginia was granted exclusive rights to export tobacco to England, making it as valuable as silver by weight in 1624. Smoking tobacco in pipes was popularized in England by among others, Queen Elizabeth I, and in the 18th century, snuff became popular, but in the colonies, most tobacco was actually chewed until the mid-19th century. Cigarettes were not introduced to the UK until the early 19th century by soldiers returning from the Napoleonic campaigns in Iberia. Later, Americans touring Europe brought cigarette smoking to the US, and all forms of tobacco use increased during and after the Civil War. By 1880, 1.3 billion cigarettes were consumed annually in the US, which had a population of 50 million.

The health impacts of smoking were noted early on. When James I took the throne in the UK in 1603, he discouraged tobacco use by displaying the blackened organs of smokers' corpses and by a 40-fold increase in tobacco tax (Ravenholt, 1990). In the US, where smoking was not popular until after the Civil War, the anti-tobacco movement took shape in the 1890s and early 1900s. It was led by Lucy Page Gaston and the Women's Christian Temperance Movement. By 1900, it had resulted in 12 states passing legislation to ban cigarette smoking.

Legislative and popular efforts to ban cigarette smoking were undermined by the US federal government during WWI when it included cigarettes in soldiers' rations (Ravenholt, 1990). After the war, aggressive and unregulated radio and cinema advertising campaigns helped double cigarette consumption in the US during the 1920s. The US government further promoted tobacco interests by establishing a federal tobacco quota program in 1938 to protect tobacco farmers (Tiller, Feleke, and Starnes, 2010). US cigarette consumption doubled again between 1940 and 1945 when the US government gave soldiers and civilian groups cigarettes during WWII (Ravenholt, 1990).

With the federal government promoting cigarette smoking and tobacco production, by 1950, smoking prevalence in the US was at its highest and there was an epidemic of lung cancer. This same year, the link between smoking and lung cancer was established scientifically (Ravenholt, 1990). A seminal report to the US Surgeon General confirmed that cigarette smoking caused lung cancer in 1964. In response, tobacco companies intensified their advertising campaigns. While the US Department of Agriculture was promoting tobacco production, the US Federal Communications Commission (FCC) applied the Fairness Doctrine in 1967 to require that radio and TV advertising be balanced with anti-smoking information. The result was that tobacco companies reduced their radio and TV advertising to avoid anti-smoking ads. However, tobacco sales in the US continued at record levels in the 1970s. In 1977, Joseph Califano was appointed US Secretary of Health, Education, and Welfare. He was so effective at using the resources of the agency to promote anti-smoking that tobacco interests pressured President Carter to fire him in 1979.

Not until 2004 did the US government end its federal program to protect tobacco farmers, 40 years after the US Surgeon General's report about lung cancer and smoking. The Fair and Equitable Tobacco Act of 2004 gave US$ 10 billion in taxpayer's money to tobacco quota owners and tobacco growers (Tiller, Feleke, and Starnes, 2010). Far from being motivated by 54 years of scientific knowledge that tobacco caused lung cancer, the Act was created because tobacco growers were losing their global market share and demand; US tobacco prices were 50% above global prices, discouraging domestic cigarette manufacturers from using US-produced tobacco and reducing exports of US tobacco. The 2004 Act brought US tobacco prices closer to global prices and encouraged smaller, less productive tobacco farms to leave tobacco farming. The number of US tobacco farms fell by 72% between 2002 and 2007. The result was tobacco farms got larger and the total US tobacco production actually increased. The US is now the fourth-largest producer of tobacco in the world, with North Carolina and Kentucky accounting for 70% of US production (CDC, 2019a).

The link between smoking and cancer has been used to justify raising taxes on cigarettes and suing tobacco companies. Ostensibly, this money was supposed to be used by states to fund programs to prevent smoking and help smokers quit. In FY 2019, states collected US$ 27.3 billion from tobacco taxes and court settlements, but spent only 2.4% of that on anti-smoking efforts (CDC, 2019b). Over 97% of the collected funds were used to fund other state activities or cut state taxes. In other words, almost all the tobacco taxes and settlements were not used for their stated purpose. This means that those who want to quit smoking must turn to private or non-profit efforts for assistance. Why in the world should non-profits step in to do the job that state governments have collected taxes and settlements for, yet have refused to use the money they have collected to do the job? Would anyone suggest that we ask non-profits to raise money to build or repair roads because state governments allocated nearly all their highway funds for purposes other than roads? Clearly, states are shirking their responsibility by not using the money collected to prevent and treat smoking for those very purposes.

With over US$ 170 billion in direct medical costs, one would expect health care providers to be motivated to help smokers quit. Yet while over 80% of health care providers have adopted at least one recommended strategy to treat tobacco addiction, less than 6% have adopted all eight recommended strategies (McMenamin et al., 2010). This means medical treatment is far less effective than it could be at treating tobacco addiction. If health care providers are not using the tools available to treat addiction, why should non-profits fill the gap? And why should individuals be blamed when experts are not using the tools available to them to help their patients fight tobacco addiction?

Tobacco illustrates that, far from being a personal failing, smoking in the US is the result of systemic government policies. The upshot is that the US federal government has protected, promoted, and subsidized tobacco production and cigarette demand, well into the 21st century; state governments are currently using over 97% of tobacco taxes and settlements for purposes other than smoking prevention and treatment of tobacco addiction; and less than 6% of health care providers are using best practices to treat tobacco addiction. Meanwhile, US$ 9 billion is still being spent annually on tobacco advertising in the US (CDC, 2019a). It is generous to call US policy toward tobacco addiction and deaths a policy failure. Rather, US policies have been deliberately aimed at promoting tobacco addiction, ignoring the scientifically proven link between tobacco use and deaths, not using money generated for addiction prevention and treatment for those very purposes, and not using best practices in treating addicts. Failure is too mild a word to describe US tobacco policies.

We need to change the policies that cause the problems in the first place

While non-profits have engaged in many noble efforts, the continued reliance on non-profits to solve systemic policy issues in the US is misguided. We need changes in government policies, not projects that address symptoms. Non-profits need to advocate policy changes that address the problems they were founded to solve. They must be political to be effective. Non-profits that merely distribute food will not solve hunger; only higher wages and policies to make housing, health care, and education more affordable will solve hunger in America.

Non-profits promoting healthy lifestyles will not solve the obesity crisis because they are only addressing the symptoms. However, advocating the removal of policies that make unhealthy foods cheap and healthy foods expensive will incentivize individuals to make better decisions. Asking people to use their willpower to overcome structural market issues is like putting shackles on someone and asking them to run; take off the shackles if you want them to run. Building communities that incorporate exercise and reduce the amount of time being sedentary will also help reduce overweight and obesity. These are the purviews of local government: zoning and design to encourage, rather than impede, exercise.

Non-profits will not solve environmental problems unless they address the specific policies that have created the problems in the first place. US agricultural policies have resulted in the loss of habitat, the degradation of soil, the pollution of water, and the poisoning of people and other species. They have done this while reducing the number of families who can make a living farming and creating a food system that is encouraging Americans to eat themselves to death.

Tobacco illustrates how non-profits cannot solve addiction issues unless they hold governments accountable for creating the addictions in the first place, and use the monies they are collecting for prevention and treatment. The federal government worked assiduously for over a century to promote tobacco smoking, and even longer to promote tobacco production, so there is reason to believe it could be just as effective at eliminating it, given the time and resources to do so. Furthermore, states have worked very hard to extract money from tobacco sales and tobacco companies; they have the resources needed to prevent and treat tobacco addiction, but have chosen not to use the money they have collected for those purposes. There is no doubt that if states were to use more than 3% of the money they collected on prevention and treatment, tobacco would not kill nearly half a million Americans each year.

Tobacco serves as an example of how government policies have created a health problem, and how changes in government policies are needed to address the problem created by government policies. Agriculture is another example of how government policies have fostered the environmental and health problems we are experiencing. Yet, Americans want to rely on individuals and non-profits to solve problems, even when those problems were created by the government. We want to see social problems as personal failings, but social problems require social policies to solve them. That is why government exists—to address social needs and problems. We can start by changing the policies that are creating and exacerbating the environmental and health problems in the first place.

Exercise: Look at the policies

Identify one social issue that concerns you. Identify government policies that affect the issue. What policies at federal, state, or local level might solve the problem, not just address the symptoms?

References

Akers, J. and Seymour, E. 2018. Instrumental exploitation: Predatory property relations at city's end. Geoforum, 91, 127–140.

Association of Statisticians of American Religious Bodies. 2012. 2010 US religious census. http://usreligioncensus.org, accessed June 28, 2019.

Brown, D. A. 2018. Homeownership in black and white: The role of tax policy in increasing housing inequity. University of Memphis Law Review, 49, 205–228.

CDC. 2018. Health effects of cigarette smoking. https://www.cdc.gov/tobacco/data_statistics/fact_sheets/health_effects/effects_cig_smoking/index.htm, accessed August 20, 2019.

CDC. 2019a. Economic trends in tobacco. https://www.cdc.gov/tobacco/data_statistics/fact_sheets/economics/econ_facts/index.htm, accessed August 20, 2019.

CDC. 2019b. Fast facts. https://www.cdc.gov/tobacco/data_statistics/fact_sheets/fast_facts/index.htm, accessed August 20, 2019.

Development Initiatives. 2018. 2018 global nutrition report: Shining a light to spur action on nutrition. https://globalnutritionreport.org/reports/global-nutrition-report-2018/, accessed October 22, 2020.

FAO. 2011. Global food losses and food waste—Extent, causes and prevention. http://www.fao.org/3/a-i2697e.pdf, accessed March 22, 2019.

FAO. 2017. The future of food and agriculture: Trends and challenges. http://www.fao.org/3/a-i6583e.pdf, accessed April 3, 2019.

Feeding America. 2008. America's Second Harvest changes name to Feeding America. September 5. https://www.feedingamerica.org/about-us/press-room/americas-second-harvest-changes-name-to-feeding-america, accessed June 28, 2009.

Fisher, A. 2017. Big Hunger: The Unholy Alliance between Corporate America and Anti-Hunger Groups. Cambridge, MA: The MIT Press.

Horton, R. 2018. GBD 2017: a fragile world. The Lancet, 392(10150), 1683. https://doi.org/10.1016/S0140-6736(18)32858-7, accessed October 22, 2020.

Li, Y., Pan, A., Wang, D. D., Liu, X., Dhana, K., Franco, O. H., Kaptoge, S., Di Angelantonio, E., Stampfer, M., Willett, W. C., and Hu, F. B. 2018. Impact of healthy lifestyle factors on life expectancies in the US population. Circulation, 138(4), 345-355. https://www.ahajournals.org/doi/pdf/10.1161/CIRCULATIONAHA.117.032047, accessed October 22, 2020.

McKeever, B. 2018. The non-profits sector in brief 2018. National Center for Charitable Statistics, December 13. https://nccs.urban.org/publication/non-profit-sector-brief-2018#the-non-profit-sector-in-brief-2018-public-charites-giving-and-volunteering, accessed June 28, 2019.

McMenamin, S. B., Bellows, N. M., Halpin, H. A., Rittenhouse, D. R., Casalino, L. P., and Shortell, S. M. 2010. Adoption of policies to treat tobacco dependence in US medical groups. American Journal of Preventative Medicine, 39(5), 449–456.

Ravenholt, R. T. 1990. Tobacco's global death march. Population and Development Review,16(2), 213–240.

Reilly, J. F. and Braig Adam, B. A. 2003. Political campaign and lobbying activities of IRS 501(c)(4), (c)(5), and (c)(6) organizations. Exempt Organizations-Technical Instruction Program for FY 2003. https://www.irs.gov/pub/irs-tege/eotopicl03.pdf, accessed June 28, 2019.

Robinson III, J. N. 2017. Negotiating the (legal) right to the city: Public housing demolition and the federal courts in two postindustrial US cities. Journal of Urban Affairs, 39(2), 277–290. http://dx.doi.org/10.1080/07352166.2016.1245077, accessed October 22, 2020.

Roser, M. and Ritchie, H. 2018. Yields and land use in agriculture. https://ourworldindata.org/yields-and-land-use-in-agriculture, accessed March 18, 2018.

Second Harvest. n.d. Who we are. https://secondharvest.ca/who-we-are/, accessed June 28, 2019.

Tiller, K. J., Feleke, S. T., and Starnes, J. H. 2010. Exits among US burley tobacco growers after the end of the federal tobacco program. Journal of Agricultural and Applied Economics, 42(2), 161–175.

Toqueville, Alexis de. 2004. Democracy in America. Translated by A. Goldhammer. New York: The Library of America.

UNEP. 2019. Global Environmental Outlook - GEO-6: Healthy planet, healthy people. https://wedocs.unep.org/bitstream/handle/20.500.11822/27539/GEO6_2019.pdf?sequence=1&isAllowed=y, accessed June 3, 2019

US Census Bureau. 2018. Income and poverty in the US: 2017. Table A-1. Households by Total Money Income, Race, and Hispanic Origin of Householder: 1967 to 2017. https://www.census.gov/data/tables/2018/demo/income-poverty/p60-263.html, accessed July 10, 2019.

US Internal Revenue Service. 2018. Measuring lobbying: Substantial part test. https://www.irs.gov/charities-non-profits/measuring-lobbying-substantial-part-test, accessed June 28, 2019.

US Internal Revenue Service. 2019. Publication 1828, Tax Guide for Churches and Religious Organizations. https://www.irs.gov/pub/irs-pdf/p1828.pdf, accessed June 28, 2019.

World Food Programme. 2013. What causes hunger? November 5. https://www.wfp.org/stories/what-causes-hunger, accessed February 4, 2019.

Zepeda, L. 2018. Hiding hunger: Food insecurity in middle America. Agriculture and Human Values, 35(1), 243–254. doi: 10.1007/s10460-017-9818-4.

Zepeda, L. and Reznickova, A. 2018. Potential demand for local fresh produce by mobile markets. US Department of Agriculture, Agricultural Marketing Service Research Publication. http://localandorganicfood.org/wp-content/uploads/2018/05/Potential-Demand-for-Local-Fresh-Produce-by-Mobile-Markets-05-18-1.pdf, accessed October 22, 2020.

CHAPTER EIGHT

NO REALLY, HOW DO WE FIX THIS?

The US has pursued agricultural, land, and nutrition policies that have been detrimental to human health, social equity, and the environment. From its inception, the US has fostered policies to distribute lands, taken from indigenous peoples, to wealthy White men to grow export crops using slave labor. The sale of public lands was the primary means of funding the federal government for over 125 years. The 1796 Public Land Act codified the role of the federal government in concentrating land in the hands of the wealthy. It established that the minimum sale size of public land was 640 acres (259 hectares) at US$ 2 per acre (less than US$ 5 per hectare) (Spielmaker, 2018). At the time, the minimum purchase price of US$ 1,280 was beyond the means of all but the very wealthy and the tracts of land were so large that they could only feasibly be worked by slaves or partitioned and sold by land speculators. The result of this policy was an agricultural economy oriented to producing non-food export crops: first tobacco, then cotton.

Throughout the 19th century, there was pressure to distribute the vast tracts of federal land acquired through purchase, war, and conquest more equitably…at least among White men. However, the Senate fought the Homestead Act throughout the 1850s and it was vetoed by President Buchanan in 1860 (US National Archives and Records Administration, 2016). Those in power did not want to distribute wealth in the form of land. So, the Homestead Act did not pass until during the Civil War in 1862, when Lincoln was President and many of the Representatives and Senators of the Southern States did not participate in Congress. Securing title to the160-acre (65-hectare) parcels distributed through the Homestead Act required five years of continuous cultivation of the land (USDA, National Agricultural Library, 1862). However, few people could actually afford to make the trip west with the needed provisions and tools. So, rather than achieve the stated intent of more equitable land distribution, the Homestead Act was, in fact, a mass transfer of public wealth to private and wealthy interests. By 1904, 84% of the 500 million acres (202 million hectares) dispersed through the Homestead Act went to speculators, railways, cattlemen, miners, and lumbermen (Our Documents, n.d.).

Like so much legislation in the US, the Homestead Act provided cover for policies that benefited the wealthy. The Homestead Act was associated with pioneers, and the building of an American middle class. While the largest beneficiaries were the speculators, railways, cattlemen, miners, and lumbermen, it did provide some wealth transfer in the form of land to middle-class Whites. These farms were large by international standards and focused on commodities. However, they were somewhat diversified through the beginning of the 20th century, simply because farm families needed to grow some of their own food. In 1920, the average farm in the US grew five crops and had 20 livestock (Kirwan, 2017).

US agricultural policy: Farm Bills, farm operators, and what is produced

Until 1934, the primary means the US federal government used to subsidize agricultural production was through the sale and grants of federal land. Cheap rental of approximately 229 million acres (92.7 million hectares) of federal lands in the western US for grazing represents an ongoing subsidy for livestock production. The federal government spends in excess of US$ 125 million more a year managing the rangelands than it receives from grazing fees (Glaser, Romaniello, and Moskowitz, 2015). In addition, grazing on these public lands has had devastating environmental consequences. The nature of these land giveaways and subsidized grazing lands has favored the already wealthy, promoted commodity production, and subsidized exports.

Direct monetary subsidies to US farmers occurred during WWI to encourage the production of wheat; the US government created its first direct commodity subsidies by doubling the domestic price of wheat. However, the first permanent US government program to subsidize farm incomes occurred with the first Farm Bill in 1933. The US federal government created an ongoing policy of direct monetary subsidies to farmers by paying them for certain commodities (Farm Policy Facts, 2018). The Farm Bills were so successful at stimulating the production of subsidized crops that they created vast surpluses. These surplus commodities were used to feed the poor in the US, as aid to developing countries, and as in-kind subsidies to promote trade to develop foreign markets. Later Farm Bills tried to reduce the costs of the program by curbing production. This approach raised farm prices and hence farm incomes. At times, the government even encouraged conservation by paying farmers not to farm some of their most vulnerable lands. One effect of the Farm Bills was to make US farms highly specialized, either as crop or livestock farms, with crop farms growing an average of two crops and livestock having over 130 head (Kirwan, 2017).

The 1996 Farm Bill attempted to remove all subsidies to US farmers, but a drop in farm prices led to legislation for emergency assistance to farmers in 1998-99 (Spielmaker, 2018). Subsequent Farm Bills continued to pay farmers not to grow crops on marginal lands through a conservation program, but provided farmers with crop insurance, and provided subsidies for corn (maize), soybeans, wheat, rice, cotton, peanuts, oats, barley, sorghum, and oilseeds. In FY 2016, 71% of the US$ 6.9 billion cost of the two commodity support programs went on subsidizing corn (43.3%) and wheat (27.7%) (Angadjivand, 2018). Corn (maize) is largely used for animal feed and ethanol, while wheat is consumed by humans. Since significant amounts of both crops are exported, US agricultural policies essentially function to subsidize and promote agricultural exports.

Federal agricultural subsidies make up an important part of US farmers' incomes. In 2018, US government payments to farmers represented 17% of farm incomes (USDA ERS, 2018a). The distribution of subsidies is concentrated among the largest farms, who are much more likely to receive subsidies, and these subsidies are much larger than those received by smaller farms. Farms with over US$ 1 million in sales represent 1.7% of all farms in the US and 79% of these farms receive subsidies, averaging nearly US$ 57,000 annually, while farms with sales under US$ 10,000 a year represent 57% of all farms in the US, but only 18% receive subsidies and these average only US$ 439 per year (Kirwan, 2017).

Taken as a whole, nearly a fifth of farm income in the US comes from government support, yet despite this, the number of farms has steadily decreased since 1920 (USDA NASS, 2019; USDA NASS, 2018). The number of farms would be even less if the US government used a consistent definition for a farm. The change in the definition of a farm creates the illusion that there are more than twice as many farms now as there would be if the definition had stayed the same as in 1870. Adjusting for inflation, the current number of farms would be less than 850,000, rather than over 2 million using the current definition of "farm." Average farm size in the US in 1860 was over 80 hectares; today, using the revised definition of a farm, it is officially over 180 hectares. The official average farm size would be even larger had the definition of a farm remained constant over time.

Who farms in the US and, therefore, receives government subsidies reflects centuries of policies that have protected and privileged the few. Today, as during its inception, land in the US is concentrated in the hands of old White men: 67.8% of all principal agricultural producers are White men averaging 58.6 years old (USDA NASS, 2019). Yet, non-Hispanic White men, 60 years and older, make up only about 6.5% of the total US population (US Census Bureau, 2019).

In contrast, African American men make up 6.2% of the US population (US Census Bureau, 2019), but only 1.1% of all principal agricultural producers (USDA NASS, 2019). African Americans have lost over 12 million acres (4.9 million hectares), or 98% of the land they owned over the last century (Newkirk, 2019). Lack of access to credit available to White farmers through federal programs, discriminatory lending and foreclosure practices by banks, blocking of market and sales access, as well as strong-arm tactics and scams have been used to extract land from Black farmers (Sewell, 2019). Agricultural land ownership is emblematic of social and economic inequality in the US.

How we use land in the US is also reflective of our attitudes toward the environment and human health. Currently, animal production dominates the US landscape. Nearly 93% of US agricultural land in the lower 48 states is allocated to the production of animals, their feed, and ethanol, and about 6% to wheat and rice, used for human consumption (Bigelow and Borders, 2017). The remaining 1% of agricultural land includes not only FAV, but also pulses, beans, oils, and sugars for human consumption.

Economically, the US food system is essentially designed to produce animal products. In 2018, it is estimated that US agriculture generated US$ 374.8 billion in cash receipts to farmers (USDA ERS, 2018b). Of this amount, 62.3% were for animal products or animal feeds. Despite the allocation of resources to animal production, animal-derived foods provided less than one-quarter of the energy and less than half the protein available for human consumption in the US (White and Hall, 2017). The immense resources of the US are being squandered to grow cheap animal feeds without taking into account the environmental costs of water depletion and pollution, soil erosion and contamination, habitat loss, and human health impacts.

End policies that subsidize unhealthy foods, pollute, and promote fewer, bigger farms

The composition of agricultural production in the US is a direct result of government policies that promote and subsidize a few commodities, as well as animal production. These policies have made the ingredients for processed foods and animal products artificially abundant and cheap. Thus, processed foods and animal products are produced cheaply, making them less costly relative to healthy foods like FAV. As a result of emphasizing processed foods and animal products, agricultural ingredients make up less than 10% of the value of the food system (USDA ERS, 2018b; US Census Bureau, 2018). The impacts of US agricultural policies are global because one-third of the value of US agricultural products is exported: US$ 138.4 billion in 2017 (USDA FAS, 2018). Hence, US policies subsidize processed foods and animal products globally.

The effect of making processed foods and animal products cheap relative to healthier foods is to make it economically rational to choose an unhealthy diet. Recommendations to eat fewer animal products, and more whole grains, nuts, seeds, pulses, and FAV (Carrington, 2019) are countermanded by government policies that have made these healthier foods expensive relative to processed foods and animal products. To promote healthy eating, the first order of any nutrition policy in the US, and globally, requires the removal of all agricultural programs that create artificially cheap, unhealthy foods. In other words, ending current agricultural subsidy programs. Doing so would shift production and change relative prices, making healthy foods relatively cheaper. This would level the playing field by taking away economic incentives for consumers to eat unhealthy foods. Even if the impact of relative price changes at the retail level is small, there is simply no rational justification for subsidizing products that are antithetical to public health.

Existing agricultural policies in the US have been detrimental to farmers themselves; their numbers continue to fall, despite billions of dollars in subsidies. As long as US policies are tied to production, they create an incentive to increase farm size to gain more subsidies; the largest farms are four times as likely to receive subsidies and those subsidies are more than 100 times larger than the smallest farms (Kirwan, 2017). This has created incentives for fewer, larger farms. Agricultural policies must be decoupled from output if we want to stop a decline in farm numbers.

We need to rethink agricultural policies so that they will provide a livelihood to farmers, promote health, and protect the land and water. What would those policies look like? What effects would they have on land and water use?

First, agricultural policies need to focus on farm income rather than farm output. Second, policies need to promote soil and water conservation, avoid water contamination, reduce GHG emissions, and capture carbon. Third, policies need to promote the production of foods that improve people's diets, making these foods relatively cheaper and hence providing consumers with incentives to choose healthy foods. Our current policies do the opposite; they result in fewer and larger farms, land and water degradation and pollution, and a food supply in which FAV are more expensive than candy. Why are we using government policies and subsidies to create these social, environmental, and health problems? Public policy should promote public goods and services, not public problems.

Simply ending current subsidy programs would reduce the incentives for fewer and larger farms, environmental degradation, and a food supply that makes unhealthy foods relatively cheap. Removing subsidies for commodity crops would make them less profitable, hence increasing the diversity of crops planted. Removal of production subsidies would remove incentives to have fewer and larger farms, stemming the decline of rural economies. Currently, most of the US agricultural program support goes to corn (maize) and wheat. Meat production is supported not just through feed subsidies, but through subsidized grazing on public lands. Grazing puts pressure on the habitat in general and wild animals in particular, as well as contaminating water resources (Glaser, Romaniello, and Moskowitz, 2015). As regards farmland, if less land were used for animal feed, more land would be available for human foods like grains, pulses, seeds, oils, and FAV, not to mention habitat restoration.

Removal of subsidies and incentives to produce animal feeds and products would reduce mono-cropping, the use of chemicals, and animal waste, all of which affect water quality. Further reductions in contamination could be created by having polluters pay. Applying a polluter pay tax, that took into account production methods to cover the costs of clean up, would create incentives to farm sustainably. This would encourage reduced chemical usage, which is polluting water, soil, and adversely affecting human health. Animal waste applied to land below a sustainable threshold would be exempt. Pollution payments could rise with application rates, and be adjusted for time of year, weather, and nearness to water sources. Since any costs would be passed on to consumers, unsustainably produced products would cost more than those produced sustainably. The opposite is true now. If prices reflected the true cost of farm products, the demand for unsustainably produced products would decline. Many of these same unsustainably produced foods are also responsible for food-related illnesses. Therefore, removing subsidies would benefit the environment and public health.

Alston and Okrent (2017) criticize this approach. They dismiss government subsidies, R&D, and government nutrition programs as having any impact on obesity. They argue that commodities make up such a small proportion of retail food costs and that people's food habits are so inelastic, that changing relative prices will not change behaviors. Yet, they concede that policies have generally made food cheaper, especially processed foods, and this is due to increases in productivity and farm policies that have made these ingredients cheaper, as well as increases in competition in retailing. They argue that the real prices of commodities have declined by 50% since 1950, due mostly to government R&D investments and the granting of private intellectual property rights for discoveries funded with public research monies. Real prices of food grains, mostly rice and wheat, have fallen by 50%, while real prices of animal products have fallen by 40-75%, mostly due to cheaper feed grains. In contrast, the prices of fruits and tree nuts have fallen by only 20%, and vegetables and melons by only 10%. The result has been to make the relative prices of unhealthy foods cheaper than healthy foods. This begs the question, why should any government funds be used to distort prices to make unhealthy foods cheap relative to healthy foods? Even if Alston and Okrent are correct about the impact of removing subsidies on obesity, from a public welfare perspective, it makes no sense to use public monies to foster public problems.

Taken a step further, policies and existing agricultural budgets could be used to actually promote farming, environmental stewardship, and public health. The current budget for farm programs could be used to support farm incomes, promote sustainable farming practices, encourage the production of healthier foods, and capture carbon.

For those worried about having enough food, there are several responses. First, removing subsidies would free up land currently used to produce animal feed and fuel so that it could produce food for humans. Reducing resources allocated to animal production would increase the resources available to produce food for humans because so much of US land and water is used to produce animal feed and ethanol. Second, we already produce more than enough food for everyone, but it is distributed inequitably; the lack of income, not food, is the problem. Third, we waste a huge proportion of what we do produce; 40% of what is harvested in the US is wasted. That does not count food that rots in the fields because it was not harvested. Focusing on reductions in food waste could greatly increase food availability.

Reorienting agricultural policies to encourage sustainable production would also promote public health. More than 140,000 chemicals and pesticides have been introduced into agriculture since 1950 (Landrigan et al., 2018). Exposure to agrochemicals like organochlorines has decreased due to regulations, but these chemicals are ubiquitous in the environment, our food, and our bodies, while the health effects are difficult to determine, especially in combination with other chemicals (Ekins, Gupta, and Boileau, 2019). However, studies suggest that Parkinson's disease and breast cancer are related to exposure to pesticides and show that farmers have especially high rates of non-Hodgkin's lymphoma. Pesticide exposure is associated with cancers, reproductive and endocrine problems, decreased cognitive scores, and attention and behavioral problems in children (Hyland et al., 2019). About half of the food in the US has detectible levels of pesticide residues. Hence, diet is the primary source of organophosphate exposure and a major source of exposure to other pesticides like pyrethroids, neonicotinoids, and 2,4-D. Chlorpyrifos was the most widely used organophosphate in US agriculture between 2007-2012. It was banned from residential use in 2000 because it is a neurotoxin that has documented adverse impacts on children's brains (Wallace and Kaufman, 2019). In 2018, a court ordered the US EPA to review its use in agriculture, but the EPA has refused to ban it. While organophosphate use has declined in US agriculture, the use of pyrethroids and neonicotinoids has increased (Hyland et al., 2019). Pyrethroids are also widely used in residential and business structures. Neonicotinoids are systemic, so they cannot be washed off.

However, there is a solution to pesticide exposure. Consistent with other studies, Hyland et al. (2019) found that just six days on an organic food diet significantly reduced 13 out of 14 pesticides and pesticide metabolites in the urine of all of their study participants. Currently, most organic foods are more expensive than those produced with synthetic pesticides, which begs the question, as articulated by a focus group participant, "If organic is good, and the government knows it, and the USDA continues to subsidize some food, why can't they subsidize organic food in such a way so that when you go to the supermarket, across the board, it's the same price for the rich and the poor?" (Zepeda, Chang, and Leviten-Reid, 2006, p. 392).

Reorienting agricultural policies to remove subsidies for processed foods and animal products is also a way to improve diets and reduce health care costs. Americans have increased calorie consumption from 1970 to 2010 by over 500 calories per person per day (Alston and Okrent, 2017). Much of the food they eat is highly processed, low quality, and full of empty calories. The result is that two-thirds of adults in the US are overweight or obese. The private costs of obesity and overweight in the US are estimated at US$ 113 billion or 4.8% of all medical expenditures, while the public costs of obesity and overweight for Medicare and Medicaid[6] are estimated at US$ 166 billion annually. The cost of private weight loss programs adds another US$ 63 billion a year. Further indirect costs include absenteeism, on the job injury, lower productivity at work, and higher insurance costs. The results are higher medical costs for everyone, greater public costs for taxpayers, and added costs for employers.

Our current agricultural policies make processed foods cheap. As a result, the proportion of food we eat that is processed, as well as food eaten away from home, has increased, while the consumption of unprocessed foods and FAV has fallen (Alston and Okrent, 2017). In addition, there has been an increased tendency to skip breakfast but eat snacks more frequently, with about one-fifth of calories coming from snacks, which are often processed foods with empty calories. Consumption of highly processed foods has adverse health impacts. In a five-year study involving over 105,000 people, eating ultra-processed food[7] significantly increased the risk of cardiovascular disease, the leading cause of death worldwide, even after controlling for

[6] Medicare is a government health care program in the US for those aged 65 years and older. Medicaid is a government health care program for low income Americans. Most other Americans get health care through the private sector, often paying for health insurance through their employers. However, 8.5% of Americans had no health insurance at all in 2018 (Berchick, Barnett, and Upton, 2019).

[7] Ultra-processed foods include sugary foods, breakfast cereals, salty snacks and chips, sodas, fruit and sugared drinks, processed meats, instant soups, pizza, margarine, mayonnaise, and distilled alcoholic beverages. Bread, beer, wine, and cheese are considered processed foods, while sugar, salt, oil, butter, and lard are considered processed culinary ingredients, and FAV, natural juice, legumes, milk and fermented milk products like yoghurt, meat, poultry, seafood, grains, coffee, and water are considered minimally or unprocessed foods.

other risk factors (Srour et al., 2019). Ultra-processed foods also increased cancer risk in general, and breast cancer in particular (Fiolet et al., 2018). In another study, that involved nearly 20,000 people over four years, eating at least four servings of ultra-processed foods per day increased the risk of dying from chronic disease, mostly cancer, by 62%, after controlling for other risk factors like smoking and BMI (Rico-Campà et al., 2019). Each additional serving per day of ultra-processed foods increased the risk of dying from a chronic disease by 18%.

The health impacts of our agricultural policies on the young are particularly startling. Abeysekera et al. (2019) found a much higher prevalence of liver disease among 24-years-olds than previously expected; 20% had non-alcoholic fatty liver disease, putting them at risk of liver cancer, type 2 diabetes, and heart attacks. Young people are rarely tested for liver disease, creating a hidden public health problem. Most who had this disease were overweight and 60% were obese, meaning that doctors have a means of identifying who is at risk. However, this requires making health care providers aware of fatty liver disease among the young who are overweight or obese. Since fatty liver disease can be reversed through diet, there is an incentive to get an early diagnosis. Yet to change one's diet in the current environment requires tremendous fortitude; one simply cannot eat most of the foods available in stores or restaurants.

Our unhealthy food environment is created by current policies

Getting people to change eating habits and exercise is difficult. Even when motivated and paying for weight loss, the only commercial weight loss program that has been shown to be effective in the US is Weight Watchers, and it has resulted in only a 5% weight loss (Tsai and Wadden, 2005). Why are weight loss programs so ineffective, especially at a time when the number of overweight and obese adults has risen to two-thirds of the US population? Blaming the rise of overweight and obesity on individual failings ceases to make sense when these problems affect the vast majority of the population. This is a systemic problem that requires examining how the system can be changed to alter the outcomes.

First, we know that Americans need to eat fewer calories and get more exercise. They also need to change the type of food they eat and how they eat. Improving eating habits involves not just how much people eat, but the quality of their food and how processed it is, as well as the timing and the frequency of eating. It is not simply a matter of eating more healthy foods, but also reducing the amount of unhealthy foods eaten, reducing sedentary behaviors, reducing screen time, increasing exercise, and getting enough sleep. Americans are 43% more sedentary, they perform less physical activity at work and home, and they walk 71% less than in 1950, and over the past 50 years, their sleep has declined by 1.5 to 2 hours per night (Alston and Okrent, 2017). All these things have helped us put on weight.

The assumption is that the individual is at fault for having a lifestyle that leads to poor eating habits, lack of exercise, and food-related health problems. For example, many economists urge "nudging" consumers to make better choices. Yet economists fail to recognize the existing contextual environment, which includes agricultural policies, R&D investments, transportation policies, and land use planning, that have made processed foods and animal products cheap relative to healthy foods, and made exercise expensive. These factors have created our unhealthy lifestyles in the first place. Providing nudges to "make better choices" without recognizing the environment those choices are made in is akin to asking someone to swim harder against a riptide.

Government policies have been instrumental in promoting unhealthy lifestyle choices. While farm commodities represent less than 20% of food costs in retail stores and far less for food eaten away from home (Alston and Okrent, 2017), current policies create an environment where processed foods are relatively cheaper than they would be otherwise. The effects of subsidies on prices may seem small, but agricultural policies have made the ingredients of highly processed foods cheap relative to healthy foods like whole grains, fish, legumes, seeds, nuts, and FAV. Investments in R&D have also promoted monocultures that require high levels of chemical inputs that affect human health, pollute water, and adversely affect the environment (Vanloqueren and Baret, 2009). Policies on intellectual property rights have granted private interests the right to profit from discoveries funded by public monies (Cervantes, n.d.). Federal communications policies have done little to inhibit the advertising of highly processed, low nutrition foods, especially to children; this fosters a lifetime of bad eating habits (Story and French, 2004). Federal nutrition policies have set nutrition standards and labels that have been ineffective by design in communicating health information to consumers (Nestle, 2002). City and federal planning and transportation policies have promoted and subsidized driving, making the US highly dependent on personal cars (Buehler, 2014). Our reliance on cars has made Americans more sedentary, which is linked to increased cardiovascular disease and mortality (Warren et al., 2010). Government wage and labor policies have made many Americans "time poor" because they work more hours and need to have more jobs to try to maintain living standards. This impedes both meal preparation and exercise by making them more costly in terms of time. Since most prepared food is highly processed, cooking your own food is one of the only ways to ensure that you can eat healthily; prepared foods and food eaten away from home often consist of highly processed and unhealthy ingredients.

Taken together, these "nudges" have created an environment where eating highly processed, prepared foods is considered normal. Indeed, Americans accept that children's foods are the most highly processed foods: hotdogs, french fries, soda, and breakfast cereals. Rather than feed their children the healthiest foods, Americans stuff their children with sweets and processed meats as though they were the witch feeding Hansel and Gretel. American adults routinely state that children do not eat vegetables…in front of their children. The fact is, children eat the food that they are given; they learn eating habits from their parents, as well as advertisers. So, if all they are offered is highly processed food, that is what they will eat. And if all they eat is highly processed food, they are likely to become overweight, experience diet-related health problems, and have a shortened life expectancy. One day, feeding children processed foods will be viewed as a form of child abuse, but currently, it is too ubiquitous, just as using a belt or a switch to punish a child was considered normal in the past.

Our unhealthy food environment is reinforced at nearly every level of society and policy. It has so normalized unhealthy eating habits among us, that many people believe their diets to be healthy. They maintain that belief even when completing written food diaries, although they are more likely to see that what they have eaten is unhealthy when they look at photos of what they ate, rather than simply writing down what they ate (Zepeda and Deal, 2008). Americans often have very distorted views of what they should eat, thinking that only animal products have protein, that their protein needs are much higher than is recommended, and that serving sizes are much larger than is recommended. Eating "healthier" in the minds of many Americans involves adding a salad or a piece of fruit rather than reducing the amount of sugar, highly processed foods, and alcohol in their diets. It is as though they believe a few lettuce leaves will absorb or offset sugars, alcohol, and processed foods.

To eat healthier, we not only need to eat FAV, whole grains, seeds, nuts, and pulses, but we also need to consume fewer processed foods, animal products, and alcohol. This is extremely hard to do if one eats food away from home, which makes up a large portion of Americans' diets. Most restaurants simply do not offer healthy options. Serving sizes of meats are too large, vegetables are added as mere decorations, and whole grains are largely absent. Choosing a salad at a restaurant as a meal generally means tasteless greens covered in cheese and salad dressing, and it may even have more calories than choosing a hamburger. Chefs claim they cannot offer foods that comply with nutrition recommendations because they do not sell. Healthy food simply cannot compete because it is an aberration. Who is going to choose such food when they have been conditioned to choose highly processed foods, because that is all they have ever been offered?

Homes are no better. Americans have never had a great culinary tradition. This is the result of colonization: transplanting a culture to a new land and lacking knowledge or interest in the local ecology. Early colonists starved to death (in Jamestown) or nearly did so (in Plymouth) because they simply had no idea they were surrounded by food. The native peoples had to show colonists what to eat and how to cultivate new crops, but the colonists stuck stubbornly to the culinary traditions they brought with them, converting corn to alcohol and pork, while avoiding FAV. Processed foods like salt pork and milled flour were central to American diets throughout the western expansion and America's industrial development. During the 20th century, as nutrition knowledge grew, the American diet became increasingly unhealthier. For decades, few Americans have cooked from scratch; it is considered too difficult and time-consuming. Ironically, we now spend far more time eating than before. We also spend far more money on prepared and processed foods and foods eaten away from home, as well as spending far more on health care costs due to our diets. Literally, the cheapest and quickest thing we could do for our health is cook, but we are convinced otherwise.

Again, one can blame the individual for this, but that only makes sense if the individual is doing something different from everyone else. When eating pizza seven days a week is normal, when eating even a single meal a day with one's family is highly unusual when people get one-fifth of their calories from snacks, 34% of their calories from food away from home (Saksena et al., 2018), and only 50% of Americans get the minimum recommended exercise (150 minutes a week of moderate activity) (Centers for Disease Control and Prevention, 2019), how is this a matter of individual choice? This is a social problem. Our public policies have fostered and reinforced unhealthy lifestyles.

Therefore, the solution is to change the “nudges,” to change the environment in which we operate. We need to start by having agricultural policies that remove all subsidies of unhealthy foods to create a level playing field. Any subsidies should only be for healthy foods, to create incentives to eat healthier. We need labor and wage policies that allow us time for basic self-care: cooking and exercise. We need land use and transportation policies that encourage and facilitate human movement, which is essential for our health. Our health and educational institutions need to provide healthy meals and education about healthy eating and cooking. We can only make healthy choices when we are faced with healthy options. We cannot expect people to make healthy choices when all their options are bad.

The US Farm Bill

The current US Farm Bill, the 2018 Farm Act, is in effect from 2019 to 2023. It will cost US$ 428 billion over five years (CRS, 2019). Over two-thirds, 76% or US$ 326 billion, of the budgeted expenses are for nutrition programs. Despite this, prior to the COVID-19 pandemic, when the economy was strong and unemployment was below 4%, the prevalence of food insecurity in the US remained stubbornly at one in eight Americans. However, rather than alleviating structural poverty by setting a living wage, providing universal health care, supporting K-12 education, and affordable higher education, US politicians on both sides of the aisle prefer to rally around miserly government nutrition programs, which provide, at most, a few hundred dollars a month to buy food (Fisher, 2017).

The pandemic has only magnified the shortcomings of US policies. Unemployment climbed to nearly 15% in April of 2020, and by September, it was still twice what it had been pre-pandemic (US BLS, 2020). Food insecurity has doubled for US households because of the pandemic, and tripled for households with children (Schanzenbach and Pitts, 2020). Nearly one-quarter, 23%, of all US households reported being food insecure, with 92% of the increase in food insecurity due to unemployment. Food banks and food pantries are straining to deal with the increased demand (Smith, 2020), while participation in the SNAP program increased by 17 percent between February and May 2020 (Rosenbaum, 2020).

Despite its name, the Supplemental Nutrition Assistance Program does not necessarily promote good nutrition. The lack of limitations on SNAP purchases means recipients purchase what is prevalent and cheapest due to the structure of our food system and our agricultural subsidies: highly processed foods. So, is it any wonder that the poorest Americans have a higher prevalence of food-related health problems?

Over one-fifth (22.6%) of food purchases by SNAP recipients are for sugary beverages, desserts, salty snacks, candy, and sugar (USDA FNS, 2016). Of the US$ 60.4 billion spent in 2019 by SNAP recipients (Tiehen, 2020), that means US taxpayers handed over US$ 13.7 billion in subsidies to the producers and retailers of unhealthy foods in the guise of a nutrition program.

Unsurprisingly, food industry lobbyists have opposed any restrictions that would limit SNAP purchases to healthier foods. They argue that SNAP recipients should not be denied the same foods as other households. Indeed, households that do not receive SNAP spend a similar percentage on these items (19.6%), but spend much more overall. However, by that argument, we should provide benefits for alcohol, tobacco, and meth so that SNAP recipients could spend the same proportion on these items as non-recipients.

Along with transferring billions of dollars to the food industry for junk food, nutrition programs provide cover for US agricultural policies. Since all states in the US have large numbers of people who are food insecure, the inclusion of nutrition programs with farm subsidies ensures broad support for Farm Bills. However, farm subsidies have the largest benefits for a few commodities produced by the largest and wealthiest farmers in just a few states. Farms with over US$ 1 million in sales are only 1.7% of all farms in the US, but average nearly US$ 57,000 annually in direct farm subsidies, while farms with sales under US$ 10,000 a year represent 57% of all farms in the US, but average only US$ 439 in direct farm subsidies per year (Kirwan, 2017). Clearly, most of the farm subsidies are going to the largest and wealthiest farmers.

Direct payments to farmers were US$ 11.5 billion in 2017, but have risen since, largely to compensate farmers for the effects of President Trump's trade wars. They rose to US$ 13.8 billion in 2018 and US$ 19.5 billion in 2019 (USDA ERS. 2019a). Direct payments are an important part of farm income; they were 14.8% of average net farm income in 2017, rose to 16.3% in 2018 and are estimated at 22.1% for 2019 (USDA ERS, 2019b).

However, they are not distributed equally; 34.5% of all direct farm payments went to producers in just five states: Iowa, Illinois, Texas, Minnesota, and South Dakota (USDA ERS, 2019c).

Three farm programs made up 96% of the US$ 102 billion allocated to farm subsidies: crop insurance, commodity programs, and conservation programs (CRS, 2019). The budget for crop insurance is US$ 38 billion or 9% of the total Farm Bill. The commodities programs are budgeted at US$ 31 billion, and the conservation program US$ 29 billion, each about 7% of the total Farm Bill.

The crop and livestock insurance program is actually a wealth transfer from taxpayers to private insurance companies and private insurance agents who collect large commissions for selling insurance to farmers. Rather than offer insurance directly to farmers, the USDA Risk Management Agency (RMA) designates approved private companies to provide farmers with insurance (USDA RMA, 2016). These companies receive administrative and operating subsidies from the US government. The US government also underwrites part of the risk, and is ultimately responsible for payouts if the private companies are mismanaged and become insolvent. In years when the private insurance companies pay out more than their premiums, US taxpayers cover the difference. However, when payouts are less, private insurance companies keep the profits (Babcock and Hart, 2006). In addition, taxpayers pay 55-80% of farmers' insurance premiums, while farmers pay the residual amount (USDA RMA, 2019c). In other words, private insurance companies are guaranteed profits to provide insurance that the government largely pays for, underwrites, and is ultimately responsible for.

While about 80% of farmers are insured (Babcock and Hart, 2006) and insurance covers over 100 crops, including tobacco and now hemp (CRS, 2018), 77% of the government's direct subsidies to producers for crop insurance goes on just four crops: corn (maize) (37%), soy (18.6%), wheat (11.1%), and cotton (10.4%) (USDA RMA, 2019a). RMA also offers three types of insurance for livestock: revenue insurance to milk producers; gross margin insurance to dairy, cattle, and swine producers; and risk protection insurance to cattle, lamb, and swine producers (USDA RMA, 2019b). The Dairy Revenue Protection program provides insurance to milk producers against yield and price declines. The Livestock Gross Margin program ensures that CAFO dairy, feeder or fed cattle, and swine producers are profitable. For dairy producers, this insurance guarantees a specific gross margin between milk price and the prices of corn (maize) and soybean meal.

For cattle, the gross margin is based on cattle and corn (maize) prices, while for swine, the gross margin also includes soybean prices in feed costs. Clearly, this insurance does not apply to pasture-fed animals, putting environmentally more sustainable pasture operations at an economic disadvantage to CAFOs, which are environmentally harmful. The Livestock Risk Protection program provides insurance against price decreases for feeder cattle, fed cattle, lamb, and swine.

Babcock and Hart (2006) found that the RMA public-private partnership is highly inefficient, costing US$ 3.31 for each US$ 1 paid out to farmers. They argue that the cost to taxpayers would be greatly reduced if the public-private partnership were eliminated and the government operated the program by itself. This would eliminate lucrative commissions to private agents and the government could keep gains when payouts were less than premiums to offset the costs of the programs.

Babcock and Hart (2006) also question why farmers need to receive such large subsidies to buy insurance in the first place. They conclude that given farmers' other risk and diversification strategies, such as commodity futures markets, off-farm income, multiple crops and or livestock, not to mention emergency bailouts by Congress during natural disasters, that the actual risks farmers face are too small for them to buy insurance unless they are subsidized to do so. This is supported by the fact that farmers get more money from insurance payouts than they pay in premiums. What kind of insurance company could operate by paying out more than it took in every year? As a farm program, these insurance programs are simply a way of transferring taxpayer money, very inefficiently, to farmers, as well as to private insurance agents and private insurance companies.

The second-largest farm program, the commodities program, will cost over US$ 31 billion over five years (CRS, 2019). Most of the cost, 67%, is for the Price Loss Coverage (PLC) program. The PLC covers wheat, corn (maize) and other feed grains, rice, soy, other oilseeds, peanuts, and pulses (USDA ERS, 2017). The PLC enrollees receive payments when market prices fall below set price floors, multiplied by their farm's historical yields, multiplied by 85% of their farm's base acreage in the commodity. The 2018 Farm Bill allows producers to update their historical yields and switch to the Agriculture Risk Coverage (ARC) program on a crop by crop basis. The ARC covers the same crops as the PLC (CRS, 2018). In the ARC, a producer chooses between county or individual coverage and receives payments when county (individual) revenue is below 86% of a county (individual) revenue benchmark (USDA ERS, 2017). The ARC is the second largest commodity program, representing 19% of the budget (CRS, 2018). So, 86% of the commodity program budget is for the PLC and the ARC programs, both of which pay out differences between actual and target prices based on past yields and output. Clearly, under these programs, the more you produce and the higher your yield, the more you get. This is a highly regressive program, rewarding the largest farms and, therefore, creating incentives for farms to become larger.

In theory, payment limits were implemented to make the commodities programs less regressive. However, payment limits are high and correspond to individuals on a farm, not a farm as a whole. Payment limits remained the same for the 2018 Farm Bill: US$ 125,000 per individual or US$ 250,000 per married couple. Congress expanded the number of individuals on a farm who can receive these payments. In addition to one's spouse, adult children and grandchildren and their spouses, siblings and their spouses, parents, and grandparents, the 2018 Farm Bill allows adult first cousins, nieces, and nephews each to receive up to US$ 125,000 per year (CRS, 2019). Hence, payments per farm are "limited" to US$ 125,000 times the number of adult extended family members. So, if Jo and Chris are a married couple in their 60s with two adult children who are married and each have two adult children who are married, government payments to a single farm prior to the 2018 Farm Bill would have been "limited" to US$ 1.75 million for a single farm. If Jo and Chris each have two nieces or nephews and each is married, and Jo and Chris also each have two cousins, each of whom is married, then that is another 16 relatives who can get subsidies, or another US$ 2 million, allowing for this one farm to receive US$ 3.75 million in taxpayer subsidies. Clearly, the program creates incentives for farms to be as large as possible to get the most government payments. Given that the smallest 57% of farmers receive less than US$ 500 in subsidies annually (Kirwan, 2017), not only is this unfair to US taxpayers, but this distribution of commodity subsidies is also clearly unfair to most farmers.

The third large farm program is conservation. There are many programs within the US$ 29 billion conservation budget that give financial incentives to producers to reduce their impact on soil erosion, water quality, and habitat destruction. The three largest are: the Environmental Quality Incentives Program (EQIP), US$ 11 billion; the Conservation Reserve Program (CRP), US$ 10 billion; and the Conservation Stewardship Program (CSP), US$ 5 billion (CRS, 2018). The EQIP subsidizes and provides technical assistance for conservation management practices, while the CSP provides incentives and assistance to maintain, improve, and expand existing conservation practices. The CRP pays producers to replace crops with conservation plantings on erodible land, with the 2018 Farm Bill expanding enrollment from 24 million acres (9.7 million hectares) to 27 million (10.9 million hectares) by 2023.

What if the Farm Bill promoted health, the environment, and farm incomes?

Clearly, the purpose of a nutrition program should be to promote nutrition. SNAP purchases should be restricted to healthy foods. Taxpayer money should not be used to subsidize purchases of foods that are contributing to a public health crisis of food-related illnesses. Indeed, the USDA's Special Supplemental Nutrition Program for Women, Infants, and Children (WIC) restricts benefits to purchases of healthier foods, and even SNAP has restrictions on prepared foods, alcohol, and household items, which are generally purchased at grocery stores.

In terms of farm insurance programs, a far more efficient and honest program would simply provide direct income transfers to support farmers. However, the current program allows politicians to hide the fact that they are transferring tens of billions of taxpayer dollars to mostly the very largest and wealthiest farmers, as well as to private insurance agents and companies. One-third of all insurance payouts go to operators with a gross cash farm income of over US$ 1 million a year (McFadden and Hoppe, 2017). These represent less than 2% of all farms (Kirwan, 2017) and in 2018, almost one-fifth of all insurance payments went to one state: Texas (USDA ERS, 2019c). "Insurance" sounds so benign and helpful. It hides the fact that the program is highly inefficient, costing over three dollars for every dollar paid out; inequitable, giving the most benefits to the largest and wealthiest farmers; a scam, since farmers get more than they pay in; and unneeded, since farmers have to be bribed to use it. At the very least, the program could be run more cost-effectively if public-private partnership were eliminated and subsidies for premiums were reduced, if not eliminated.

The commodity programs not only create incentives to produce the crops subsidized by the programs, but they also provide incentives for farms to become as large as possible, since payments increase with output. The largest payments go to the farms with the most production and hence highest incomes. This is highly regressive and contributes directly to increasing farm size, loss of farmers, and destruction of rural communities. The loss in the number of farmers can be partially hidden by incentives to count cousins, nephews, and nieces as farm operators at a cost of US$ 125,000 per relative to taxpayers, however, it is hardly an efficient method of "creating" new farmers. Clearly, there needs to be meaningful limits to taxpayers' subsidies that foster a healthy farm economy, one that does not concentrate the bulk of the subsidies on less than 2% of the farms. Such a program would have meaningful caps on payments and a distribution requirement that ensured that payments were distributed widely to all farms. A progressive farm subsidy program would distribute the subsidies to the lowest earners, rather than the highest.

The need for conservation programs is the direct result of the US government's farm insurance and commodity programs. The farm insurance and commodity subsidies increase with output and yields; this creates incentives to produce as much as possible, as cheaply as possible, to reap the largest subsidies from taxpayers. The US farm insurance and commodity programs incentivize planting fencepost to fencepost to extract as much yield as possible, without regard to soil erosion and health, or water conservation and quality. Thus, the conservation programs act as a makeshift solution to address the ills created by the insurance and commodity programs. Again, if farm payments were tied to farm incomes, rather than output, and were distributed to farmers who need them the most, rather than those who are the largest and wealthiest, farmers would not be under pressure to extract as much as they can without regard to land, water, and habitat resources. The conservation programs have been made necessary because of the commodity and insurance programs.

Limiting payments to farms rather than individuals could reduce incentives to increase farm size, at least on paper. However, it could also create incentives to break up farms on paper, into the hands of extended family so they can each continue to receive taxpayer subsidies. Thus, creating a more equitable system would also require reducing the payment limit of US$ 125,000 to any entity. It makes no sense that individuals can receive taxpayer-funded payments worth more than twice the US median family income. If the purpose of commodity programs is to help family farms, then clearly the income transfers to farm families should not be more than the median family income of the taxpayers paying for those subsidies. Finally, from a public health perspective, subsidies should be granted only for healthy foods, specifically, FAV, pulses, nuts, fish, and whole grains for human consumption. This would justify taxpayer subsidies to farms based on nutrition and public health.

The sheer complexity of existing US agriculture and food policy programs hides the fact that not only do they not help achieve stated policy goals, in fact, they often do just the opposite. For example, farmers not only do not have to pay for the damage they have done to others from practices that have resulted in erosion, soil fertility loss, habitat loss, water depletion, water pollution, and chemical and manure contamination, but they have actually been incentivized to use these practices to gain more subsidies from taxpayers. To promote environmental goals, subsidies could be reserved for farmers who manage their land and water sustainably, reduce GHG, and or sequester carbon. Furthermore, since the smallest operators receive such tiny subsidies, their incentives are small; it is the largest recipients who have the largest incentives. Rather than giving the most subsidies to the largest producers, who are causing the most environmental damage to make foods that are contributing to the obesity and diabetes crises, subsidies should be allocated to support the farm incomes of the majority of farmers to produce healthy foods in a more sustainable way. In other words, policies should promote policy objectives. The current US farm programs are simply exacerbating the demise of the family farm, as well as being destructive to the environment and public health. A sane farm program would align spending with social, environmental, and health goals.

Exercise: Voice your support or opposition to policy

Identify one food or agriculture policy goal you support or oppose. Write a letter or email or make a call explaining why you support or oppose it to your relevant elected official.

References

Abeysekera, K., Fernandes, G., Hammerton, G., Gordon, F., Portal, A., Heron, J., and Hickman, M. 2019. GS-08 The prevalence of non-alcoholic fatty liver disease in young adults: An impending public health crisis? Journal of Hepatology, 70(1, Supplement, April), e45. doi: 10.1016/S0618-8278(19)30080-5.

Alston, J. M. and Okrent, A. M. 2017. The effects of farm and food policy on obesity in the United States. New York: Palgrave Macmillan. doi: 10.1057/978-1-137-47831-3.

Angadjivand, S. 2018. U.S. farm commodity support: An overview of selected programs. Congressional Research Service, CRS Report, April 17. https://fas.org/sgp/crs/misc/R45165.pdf, accessed February 11, 2019.

Babcock, B. A. and Hart, C. E. 2006. Crop insurance: A good deal for taxpayers? Center for Agriculture and Rural Development, Iowa Ag Review, 12(3). https://www.card.iastate.edu/iowa_ag_review/summer_06/article1.aspx, accessed December 15, 2019.

Berchick, E. R., Barnett, J. C., and Upton, R. D. 2019. Health insurance coverage in the United States: 2018. US Census Bureau, Current Populations Report P60-267(RV). https://www.census.gov/content/dam/Census/library/publications/2019/demo/p60-267.pdf, accessed October 20, 2020.

Bigelow, D. P. and Borders, A. 2017. Major uses of land in the United States, 2012. USDA ERS, Economic Information Bulletin Number 178, August. https://www.ers.usda.gov/webdocs/publications/84880/eib-178.pdf?v=0, accessed February 8, 2019.

Buehler, R. 2014. 9 reasons the US ended up so much more car-dependent than Europe. Citylab. https://www.citylab.com/transportation/2014/02/9-reasons-us-ended-so-much-more-car-dependent-europe/8226/, accessed December 11, 2019.

Carrington, D. 2019. New plant-focused diet would 'transform' planet's future say scientists. The Guardian, January 16. https://www.theguardian.com/environment/2019/jan/16/new-plant-focused-diet-would-transform-planets-future-say-scientists?CMP=Share_iOSApp_Other, accessed January 17, 2019.

Centers for Disease Control and Prevention. 2019. Data, Trend and Maps. National Center for Chronic Disease Prevention and Health Promotion, Division of Nutrition, Physical Activity, and Obesity. https://www.cdc.gov/nccdphp/dnpao/data-trends-maps/index.html, accessed September 16, 2019.

Cervantes, M. n.d. Academic patenting: How universities and public research organizations are using their intellectual property to boost research and spur innovative start-ups. World Intellectual Property Organization.

https://www.wipo.int/sme/en/documents/academic_patenting.html, accessed December 11, 2019.

CRS (Congressional Research Service). 2019. The 2018 Farm Bill (P. L. 115-334): Summary and side-by-side comparison. CRS Report R45525, February 22. https://crsreports.congress.gov/product/pdf/R/R45525, accessed October 24, 2019.

Ekins, P., Gupta, J., and Boileau, P. 2019. Global environment outlook (GEO-6): Healthy planet, Healthy people. UNEP. Cambridge, UK: Cambridge University Press. doi: 10.1017/9781108627146.

Farm Policy Facts. 2018. Farm Bill: a short history and summary. https://www.farmpolicyfacts.org/farm-policy-history/, accessed February 15, 2019.

Fiolet, T., Srour, B., Sellem, L., Kesse-Guyot, E., Allès, B., Méjean, C., Deschasaux, M., Fassier, P., Latino-Martel, P., Beslay, M., Hercberg, S., Lavalette, C., Monteiro, C. A., Julia, C., and Touvier, M. 2018. Consumption of ultra-processed foods and cancer risk: results from NutriNet-Santé prospective cohort. British Medical Journal (Clinical research ed.), 360, k322. doi: 10.1136/bmj.k322.

Fisher, A. 2017. Big Hunger: The Unholy Alliance between Corporate America and Anti-Hunger Groups. Cambridge, MA: The MIT Press.

Glaser, C., Romaniello, C., and Moskowitz, K. 2015. Costs and consequences: The real price of livestock grazing on America's public lands. The Center for Biological Diversity.
https://www.biologicaldiversity.org/programs/public_lands/grazing/pdfs/CostsAndConsequences_01-2015.pdf, accessed December 11, 2019.

Hyland, C., Bradman, A., Gerona, R., Patton, S., Zakharevich, I., Gunier, R. B., and Klein, K. 2019. Organic diet intervention significantly reduces urinary pesticide levels in US children and adults. Environmental Research, 171, 568-575. doi:10.1016/j.envres.2019.01.024.

Key, N., Burns, C., and Lyons, G. 2019. Financial conditions in the US agricultural sector: Historical comparisons. USDA ERS, Economic Information Bulletin 211, October.

https://www.ers.usda.gov/webdocs/publications/95238/eib-211.pdf?v=8745.1, accessed October 25, 2019.

Kirwan, B. E. 2017. US farm dynamics and the distribution of US agricultural subsidies. Applied Economics Letters, 24(3), 207–209. doi:10.1080/13504851.2016.1178837.

Landrigan, P. J., Fuller, R., Acosta, N. J. R., Adeyi, O., Arnold, R., Basu, N., Baldé, A. B., Bertollini, R., Bose-O'Reilly, S., Boufford, J. I. et al. 2018. The Lancet Commission on pollution and health. The Lancet, 391(10119), 462-512. https://doi.org/10.1016/S0140-6736(17)32345-0, accessed August 27, 2019.

McFadden, J. R. and Hoppe, R. A. 2017. The evolving distribution of payments from commodity, conservation, and federal crop insurance programs. USDA ERS, Economic Information Bulletin 184, November. https://www.ers.usda.gov/webdocs/publications/85834/eib-184.pdf?v=43068, accessed October 25, 2019.

Nestle, M. 2002. Food Politics: How the Food Industry Influences Nutrition and Health. Berkeley, CA: University of California Press.

Newkirk II, V. R. 2019. This land was our land. The Atlantic, 324 (3, September), 74–85.

Our Documents. n.d. Homestead Act (1862). https://www.ourdocuments.gov/doc.php?flash=false&doc=31, accessed February 15, 2019.

Rico-Campà, A., Martínez-González, M. A., Alvarez-Alvarez, I., Mendonça, R. D., de la Fuente-Arrillaga, C., Gómez-Donoso, C., and Bes-Rastrollo, M. 2019. Association between consumption of ultra-processed foods and all cause mortality: SUN prospective cohort study. British Medical Journal (Clinical research ed.), 365, l1949. doi: 10.1136/bmj.l1949.

Rosenbaum, D. 2020. Boost SNAP to capitalize on program's effectiveness and ability to respond to need. Center on Budget and Policy Priorities. July 18. https://www.cbpp.org/research/food-assistance/boost-snap-to-capitalize-on-programs-effectiveness-and-ability-to-respond, accessed October 20, 2020.

Saksena, M. J., Okrent, A. M., Anekwe, T. D., Cho, C., Dicken, C., Effland, A., Elitzak, H., Guthrie, J., Hamrick, K. S., Hyman, J., Jo, Y., Lin, B. H., Mancino, L., McLaughlin, P. W., Rahkovsky, I., Ralston, K., Smith, T. A., Stewart, H., Todd, J., and Tuttle, C. 2018. America's eating habits: Food away from home, EIB-196, M. Saksena, A. M. Okrent, and K. S. Hamrick, editors. US Department of Agriculture, Economic Research Service, September. https://www.ers.usda.gov/webdocs/publications/90228/eib-196.pdf, accessed September 16, 2019.

Schanzenbach, D. and Pitts, A. 2020. How much has food insecurity risen? Evidence from the Census Household Pulse Survey. Institute for Policy Research Rapid Research Report. https://www.ipr.northwestern.edu/documents/reports/ipr-rapid-research-reports-pulse-hh-data-10-june-2020.pdf, accessed October 20, 2020.

Sewell, S. 2019. There were nearly 2 million black farmers in 1920. Why have they disappeared? The Guardian. April 29. https://www.theguardian.com/environment/2019/apr/29/why-have-americas-black-farmers-disappeared?CMP=Share_iOSApp_Other, accessed September 4, 2019.

Smith, J. 2020. Pandemic, growing need strain US food bank operations. The Wall Street Journal, July 16. https://www.wsj.com/articles/pandemic-growing-need-strain-u-s-food-bank-operations-11594891802, accessed October 20, 2020.

Spielmaker, D. M. 2018. Growing a nation: Historical timeline. March 21. https://www.agclassroom.org/gan/timeline/index.htm, accessed February 15, 2019.

Srour, B., Fezeu, L. K., Kesse-Guyot, E., Allès, B., Méjean, C., Andrianasolo, R. M., Chazelas, E., Deschasaux, M., Hercberg, S., Galan, P., Monteiro, C. A., Julia, C., and Touvier, M. 2019. Ultra-processed food intake and risk of cardiovascular disease: prospective cohort study (NutriNet-Santé). British Medical Journal, 365 (May), l1451. doi: 10.1136/bmj.l1451.

Story, M. and French, S. 2004. Food advertising and marketing directed at children and adolescents in the US. International Journal of Behavioral Nutrition and Physical Activity, 1, 3. doi: 10.1186/1479-5868-1-3.

Tiehen, L. 2020. Taking a closer look at Supplemental Nutrition Assistance Program (SNAP) participation and expenditures. Amber Waves, USDA ERS, August 3. https://www.ers.usda.gov/amber-waves/2020/august/taking-a-closer-look-at-supplemental-nutrition-assistance-program-snap-participation-and-expenditures/, accessed September 14, 2020.

Tsai, A. G., and Wadden, T. A. 2005. Systematic review: An evaluation of major commercial weight loss programs in the United States. Archives of Internal Medicine, 142, 56–66.

US Bureau of Labor Statistics. 2020. The employment situation - September 2020. https://www.bls.gov/news.release/pdf/empsit.pdf, accessed October 20, 2020.

US Census Bureau. 2018. American Fact Finder. 2012 Economic census, all sectors, economy wide key statistics, released April 19. https://factfinder.census.gov/faces/nav/jsf/pages/download_center.xhtml, accessed February 7, 2019.

US Census Bureau. 2019. American Fact Finder, Community statistics on age and gender and on race. https://factfinder.census.gov/faces/tableservices/jsf/pages/productview.xhtml?src=CF, accessed August 26, 2019.

USDA ERS. 2017. Crop commodity programs. https://www.ers.usda.gov/agricultural-act-of-2014-highlights-and-implications/crop-commodity-programs/, accessed October 28, 2019.

USDA ERS. 2018a. Farm income and wealth statistics, net cash income. November 30. https://data.ers.usda.gov/reports.aspx?ID=17831, accessed February 8, 2019.

USDA ERS. 2018b. Cash receipts by commodity, 2010-2018F. Nominal (current dollars). https://data.ers.usda.gov/reports.aspx?ID=17845, accessed February 4, 2019.

USDA ERS. 2019a. Government farm program payments. https://data.ers.usda.gov/reports.aspx?ID=17833, accessed October 25, 2019.

USDA ERS. 2019b. Summary of US farm income financial indicators. https://www.ers.usda.gov/data-products/farm-income-and-wealth-statistics/data-files-us-and-state-level-farm-income-and-wealth-statistics/, accessed October 25, 2019.

USDA ERS. 2019c. Farm income atlas, Insurance indemnities by state in 2018. https://www.ers.usda.gov/data-products/farm-income-and-wealth-statistics/charts-and-maps-of-us-farm-income-statement-data.aspx, accessed October 28, 2019.

USDA FAS. 2018. US agricultural exports 2017. March 23. https://www.fas.usda.gov/data/top-us-agricultural-exports-2017, accessed February 12, 2019.

USDA FNS. 2016. Foods typically purchased by Supplemental Nutrition Assistance Program (SNAP) households (Summary). November. https://fns-prod.azureedge.net/sites/default/files/ops/SNAPFoodsTypicallyPurchased-Summary.pdf, accessed September 14, 2020.

USDA National Agricultural Library. 1862. Homestead Act. https://www.nal.usda.gov/homestead-act, accessed February 15, 2019.

USDA NASS. 2018. Table 1. Historical highlights: 2012 and earlier census years. https://www.nass.usda.gov/Publications/AgCensus/2012/Full_Report/Volume_1,_Chapter_1_US/st99_1_001_001.pdf, accessed March 22, 2019.

USDA NASS. 2019. 2017 Census of Agriculture. Report AC-17-A-51, April. https://www.nass.usda.gov/Publications/AgCensus/2017/#full_report, accessed May 17, 2019.

USDA RMA (Risk Management Agency). 2016. About the Risk Management Agency. August. https://www.rma.usda.gov/Fact-Sheets/National-Fact-Sheets/About-the-Risk-Management-Agency, accessed October 25, 2019.

USDA RMA (Risk Management Agency). 2019a. Prepared national reports. https://prodwebnlb.rma.usda.gov/apps/SummaryofBusiness/PreparedReports, accessed October 24, 2019.

USDA RMA (Risk Management Agency). 2019b. Livestock insurance plans. https://www.rma.usda.gov/Topics/Livestock, accessed October 24, 2019.

USDA RMA (Risk Management Agency). 2019c. Whole-farm revenue protection plan. August 30. https://www.rma.usda.gov/en/News-Room/Frequently-Asked-Questions/Whole-Farm-Revenue-Protection-Plan-2020, accessed October 25, 2019.

US National Archives and Records Administration. 2016. The Homestead Act of 1862. https://www.archives.gov/education/lessons/homestead-act, accessed February 15, 2019.

Vanloqueren, G. and Baret, P. V. 2009. How agricultural research systems shape a technological regime that develops genetic engineering but locks out agroecological innovations. Research Policy, 38, 971–983.

Wallace, G. and Kaufman, E. 2019. EPA refuses to ban pesticide tied to children's health problems. CNN, July 18. https://www.cnn.com/2019/07/18/politics/epa-chlorpyrifos/index.html, accessed September 5, 2019.

Warren, T. Y., Barry, V., Hooker, S. P., Sui, X., Church, T. S., and Blair, S. N. 2010. Sedentary behaviors increase risk of cardiovascular disease mortality in men. Medicine and Science in Sports and Exercise, 42(5), 879–885. doi: 10.1249/MSS.0b013e3181c3aa7e.

White, R. R. and Hall, M. B. 2017. Nutritional and greenhouse gas impacts of removing animals from US agriculture. PNAS, November 13, E10301–E10308. doi:10.1073/pnas.1707322114.

Zepeda, L., Chang, H.-S., and Leviten-Reid, C. 2006. Organic food demand: A focus group study involving Caucasian and African-American shoppers. Agriculture and Human Values, 23, 385–394. doi:10.1007/s10460-006-9001-9.

Zepeda L. and Deal, D. 2008. Think before you eat: Photographic food diaries as intervention tools to change dietary decision-making and attitudes. International Journal of Consumer Studies, 32, 692–698.

CHAPTER NINE

EPILOGUE

Globally, we have a food system that is contributing to resource depletion, pollution, climate change, social injustice, economic hardship for small and medium farms, and a public health crisis. The costs of this current system are not fully acknowledged: the loss of farms, the loss of soil fertility, the depletion of water, habitat and species, water pollution, climate change, obesity, overweight, type 2 diabetes, heart disease, strokes, diet-related cancers, mental health problems, and food insecurity. The health costs alone are huge: one in five deaths globally is diet-related (GBD 2017 Diet Collaborators, 2019). Furthermore, current policies do not adequately address these issues, so we can expect a continued rapid decline in biodiversity, more people living in water-stressed areas, more food systems that are stressed, and more malnourished people (UNEP, 2019).

In terms of environmental problems, the greatest threat to global land and freshwater ecosystems is land use change, most of which has been for agricultural expansion (IPBES, 2019). Land degradation from agricultural expansion and practices has reduced productivity on 23% of the world's land surface, while 85% of the area of global wetlands has been lost, and 25% of animal and plant species are threatened, mostly due to habitat loss because of agriculture, leaving about one million species facing extinction. By 2100, we will lose 38% of all vertebrate species due to climate change and habitat loss (UNEP, 2019). In addition, fewer types of crops and fewer crop varieties and animal breeds are being produced, exposing our vulnerable food system to climate change, pests, and diseases (IPBES, 2019). Our food system is also responsible for significant greenhouse gas emissions, and is energy inefficient (UNEP, 2019). Manmade climate change further exacerbates the impacts of biodiversity and ecosystem loss. So, in addition to the environmental costs, all of this is putting more people's livelihoods at risk, increasing conflict, and reducing access to food.

Our current food system is touted as productive and the only solution to feeding future generations, yet it does not feed the hungry now, nor is it healthy for those with enough food. Current policies are "second best, small-scale and focus on technological solutions," when what we need is structural change (UNEP, 2019). There is plenty of food in the world, even despite one-third of what is produced being wasted; yet 11% of the global population are undernourished and 20% of the world's preventable deaths are diet-related (IPBES, 2019). This is because hunger is not due to the lack of food production. The problem is that people cannot access food, either because of conflict and/or lack of income. Reducing conflict (Sen, 1999), reducing food waste, and more equal distribution of income will reduce hunger (IPBES, 2019). Producing more food will not increase people's access if they have no means to buy it or conflict prevents access. Indeed, resource scarcity and environmental degradation are a major source of conflict, war, and migration (UNEP, 2019). Thus, increasing production could simply lead to more externalized production costs: soil degradation, habitat loss, water depletion and pollution, and lower farm incomes, which will mean fewer farmers, as well as more conflict, migration, and hunger.

Given there is plenty of food to feed everyone now, the unequal distribution of income and wealth is at the root of hunger, resource depletion, waste, and conflict. Furthermore, inequality exacerbates conflict, which causes more resource degradation (UNEP, 2019). Just as there is plenty of food, there is plenty of money in the world for everyone to eat. Global gross national income (GNI) per capita in 2018 was US$ 11,098 (World Bank, 2019). That is more than twice what 84.1% of adults in the world earned in 2018: US$ 4,836 GNI per capita. In contrast, less than 16% of the world's adult population earned 63.4% of all global income. Per capita income in the US is US$ 62,850, nearly 13 times what 84% of the world's population earns.

Looking at wealth, there is even greater global inequality. In 2019, average global wealth was US$ 70,850 per adult (Credit Suisse, 2019). However, less than 1% of all adults owned 44% of all global wealth, while 57% of all adults owned less than 2% of all wealth. The bottom 90% of the world's population accounted for only 18% of global wealth, while the richest 10% owned 82%. Not only is global wealth concentrated in the hands of a few, but it is also concentrated geographically; the US has 40% of the world's millionaires, and about half the ultra-rich adults, who have more than US$ 50 million each.

While income inequality between countries has actually narrowed since 1980, it has increased within countries (UNEP, 2019). Take the US as an example. Despite the concentration of global wealth in the US, inequality in the US is pervasive. The median US household income in 2018 was US$ 63,179 (US Census Bureau, 2019a). Yet the richest 20% of US households earned an average of US$ 238,895 or 52% of all income in the US in 2018, while the poorest 20% of households averaged US$ 13,775 per household, earning only 3.1% of all income. The higher the income, the greater the concentration; the richest 5% earned 23% of all income in the US, with a mean income of US$ 416,520 in 2018.

Income and wealth inequality exists because of current policies: wage and labor laws that do not pay workers a living wage; income and property tax laws that privilege the rich (Stiglitz, 2012); lack of access to basic services like clean water, sewers, education, and health care that cut into income and well-being and contribute to debt and bankruptcy; and gender, racial, and ethnic inequality. These inequalities affect access to basic services and health. In 2015, 2.1 billion people lacked access to safe drinking water and 4.5 billion lacked access to sanitation, while 80% of global wastewater was discharged without any treatment (UNEP, 2019). Women and girls are disproportionately affected health-wise because they are often responsible for carrying water from afar (IPBES, 2019).

Gender inequality also affects resource use. When women have power over environmental decision-making, resources are more likely to be distributed for human development priorities, and when women have access to agricultural resources, food security and sustainability increase (UNEP, 2019). Despite this, environmental and agricultural policies have almost no explicit gender targets or indicators. Other gender inequities include denying women access to property, education, rights, and even control over their own bodies. Across 105 countries, the correlation between fertility rates and measures of discrimination against women was 0.66 (Doepke and Tertilt, 2018). Across 51 countries, these researchers found men on average wanted women to have more children than women wanted. Given population growth is one of the main drivers of environmental degradation (UNEP, 2019) and that placing reproductive decisions in the hands of women affects the timing and number of children, and women's access to education and employment reduce their fertility rates (UNEP, 2019), gender inequality is at the core of environmental degradation. It is also at the core of hunger: 60% of the world's hungry are women and most of the two billion people suffering from micronutrient deficiencies are women (FAO, 2017). Hence, gender equality is a key strategy to fix our food system and solve environmental, health, and social problems.

Fixing our food system requires that we understand that it is a manifestation of the policy environment in which it exists, a policy environment based on subsidizing the resource extraction and wealth accumulation of a few, mostly men, at the expense of the many, mostly women, children, and minority populations. As an example, 67.8% of all agricultural land in the US is concentrated in the hands of old White men (USDA NASS, 2019) who represent approximately 6.5% of the total US population (US Census Bureau, 2019b). In contrast, African American men of all ages make up 6.2% of the US population (US Census Bureau, 2019b), but only 1.1% of all farmers (USDA NASS, 2019). African Americans have lost over 12 million acres (4.9 million hectares), or 98% of the land they owned over the last century, mostly through discriminatory practices by banks and government agencies (Newkirk, 2019). Fixing our broken food system requires understanding where we are, how we got here, and what needs to change.

This book has argued that to change our food system, we need to promote equity, eliminate subsidies that are harmful to the environment and public health, create incentives for sustainable land and water use, and enforce regulations (IPBES, 2019). This will require structural changes in our political, economic, social, and technological systems. Business as usual is not sustainable; we would need to increase production by 50% by 2050 under current practices if we do not address waste, rising population figures, and unsustainable consumption and production (UNEP, 2019). There simply is not enough land and water to do this. In addition, nitrogen and phosphorous loads are already at unsustainable levels, and GHG emissions from agriculture alone are on a trajectory that will cause us to exceed the two degrees Celsius target set by the Paris Agreement. Our current policies are not solving our problems, they are causing them. We need "transformative change" but this requires vision, social and policy innovation, the phasing out of unsustainable practices, and opportunities to enable stakeholders (UNEP, 2019).

We are facing critical problems driven by population growth and unsustainable consumption and production (UNEP, 2019). Fortunately, the solutions to our problems regarding the environment, climate, public health, and the economy coincide. They require greater equity, fairness, and transparency. Agricultural policies need to begin by eliminating subsidies that encourage the degradation and overuse of land and water resources, and the production of foods that adversely affect public health. We cannot transform our food system and public health by making marginal changes to a broken system. The incentives that created the problems in the first place need to be eliminated. All agricultural policies need to be measured against criteria such as public health, environmental impact, and equity. They should ensure that the polluter pays, that farmers capture carbon, and that incentives are provided to produce and consume sustainably. They should result in greater diversity and equity in who receives these benefits. They should result in greater production and consumption of healthy foods, as well as reduced consumption of unhealthy foods. This does not mean eliminating animal products and processed foods from one's diet but reducing them to levels that do not kill us. Diets with low levels of animal products and high levels of FAV, pulses, whole grains, nuts, and seeds meet both environmental and health goals that will allow us to survive and have a better quality of life (UNEP, 2019).

Within the greater policy context, we need economic reforms to permit individuals to make choices that promote their health and well-being: a living wage, affordable housing, and access to health care and education that does not bankrupt families. These are policies that would reduce food insecurity by eliminating the need for people to make choices between food and paying for other needs, like rent or medical care (Zepeda, 2018). We also need to design and implement built environments that facilitate exercise and limit sedentariness. Antitrust legislation needs to be enforced to break up the concentration and power of food processors, brands, seed and chemical companies, food retailers, and food suppliers to allow consumers and producers real choices (Lauck, 1999). Farmers, workers, and consumers all benefit when there is real competition and choice regarding who to buy from, sell to, and work for (Carstensen, 2000). Furthermore, this historic level of concentration of market power has had detrimental effects on wage and labor policies, and hence on living standards (Stiglitz, 2012). It impedes our economy and society; many full-time workers cannot meet basic needs. When employees receive a living wage, they can afford basic needs that promote the well-being of their families and prevent external costs due to food-related disease, addiction, crime, and other social problems that stem from poverty and inequity. To support this, tax and financial policies need to ensure that wealth, and particularly land and property, are not concentrated in the hands of a few; taxes must be progressive (Stigliz, 2012). Furthermore, a Tobin tax on financial transactions could reduce speculation and market volatility (Palley, 2003). To foster trade, based on environmental and social impacts, the WTO needs reforms that incorporate these measures (Wolff, 2019). Across all sectors, we need to enact policies to guarantee gender and racial equity. Inequality, especially income and gender inequality, undermine the capacity for sustainability (IPBES, 2019). Finally, we need international cooperation, because environmental, social, and economic problems do not respect political boundaries. We are intertwined; we can strangle ourselves by struggling against our ties, or work together, using the ties that bind us to lift each other up.

Why we blame the individual

Our food system is killing many of us and destroying much of the natural environment. However, our health and environmental problems are blamed on the individual: each and every one of us apparently lacks the willpower, impulse control, and/or judgment to make choices that are healthy and sustainable. Reflect a minute on the conclusion that everyone is making bad choices because we are all lacking in willpower. Such a conclusion defies logic and ignores recognition of our social, economic, and political environment.

Some attribute unhealthy food choices and lack of exercise to lack of time, money, education, knowledge, or even cooking skills. However, interventions to address these issues generally fail (GBD 2017 Diet Collaborators, 2019). While each of these factors may contribute to unhealthy and unsustainable diets and lack of exercise, this book has argued that our food choices occur within a policy context, one which makes healthy and sustainable choices difficult and costly. We shop in grocery stores that offer more than 30,000 items (Food Marketing Institute, 2019), most of which are unhealthy (Access to Nutrition Foundation, 2018); yet somehow, we are supposed to ignore the vast majority of items offered and choose the few items that are healthy and sustainable. For a 100 years, Americans have been fed since early infancy on formulas and foods full of sugar, salt, and fat, which have been designed by baby food companies to be addictive (Bentley, 2014). This has created generations that are habituated to highly processed foods that contribute to our food-related diseases. In addition, most of us are paid so poorly that we have to work and commute long hours, leaving us stressed and with little time; so, we crave these ready-to-eat, familiar, comforting foods. Food brands, retailers, and restaurants are only too happy to oblige, offering a thousand variations made with high levels of a few ingredients: sugar, salt, fat, and animal products. Given the number of products available, we believe we have choices. However, most of the choices, which are offered by a handful of companies, are bad for our health, bad for the environment, and bad for most farmers. If most choices we are given are bad, how can we make good choices?

We accept the system we are in, thinking it is natural and right, because we have nothing to compare it to. However, it has been carefully constructed to privilege and enrich a few, as Chapter Three showed. In the US, land was granted to wealthy White men, and policies continue to preserve and protect their privileges. Food manufacturing was created to feed armies and then an army of poorly paid industrial workers. Investors in food manufacturing profited by exploiting workers and also from wars, by selling to the military…and they grew rich. The concentration of agricultural suppliers, food processors, and retailers has gone unchallenged by antitrust legislation in the US, leaving farmers globally with few choices regarding from whom to buy inputs and to whom to sell their products. Consumers' choices between and within stores are masked by a variety of names and brands that give us the illusion of choice; yet a few global companies control most brands. Even if we shop at multiple stores, they may actually be owned by a single large multinational.

Nearly all of our food choices are bad, yet we continue to blame the individual for lack of self-control. Self-help, diet, and exercise media and programs reinforce (and profit from) the focus on individual "failings." The irony of blaming the individual is that our individual attempts to make good choices can alienate others (Fischler, 2013). Individuals struggling to make good choices adhere to diets and exercise programs with fervor that generates incivility: keto-vegan internet wars, family meals that devolve into food fights, and guests who treat their hosts as short-order cooks. Meals have become less a place of community, and more of a battleground. Not surprisingly, we wind up eating alone; for who would wish to eat with companions who complain, each demanding their host cook them special foods? Again, reflect a moment on a society that has this result; by putting the onus on the individual, we have created a society of eaters who by exercising "choice," are demanding, thus alienating others. If the blame for our unsustainable and unhealthy food system is really on individual bad choices, then why, when we exercise what we believe to be good choices, are we all making such contradictory choices that lead to estranging others?

This is not a plea for conformity, nor for food police, in fact, it is the opposite. It is a plea to dismantle the system that has given us nothing but bad choices and then accused us of individual failings. We can level the playing field by: removing subsidies for unhealthy, unsustainable foods;

incentivizing farmers to capture carbon, produce sustainably, and produce healthy foods; breaking up the concentration of agribusiness, processors, brands, and retailers; providing workers with a living wage and benefits; designing built environments that facilitate exercise and non-sedentary behaviors; and providing accurate and easy-to-understand nutrition information. This would allow individuals to have options to make real choices, good or bad.

Leveling the playing field means that unhealthy, unsustainable food will become relatively more expensive. A level playing field means that food prices should reflect the full cost of their environmental, social, health, and economic externalities. A level playing field means that any farm subsidies promote public health and enhance environmental services and resources. A level playing field means enforcing antitrust legislation to break up industry concentration, thereby providing actual choice for consumers and farmers. A level playing field means that people get the exercise and movement needed to stay healthy in the course of their day. A level playing field means that full-time workers can afford to purchase healthy and sustainable foods for their families.

These changes will not happen if we do not demand them. They require political action. That means raising awareness, electing officials committed to changing policies, persuading those in office to make changes, organizing and lobbying to support policy changes, and getting organizations to advocate for policy changes. Change requires working together, within and between organizations, in order to be heard. Changing our diet requires changing our food system (GBD 2017 Diet Collaborators, 2019) and this is going to be difficult.

Policy changes can reduce diet-related deaths and illnesses, as well as promoting environmental sustainability (GBD 2017 Diet Collaborators, 2019). To those who think the costs of leveling the playing field are too high, reflect a minute on the costs of our current system: the billions of dollars in subsidies; the trillions of dollars in health care and environmental costs; and the resources, health, and lives lost. It is simply too expensive to continue on our current path, and it defies reason to expect people to make good choices if nearly all their options are bad, and those bad choices are made artificially cheap through government policies.

Why we look for local solutions and why we avoid policy solutions

Putting the blame on the individual deflects attention from the policies that created the problems in the first place. It also deflects from the need for individuals and non-profits to be involved in policy to solve our systemic food-related problems. If one starts with individual choice as the crux of the problem, then solutions must entail increasing consumers' options and educating them to make the "right" choices. Thus, a thousand non-profit organizations and blogs are born to address food insecurity, food deserts, and provide sustainable food options: urban agriculture, food pantries, food banks, CSAs, farmers' markets, community kitchens, etc. The sheer amount of effort, volunteer time, grants, and fundraising involved to fund this network is enormous. If even a fraction of the millions of hours of time and hundreds of millions of dollars in grants and donations were turned toward advocating change in our food policies, we would have a different food system. This is why it is so important that non-profits become involved in advocating policy changes and collaborating with other non-profits to do so, as well as asking their supporters and volunteers to act as advocates for policy changes. However, harvesting some apples from neglected trees, donating canned goods to a pantry, and growing kale in an empty lot are more straightforward, if less impactful. They seem like they have an impact, never mind how many temporal, monetary, and energy resources went into getting 40 pounds of apples, 20 cans of unwanted food, and a few dozen bunches of kale to a food bank.

The question is never raised—did the people who received the apples, canned food, or kale actually want them in the first place? Or did they accept them because that was what was available? What kind of food do they actually want? And why is it not paternalistic to provide food at food pantries or urban gardens that has been selected (if only by default) for recipients?

Clearly, there simply are not enough charities and non-profits in the world to counteract the symptoms of policies that created our food-related problems in the first place. Furthermore, until non-profits address the policies that cause these symptoms, nothing will change. As long as governments have policies that create food insecurity, obesity and other food-related illnesses, resource depletion, and unsustainable production, these problems will grow and charities will have endless opportunities to address problems without solving them.

Changing food policy is simply more complex and requires more effort and understanding than driving across town to drop off a can of unwanted soup. However, while a can of soup will do nothing to change the underlying issues of food insecurity and food-related illness, it does offer its donor the illusion of doing something about the problem, as well as getting rid of an unwanted can of soup. However, before blaming the individual for lack of political activity, reflect a minute on the fact that we have a system that makes it easier for a person to drive across town to drop off a can of soup than to speak out about changing policy, let alone have an impact on policy. On the one hand, this occurs because the environmental and social costs of resource use and inequity have been externalized, making it difficult for people to see and articulate the connections within our food system. On the other, an individual may not ask for a change to the system because they may lack information, they may not understand the role of policy, they may not believe their voice will be heard—and they may be right. An individual can easily be ignored. However, organizations and movements are more difficult to ignore. This points to a need to work collectively to change policies. This is where existing non-profits and organizations could be most useful: working together to mobilize their volunteers and supporters to demand policy changes that address the fundamental problems in our broken food system.

There are already plenty of organizations and movements, but many fail to see the connections between our problems and our policies. In addition, many non-profits eschew policy because they may confuse politics with partisanship. Being partisan means supporting candidates from a particular party. Being political means supporting particular policies. Non-profits in the US can be advocates for policy changes that are within their mission without losing their tax-exempt status. For this reason, some food banks have broadened their mission statements so they can be advocates for a living wage; they understand the link between low wages and food insecurity. Non-profits can also educate and mobilize their vast army of volunteers to act as advocates for policy changes. However, they may still choose not to because those who run non-profits benefit from the status quo and fear alienating their corporate donors (Fisher, 2017).

We do not have much time. We are running out of habitat and resources to destroy that would allow us to continue our current wasteful food system. We could live better and longer if we change the incentives that have created the problems in our food system in the first place. That requires changing agricultural, economic, and trade policies to remove subsidies for unhealthy foods and to promote sustainable, healthy foods so that we actually have choices. This can only happen if we become politically active, organized, and demand that policies be changed. If we do not put healthy, sustainable foods on the table, how do we expect individuals to choose them?

Exercise: Support a group working for change

Identify one group that is working for the change you want. How can you support their work?

References

Access to Nutrition Foundation. 2018. Access to nutrition index, 2018. Global index 2018. https://www.accesstonutrition.org/index/global.2018, accessed December 13, 2019.

Carstensen, P. C. 2000. Market concentration and agriculture: Equally harmful to producers and consumers. Conference, Visions for the Millennium: Structural Changes Facing Livestock & Grain Markets in the 21St Century, Sponsored by GIPSA, May 9-10, Kansas City, Missouri. https://www.gipsa.usda.gov/psp/publication/millennium/carstensen.htm, accessed December 13, 2019.

Credit Suisse. 2019. Research Institute: Global wealth report 2019. October. https://www.credit-suisse.com/about-us/en/reports-research/global-wealth-report.html, accessed October 31, 2019.

Doepke, M. and Tertilt, M. 2018. Women's empowerment, the gender gap in desired fertility, and fertility outcomes in developing countries. IZA Institute of Labor Economics. Discussion Paper IZA DP No. 11262, January. http://ftp.iza.org/dp11262.pdf, accessed April 3, 2019.

FAO. 2017. The future of food and agriculture: Trends and challenges. http://www.fao.org/3/a-i6583e.pdf, accessed April 3, 2019.

Fischler, C. 2013. Is sharing a meal a thing of the past? In Selective Eating: The Rise, Meaning and Sense of Personal Dietary Requirements, C. Fischler, editor. Paris: Odile Jacob.

Fisher, A. 2017. Big Hunger: The Unholy Alliance between Corporate America and Anti-hunger Groups. Cambridge, MA: The MIT Press.

Food Marketing Institute. 2019. Supermarket facts. https://www.fmi.org/our-research/supermarket-facts, accessed November 25, 2019.

GBD 2017 Diet Collaborators. 2019. Health effects of dietary risks in 195 countries, 1990-2017: a systematic analysis for the Global Burden of Disease Study 2017. The Lancet, 393, May 11. https://www.thelancet.com/pdfs/journals/lancet/PIIS0140-6736(19)30041-8.pdf, accessed November 14, 2019.

IPBES. 2019. Summary for policymakers of the global assessment report on biodiversity and ecosystem services of the Intergovernmental Science-Policy Platform on Biodiversity and Ecosystem Services. S. Díaz, J. Settele, E. S. Brondizio, H. T. Ngo, M. Guèze, J. Agard, A. Arneth, P. Balvanera, K. A. Brauman, S. H. M. Butchart, K. M. A. Chan, L. A. Garibaldi, K. Ichii, J. Liu, S. M. Subramanian, G. F. Midgley, P. Miloslavich, Z. Molnár, D. Obura, A. Pfaff, S. Polasky, A. Purvis, J. Razzaque, B. Reyers, R. Roy Chowdhury, Y. J. Shin, I. J. Visseren-Hamakers, K. J. Willis, and C. N. Zayas, editors. Bonn, Germany: IPBES secretariat. https://www.ipbes.net/global-assessment-report-biodiversity-ecosystem-services, accessed November 6, 2019.

Lauck, J. 1999. Toward an agrarian antitrust: A new direction for agricultural law. North Dakota Law Review, 75, 449–508. https://nationalaglawcenter.org/wp-content/uploads/assets/bibarticles/lauck_agrarian.pdf accessed December 13, 2019.

Newkirk II, V. R. 2019. This land was our land. The Atlantic, 324(3, September), 74–85.

Palley, T. I. 2003. The economic case for the Tobin tax. In Debating the Tobin Tax, New Rules for Global Finance, J.H. Weaver, R. Dodd, and J. Baker, editors. http://www.new-rules.org/about-new-rules/publications/136-debating-the-tobin-tax, accessed December 12, 2019.

Sen, A. 1999. Development as Freedom. New York: Anchor Books.

Stiglitz, J. 2012. The Price of Inequality. New York: W. W. Norton & Company.

UNEP. 2019. Global Environment Outlook, GEO-6: Healthy planet, healthy people. Cambridge, UK: Cambridge University Press. https://wedocs.unep.org/bitstream/handle/20.500.11822/27539/GEO6_2019.pdf?sequence=1&isAllowed=y, accessed November 4, 2019.

US Census Bureau. 2019a. Income and poverty in the United States: 2018. Report No. P60-266, September. https://www.census.gov/data/tables/2019/demo/income-poverty/p60-266.html, accessed October 31, 2019.

US Census Bureau. 2019b. American Fact Finder, Community statistics on age and gender and on race: https://factfinder.census.gov/faces/tableservices/jsf/pages/productview.xhtml?src=CF, accessed August 26, 2019.

USDA NASS. 2019. 2017 Census of Agriculture. Report AC-17-A-51, April. https://www.nass.usda.gov/Publications/AgCensus/2017/#full_report, accessed May 17, 2019.

Wolff, A. W. 2019. DDG Wolff: Acceding governments are in the vanguard of WTO reform. Global NGO Impact News, December 6. https://globalimpactnews.com/2019/12/06/ddg-wolff-acceding-governments-are-in-the-vanguard-of-wto-reform/, accessed December 12, 2019.

World Bank. 2019. GNI per capita, Atlas method (current US$). http://wdi.worldbank.org/table/WV.1, accessed October 31, 2019.

Zepeda, L. 2018. Hiding hunger: Food insecurity in middle America. Agriculture and Human Values, 35(1), 243–254. doi: 10.1007/s10460-017-9818-4.

DOPAMINE NATION TH 10-21-21 11:1